# Critical Pedagogy

**Critical Studies in Education and Culture Series**

Women Teaching for Change: Gender, Class and Power
*Kathleen Weiler*

Between Capitalism and Democracy: Educational Policy and the Crisis of the
Welfare State
*Svi Shapiro*

Critical Psychology and Pedagogy: Interpretation of the Personal World
*Edmund Sullivan*

Pedagogy and the Struggle for Voice: Issues of Language, Power, and Schooling
for Puerto Ricans
*Catherine E. Walsh*

Learning Work: A Critical Pedagogy of Work Education
*Roger I. Simon, Don Dippo, and Arleen Schenke*

Cultural Pedagogy: Art/Education/Politics
*David Trend*

Raising Curtains on Education: Drama as a Site for Critical Pedagogy
*Clar Doyle*

Toward a Critical Politics of Teacher Thinking: Mapping the Postmodern
*Joe L. Kincheloe*

Building Communities of Difference: Higher Education in the Twenty-First
Century
*William G. Tierney*

The Problem of Freedom in Postmodern Education
*Tomasz Szkudlarek*

Education Still under Siege: Second Edition
*Stanley Aronowitz and Henry A. Giroux*

Media Education and the (Re)Production of Culture
*David Sholle and Stan Denski*

# Critical Pedagogy

## AN INTRODUCTION

*Barry Kanpol*

Critical Studies in Education and Culture Series
EDITED BY
Henry A. Giroux and Paulo Freire

BERGIN & GARVEY
Westport, Connecticut • London

**Library of Congress Cataloging-in-Publication Data**

Kanpol, Barry.
    Critical pedagogy : an introduction / Barry Kanpol.
      p.  cm.—(Critical studies in education and culture series,
  ISSN 1064–8615)
    Includes bibliographical references and index.
    ISBN 0–89789–393–X (hard : alk.paper)—ISBN 0–89789–394–8
  (pbk. : alk.paper)
    1. Critical pedagogy.  I. Title.  II. Series.
  LC196.K36   1994
  370.11'5—dc20       93–49638

British Library Cataloguing in Publication Data is available.

Library of Congress Catalog Card Number: 93–49638
ISBN: 0–89789–393–X
    0–89789–394–8 (pbk.)
ISSN: 1064–8615

First published in 1994

Bergin & Garvey, 88 Post Road West, Westport, CT 06881
An imprint of Greenwood Publishing Group, Inc.

Printed in the United States of America

The paper used in this book complies with the
Permanent Paper Standard issued by the National
Information Standards Organization (Z39.48–1984).

10 9 8 7 6 5 4 3 2

## Copyright Acknowledgments

The author and publisher gratefully acknowledge permission for use of the following material:

From "Institutional and Cultural Political Resistance: Necessary Conditions for the Transformative Intellectual." *Urban Review*, Vol. 21, No. 3, 1989. pp. 163–179. Material that appears in Chapter 3.

From "Self and Community in a Fourth Grade Global Education Project: Necessary Conditions for the Emancipatory Agenda." *Urban Review*, Vol. 22, No. 4, 1990. pp. 265–280. Material that appears in Chapter 4.

From "The Politics of Similarity within Difference: A Pedagogy for the Other." *Urban Review*, Vol. 24, No. 22, 1992. pp. 105–131. Material that appears in Chapter 5.

From "Critical Curriculum Theorizing as Subjective Imagery: Reply to Goodman." *The Educational Forum*, Vol. 57, No. 3, Spring 1993. pp. 324–330. Material that appears in Chapter 5.

This book is dedicated to my three children,
Merav, Maia, and Christopher Aaron.

# Contents

# Series Foreword

Public schooling in the United States is suffering from an identity crisis. Caught amid the call for testing, privatization, and choice, the legacy of schooling as a crucial public sphere has been subordinated to the morally insensitive dictates of market forces and the ideological stridency of an alarming new cultural nativism. The allure of profit and commodification coupled with the conservative bravado of national purpose has found a hospitable place in the discourse of educational reform. One result has been the rewriting of what schools are and might become. Lost from the new discourse of educational reform is any notion of social justice and democratic community. Reduced to the language of competitiveness and individual gain, it has become difficult to relate the mission and purpose of schooling to a public discourse that addresses racism, poverty, sexism, nihilism, widespread ignorance, and cultural despair.

This extremely drastic reductionism regarding how public schooling is defined erases both the redemptive language of history as well as the productive, critical, contradictory, and democratic characteristics that speak to schools as sites of possibility, as crucial public spheres engaged in the construction of active citizens willing to struggle for a muticultural and multiracial democracy. Of course, the severity and hardness of the rhetoric and reforms that gained ascendancy during the Reagan and Bush eras did not take place without resistance from a wide variety of quarters. A number of critical educators have offered trenchant criticisms of schooling in the age of diminishing possibilities.

What is so unique about Barry Kanpol's book is that although he recognizes the importance of the language of critique, he is not willing to be bound by the moral indignation that often produces such a language. Instead, Kanpol sets his theoretical focus on a much wider terrain, one that sees critique and possibility as mutually reinforcing each other. For Kanpol, hope is the condition of agency and such agency must move beyond the boundaries that separate the personal from the political, theory from practice, and the private from the public sphere. Combining personal narratives, case studies, and concrete classroom practice, Kanpol attempts to speak to teachers about the importance of critical educational theory and its value in redefining schooling as a crucial, democratic public sphere. By narrating the ideological lineaments of his own educational journey and attitudes toward public education, Kanpol's text opens up a dialogue with teachers that asserts the importance of identity as a social consideration that is forged in history and in the shifting, contradictory terrain of struggle and self-reflection. Refusing to collapse the political into the personal, Kanpol demonstrates masterfully how knowledge, authority, and agency can be understood and transformed in a discriminating relationship between experience and critical reflection, practice and theory.

Introductory texts are often demeaning to teachers. They are generally written in a language that is superficial, paternalistic, and prescriptive. Rather than opening up a space of contestation, insight, and hope, such texts tend to diminish any sense of agency by assuming that there is no room for critical engagement between the text and the reader. Instead of being provocative and unsettling, they are often boring and dreadfully conservative. Kanpol has avoided all of these theoretical and editorial pitfalls and in doing so has redefined what it means to develop a critical text that speaks to a broad popular audience. In part, this indicates his willingness to take the notion of the public seriously; it also suggests the passion he feels and writes about in viewing schools, teachers, and educators as vital institutions and actors in the struggle over radical democracy. Without question, this is a book that will provoke, incite, and open up new spaces for understanding the diverse legacy that critical education has come to occupy within the last decade.

                                                        Henry A. Giroux

# Acknowledgments

There are many people involved in the production of this book whom I would like to thank. Henry Giroux has my gratitude for both his friendship, professional encouragement, and years of insight. Fred Yeo is more than just a friend. As a brother of mine he stands out in his personal support and honest critique. His continual probing has always provided me with an alternative view on my work. I would particularly like to thank Joe Kinchloe for his comments on an earlier draft of this manuscript. Thanks go to my department chair, Bill Henk, for providing the space to complete this work in a timely manner and to Peggy McFarlane and Diane Kling who always provided both humor and the hoops to bypass a lot of bureaucracy. Also, a special thanks to Liz Leiba and Lynn Flint who worked so diligently with me in the final production of this manuscript. The teachers who participated in these case studies are continuing sources of inspiration for me, as are my students. Although my parents are in Israel, they remain a constant source of support and encouragement. A word of gratitude to two important people in my life, Bob and Judy Cardy, for providing me with a home in troubled times. I have been blessed with a son this year from a person with whom I am sharing my life. Susan, there can be no greater gift. It is to you, Christopher Aaron and my two daughters, Merav and Maia that I dedicate this work.

# 1

# Stories and News: The Personal and the Public in Education

## INTRODUCTION

Education in the United States is in a state of crisis. Over the last ten years, ever since the influential 1983 national report *A Nation at Risk* was published, there has been much debate about the role of schools and teachers. Two major contentions emanate from *A Nation at Risk*: (a) that schools must prepare students for a competitive world economy and (b) that schools must meet the needs of diverse cultures.[1]

It has been argued in many educational journals and books that historically the primary function of schools has been an economic one—to prepare students for the work force. Although the second issue (diverse cultures) plays a small part in the report, it is largely underplayed by schools. As a result, Henry Giroux points out the following about George Bush's America 2000 plan (still in operation in the Clinton administration):

America 2000 has put forth a notion of educational leadership that is as significant for what it does not address as it is for the goals and programs it proposes. Organized around the imperatives of choice, standardized testing, and the reprivatization of public schools, it displays no sense of urgency in addressing the importance of schooling for improving the quality of democratic life . . . for instance, America 2000 ignores such problems as child poverty, unemployment, health care, teenage pregnancy, drugs, violence and racial discrimination.[2]

Giroux argues that the primary agenda of educational reform has been to further the welfare of the economy and to focus much less on cultural concerns. It is the underdeveloped issue of cultural concerns that I will focus on in this book. I will not write about standardized testing or school choice. Rather, I will focus on democratic (and cultural) issues as they pertain to the school site in particular.

With this in mind, perhaps one of the largest reforms of the U.S. school system will someday concern what in educational circles is called multicultural or diversity education. Between the devastating rate of urban dropouts[3] and the increasing numbers of minority immigrants into the United States, much thought has been and will continue to be focused on what counts as a fair and just education for so many millions of immigrant newcomers and other educationally deprived Americans. Not enough thought, however, has gone into implementing programs to equalize education for diverse groups, despite the noble efforts and minor successes of programs like Head Start. It is clear, especially after reading Jonathan Kozol's devastating book *Savage Inequalities*, that American education is in dire straits. Clearly, then, one of the largest problems facing the United States in general and education in particular is how to build a school system that is just and fair and caring and nurturing as well as democratic to its large clientele. These are the major issues within which critical social theory conceptualizes its work.

This will be a book about critical social theory and its ensuing philosophies and practices, particularly critical pedagogy. But before we begin with definitions, I would like in this introductory chapter to divert to what I describe as my personal and the public lives and thus make critical theory and critical pedagogy more manageable in Chapter 2 and the subsequent chapters. Intimately related to critical theory is my coming to terms with my school years, my preservice teacher education experiences, and some of the public's views on education. I turn my attention to this.

I was born in Australia, and I lived for ten years in Israel and one year in England. I have lived for twelve years in the United States (in the Midwest, in Columbus, Ohio; in the South, in Greensboro, North Carolina; in the West, in Orange, California; and now on the East Coast in Harrisburg, Pennsylvania). My past educational experiences as both a student, student-teacher, and teacher have profoundly affected how I view the role of schools and teachers within schools in particular. Because I am so involved in the education field, I can't help but be attracted to the specific news items about education that frequent the newspapers.

Newspapers report on former President Bush's America 2000 plan, growing poverty levels and how they affect schools, the role of the economy and education, standardized tests, gender and minority issues, and so on. All of these influence, in some way or another, how I view the role of schools socially, culturally, and politically. Despite all the media (both positive and negative), critical theorists view schools as inherently unequal places of knowledge distribution that in a large part serve to divide the United States by race, class, and gender. That is, different people divided by race, class, and gender receive and/or are privileged to receive certain forms of educational knowledge, skills, and curriculum in unequal ways. For instance, as early as 1980, a study by Jean Anyon[4] described how curriculum knowledge was distributed unequally to different groups of students in working-class, middle-class, and upper-class schools. She also described how teacher expectations for students differed in these vastly different school settings, thereby exacerbating their expectations. In short, Anyon's study depicts how unfairly class differences are reproduced.

As I reflect on my past experiences, I wonder how and if I have been a part of this problem. How I have been implicated in these educational structures is a question I always ask myself and my students as we think about the role of schools, teachers, students, and the general field of education in the larger culture. Thus, my personal experiences in education as an elementary and high school student, certification student, and public school teacher are intimately connected to the public debate in education. I ask, Who am I? Was I sexist and/or racist in my views? Am I today? Were my parents? How was I privileged? Why was I privileged? What relationships did I hold outside of the school arena and what did they look like? Why would I want to teach? Who would I like to teach? What would I like to teach?

In this chapter I will introduce the reader to some of my personal stories about education, stories divided by my experiences as a student, certification student, and teacher. I will then connect these stories to some media presentations about education.

## THE PERSONAL

My school years were spent for the most part in a middle-class suburban neighborhood in Melbourne, Australia. During this time, I attended a private Jewish day school called Mount Scopus College. As would be expected, my school years had a profound influence on me. In some ways, experiences during my formative years had a major impact on why I became an educator. I divide the following personal stories into five emerging themes: (a) authoritarianism, (b) gender, (c) fear and cheating, (d) competition, and (e) stereotype. I was in a private school, but these themes are pervasive to any system that is oppressive to either students or teachers.

### Authoritarianism

At Mount Scopus College, academic rigidity and institutional uniformity was the dominant school philosophy. Shoes had to be polished black, hair worn above the ears, girls' underwear had to be gray (and they were checked by the schools' female vice-principal monthly), and boys' ties had to be immaculate. Boys wore shorts in the summer, even if it was a cold day, and long, black slacks were worn in the winter, even if it was a warm day. As elementary school students, we lined up outside on the playground, in our designated class slots and in alphabetical order. If any one of us was out of alphabetical order, we were all sent to the male elementary school principal, Mr. Penny (name changed). I recall vividly Mr. Penny's strap as we lined up one by one to receive the sting of this leather instrument on our hands. Mr. Penny's beet-red face still makes me chuckle, as it did then. I was a little rebel. Even at that time of my life, I enjoyed being the center of attention. One way to get this attention was to deviate from simple school stipulations such as lining up correctly, coming to class on time, not learning my spelling word list by heart for every school day, and so on. Not conforming to rules was one way to alleviate the boredom of school.

The principal of the secondary school was short, thin, and balding, with a graying moustache, and scrawny lips. He almost always wore a gray or black suit. Mr. Penny always had a deep, concerned, and stern look in his eye. In 1991, eighteen years after I left the school, I visited his infamous office again. I sat outside his office door as if I were waiting for him. I recalled the fear and nervousness I had felt as a twelve-year-old waiting to be scolded and badgered. I distinctly remember how he would eye me up and down and then grimly and sarcastically scold me (as he twisted my ear) for misbehaving on the bus on the way to school (i.e., moving to another seat when I wasn't supposed to). This principal still instills fear in me, despite the social and academic positions I now hold. I remember his favorite threat: "Kanpol, I'm going to skin you alive and hang your pieces on the wall. Now pull up your socks, son, and get out of here." Eighteen years later I began to get hot and cold flushes, just recalling those events. I think, How did he have surveillance on me, even out of school? Then I add more pieces to the puzzle. When I was sixteen, he telephoned my mother: "Mrs. Kanpol, your son will not succeed in school. He takes drugs, hangs out with the wrong students, and womanizes all the girls." The implications of this statement were clear. However, I never took drugs as he described, and I was a virgin at the time. I hung out with guys who are still my friends today (and we still all laugh at this principal and poke fun at him, as we did then). Besides, I thought, who defines right or wrong behavior? And how did he know who my friends were? Did he have special investigators? I guess he did!

I was never the good academic student that this school prided itself in. I was, however, a very good Australian rules football player. This did not bode well with the principal, who was hysterically grade driven and primarily concerned with graduating students with honors. Just imagine in Australia (under the British school system) a school with a success/ pass rate of 98.5 percent, the highest in the country. In Australia, much like in Britain, it is commonly recognized that the eleventh and twelfth grades are sorting machines for defining successful and unsuccessful students, in some ways similar to college- versus non-college-bound courses in U.S. public schools, or possibly to college-bound versus vocationally-bound students. Interestingly, Jeannie Oakes[5] has written extensively on how schools institutionally track students in similar ways in the United States. The principal in my school clearly sorted out eleventh graders who weren't going to make his matriculation (twelfth-grade) pass rate increase. Indeed, I was one of the eleventh-grade victims who got jolted out of the system (as a result, my parents decided to immigrate to Israel a year earlier than anticipated).

I recall that in my eighth grade, the same principal called my parents to his office (after I had just scored 15 percent on a history exam) and commented to them as follows: "Mr. and Mrs. Kanpol, I'm sorry to tell you this, but your son will not succeed at this school. You should think of sending him to learn a profession. I think he should be a barber. Yes, that would be a good and honest profession for his talents."
I then interrupted the conversation.

*Barry*: But why did I only get 15 on my history exam?

*Principal*: Because you spelled your name correctly.

As I left the office, humiliated, I wondered what school was really about. I hated this dictator (who, as I was later to write in my diary, reminded me of Adolf Hitler, both physically and in demeanor). I realized that this story has become a part of my argument against the authoritarian elements of schools—individual teachers, grading procedures, student accountability procedures, and so on. In 1991, sitting outside the principal's office, I was soaked in feelings of fear. This principal lived inside of me!

### Gender: Male Dominance

One of my favorite school stories is about an eighth-grade math teacher. I often wondered why I was never a good math student. Maybe it's because I never learned math. I recall Mr. Twomey (name changed) as being thin, tall, slimy, with balding hair, brown teeth, and smelling of tobacco. He had a very deep and threatening voice. He would often shout directly to the males of the class: Now get to work, you morons, or I'll have your behind." The steel rod he carried with him was foreboding.

Mr. Twomey taught us math in an interesting way. As he related directions for math exercises, he always bent over a girls' table, arms around them (at one point his arms were around Lee-Ann, a childhood sweetheart of mine). If only I could be in Mr. Twomey's shoes! If only I could put my arms around Lee-Ann. We (the guys) presumed that the girls in Mr. Twomey's class loved his behavior. I once commented to one of my friends as we walked out of math class, "Surely if Mr. Twomey can put his arms all around the girls, then we stand a chance of succeeding as well!" Indeed, the guys used to joke about girls in rather demeaning ways. Admittedly, I was a major culprit myself—until one day I had the misfortune of having my jaw broken playing football—the day after I joked to all my friends about some encounter that might lead to showing off my sexual prowess. I promised myself then, not to talk about females in ugly terms. My broken jaw was like a message from God. Do not talk about girls in such ways!

Mr. Twomey had taught me a math lesson, all right. Girls can be treated like objects. None of the guys in the eighth grade questioned Mr. Twomey's peculiar methods of teaching math. We wanted to adopt his strategies. Yes, math was fun and hormones were flying, even though I could never pass the subject. Wonder why? Furthermore, treating women as objects was reinforced through the media and at the time through my social relations outside school. In the media Dobie ("Dobie Gillis") always sought after his perceived sexy girlfriend; Wilber ("Mr. Ed") was always maternally taken care of by his wife, particularly if he provided her with the materialistic items that she desired; and Fonzie ("Happy Days") always had swooning women beckoning to his call. Additionally, in my football days, locker-room talk always included parts of the female anatomy. Yes, I was trapped by this male dominance, like it or not and, threatened by it like it or not.

### Fear and Cheating

With the above experiences (especially with the principal) in mind, I lived in fear during my school days. This fear reared its head in countless ways. For example, I was sitting in my eleventh-grade British History class. It was the day before the end-of-the-year exam. Our teacher, Mr. Whacker (name changed), was renowned for failing at least 40 percent of his pupils. As the lesson prior to the final exam ended, Mr. Whacker packed his briefcase quickly and began to move out of the classroom. Before he left, I shouted out:

*Barry*: Sir, aren't you going to wish us luck for the exam tomorrow?

*Mr. Whacker*: Kanpol [pause], you don't really need luck, you need a miracle.

Readers can guess what happened to me at exam time. The passing grade was 50 percent. I received 48 percent, a failing grade.

Fear and the peer pressure at school resulted in the creation of numerous cheating systems designed and organized by the male members of my class. For instance, as we were led into the auditorium (where rows and rows of chairs were set in long, straight lines, quarter after quarter, grade level after grade level), we lined up, the smarties or brains in the front, average in the middle, and the rest (including myself) at the back; those who stereotypically weren't so academically inclined. I felt secure bringing up the rear end of the cheating line, knowing that I would be looking over the shoulders of a person who had received answers from the brains in the front of the line. Cheating became an art, even a hobby. While I laughed with my mates over our successes, I lived with the constant fear that I would fail the subject, get caught in the cheating act, drop out of school, and not live up to my image of a great guy—a sportsman who must not fail his subjects, a womanizer, and a flirt. And, finally, I would deeply disappoint my parents. Yes, cheating had its short-term perks, even though my classmate Gregory scored an 88 on his geography exam and I scored a 65. Besides, I learned that this school rarely checked the signed and returned report cards. As a result, I could change my grades for fear that my parents would enforce some punishment for low achievement. Thus, a 31 in history became an 81, or a 15 became a 75, and so on. Clearly, cheating had its short-term advantages and its long-term miseries.

I recall vividly the 250 people (my parents' friends as well as my own) in the temple who had come to celebrate my bar mitzvah. Little did I understand that my bar mitzvah also represented a fashion parade and that the place where the bar mitzvah was held had immense social status. What I remember distinctly is the fear of standing in front of all these people and talking about the Jewish traditional values of community, connectedness, and family while I also shuddered inwardly at the thought of being found out about for changing the numbers on my recent report card or that one of my friends might tell my parents that we had received our report cards (I had kept it from them until after the bar mitzvah event) or that we had had a test the day before my bar mitzvah. Instead of the bar mitzvah being a simple initiation into manhood in the Jewish tradition, it represented for me a time of great personal conflict, fear, and trepidation.

Call it fear but schools frightened me into nonconformity. I began to see that living on the edge had its short-term advantages. Yet I paid a hefty price for this life style. Parental, school, and peer pressure to achieve big was so prevalent in my life. Maybe that's why I never made it past the eleventh grade in this particular school. After all, according to the principal, I was never going to make it and would be extremely lucky to have a skilled profession. In the eleventh grade, I felt that maybe being a barber was indeed the right profession for me. If only I had listened to the principal a few years earlier!

## Competition

I want to relate three small narratives about competition. First, as elementary school students, we were often rewarded with a large, school emblem stamp in our notebooks for correct or well-completed work. After acquiring six stamps, a candy bar was awarded for strong academic efforts. We competed to see who would acquire the most candy bars in a week. The amount of candy bars received defined who was popular in the class. Competition for the bars was fierce. Students became judgmental of each other based on who had more candy bars. Additionally, at the front of the class, a large poster contained each of our names with the number of times we received school stamps and, subsequently, candy bars. Motivation for learning was both extrinsic and competitive. Reflecting back, I must have felt like Skinner's rat in a box, pushing a lever for some extrinsic and motivational reward, or Pavlov's dog salivating at the mouth. Only in this scenario I was judged critically by peers, teachers, school, and parents by the number of times the lever was pushed.

Second, I clearly recall Alan. Alan was short and stubby. I perceived him to be ugly looking. Yet he always tried hard at sports. When he was picked to be on any team, he would be totally devoted to it. However, he was clumsy and untalented at sports. I was stereotyped as the school jock and always named the team captain. Captains always picked first, and I always chose Alan last. I had to win at all costs—no matter what kind of suffering I caused any Alans of the world. The competitive ethos was so ingrained in my consciousness that human dignity was secondary. I think of Alan often. As I play competitive basketball today, there is a new immigrant Russian (someone who has very limited basketball and athletic skills) on my team. The idea of this old man's league is for everyone to play. It is still hard for me (again as captain) to let go of winning for winning's sake. I remind myself that the Russian immigrant is Alan reincarnated. And, as I think of this, I wonder if I can ever let go of the values that I have been brought up with—values that tend to damage and demean other people in some way or another.

I often ask my students how schools foster this competitive attitude, how so many cultures are all about winning and not necessarily about participating. I tell my students about my eight-year-old daughter who returns home from school crying. She comments, "Those boys always win, and they are on one team and the girls on another." One perceptive student in my Master's of Arts (M.A.) curriculum foundations class reminds me that maybe winning is different for boys than it is for girls.

Then I am reminded that schools can and should be about caring, nurturing, and connected values rather than only about the value of what I would argue to be forms of competition that belittle others. Yes, it seems that even competition is gender inflicted. And then I realize that maybe, just maybe, even though I enjoy writing, publishing also becomes another basketball game to conquer, another lever to push, or another hill to climb for the rewards promulgated by my boyhood competitive instincts. So how many publications do you possess? Where are your publications, and how many book contracts do you have?

Third, I recall Mrs. Forn (name changed), mother of my friend, Gregory. I remember a specific phone call after we received our graded geography test. "So how did Barry do on his exam?" Mrs. Forn asked my mother. "He got a 65," my mother replied. "Oh, my Gregory got an 88," answered Mrs. Forn. Parent pressure reigned supreme and enforced cutthroat competition among even the best of friends. Furthermore, I will admit to the readers of this text that the only reason I earned a 65 was because of the unique cheating system designed by my friends and me. Otherwise, I doubt if I would have scored 35!

Within the framework of fierce competition and the quest to succeed at all costs, competitiveness was instilled in my consciousness—something that came naturally to me every day of my life. It was good for some, less good for others. Obviously it backfired for me. I dropped out of high school in the eleventh grade—Gregory became a lawyer. His parents still speak of him as if he received his 88.

## Stereotyping

For many years my parents had planned on immigrating to Israel. These plans were moved forward by a year due to my dropping out of high school. In Israel I was placed in an American international high school. I remember my history teacher well. She taught a fun class, yet I received a grade of D for the course. Years later, I found myself in Columbus, Ohio, learning about the role of the school in the social order and curriculum theory, and working on my Ph.D. I also participated in events about Israel. One night my now former wife and I went to hear a group discussion about social problems in Israel. I couldn't believe it—there on the panel of discussants was my former history teacher from the American school in Israel. Yes, I was excited. Like a little boy, I felt as if I had to show her where I'd come to academically. I approached her cautiously and said, "Lucy, do you remember me?" She looked hard at me for about five to ten seconds (this, of course, seemed like minutes), and she replied, "Oh yes, you're . . . you're . . . you're the jock." I died inside. Upon reflection, I now realize how stereotyping can be so damaging, fruitless, and disheartening.

With the above in mind, I recall my experiences as an immigrant to Israel—a new culture, with new faces, different habits, and a strange language. Six years passed. I now spoke Hebrew fairly fluently, given my initial resistance to living in the culture. I recall one day speaking to a cab driver. As he dropped me off at my destination he commented (in Hebrew, of course), "You know, you'll never have the correct accent." I recall feeling alienated and worthless (as if I hadn't felt like this all these years that I was an immigrant), stereotyped as one of many who would be looked at as different. I recall the vast amount of bureaucracy I faced every day and the various stereotypes of immigrant populations: "Be careful of the Rumanians, they're sly," "The South Africans are tight with their money," or "Those Arabs will stick you in the back when you're not looking." And so the damaging stereotypes persist today.

## TEACHER EDUCATION

I recall vividly my teacher training program in Israel (which, I may add, was not very different from the ones I taught in Ohio, North Carolina, California, and Pennsylvania). There are many similarities among the programs, and some differences. I was to become an English teacher. Luckily, unlike other prospective teachers who were in training with me, I had already found employment in a high school that was in urgent need of a teacher replacement for its ninth- and eleventh-grade English language and literature classes. So the real world of teaching with various discipline problems, different student learning styles, the hustle and bustle of a busy teacher schedule and so on hit me while I was still a student at Tel Aviv University's teacher education program.

There is no doubt in my mind that I was what could be described as a snotty know-it-all. I was determined that it was going to be difficult to teach me how to teach because I perceived myself as so talented and already involved in the battlefield of discipline and the reality of teaching kids who didn't really want to learn. Yet through my initial stubbornness and obnoxious attitude, I was privy to one very important and central fact: There was a major difference between (a) what teacher educators were saying school was about, (b) state-mandated curricular guidelines handed to me, and (c) what actually went on within the four walls of the classroom. Fortunately or unfortunately, as a prospective teacher I saw through the contradictions—and it bothered me greatly.

Mrs. Haliday (name changed) was my main teacher-educator within this particular teacher education program. She was British and sixty-five years of age, with a traditional mentality, a set mind of how a class should be run—that is, *her* way. Our personalities clashed. As the only male teacher trainee among a class of thirty other females, I was intimidated enough without the antics of this woman. I believed that out in the field I experienced firsthand the discipline problems and the day-to-day pranks of kids out to initiate a beginning teacher. At the university I would prepare my so-called inductive teacher lessons (in which students cognitively arrived at conclusions through a critical process involving rules and laws) for the class and Haliday to scrutinize. I was so confident of my success that I even threw in a reality check by exposing the class to some deductive English language teaching methods (in which students are simply fed rules, laws of language, and explanations of why and how, which students need at certain times of the day—say, first period at 7:30 Monday morning). I recall Haliday telling me that the latter way was not the correct way to teach and that I would probably bore students. I complained to Haliday that in the real world outside the university walls there was a struggle with students that we were not learning in this program. I know now that I was a brash twenty-two-year-old, but I was also aware that in some part I was right about this issue. There were different learning styles in the classrooms, different cultures, different types of teacher and student and parent expectations. These issues had not so much to do with teaching as with pure sociology and/or philosophy of education. Instead of learning a whole course on Greek teachers, I felt that a course or two on cultural issues, social concerns, the disadvantaged and the advantaged would have benefited me much more. Maybe then I could have applied what was being taught to me about Plato and the good society to real-world considerations in the 1980s. Of course, not surprisingly, I received the lowest grade in the class for my efforts. I did not and could not conform to a system that undercut me. Yes, I was very confused at the time.

Believe it or not, I had to take two more courses with Haliday—the one I dreaded the most was the videotape course in which I would present a mini-lesson to be critiqued by the class. I used this lesson to talk on conflict and the feminization of teaching. How stupid of me to think that Haliday and the ten females in my class would appreciate these efforts to present a controversial issue. I learned quickly that efforts to present a conflict situation or to see various contradictions are usually smothered both in teacher education departments and at school sites. How did this class deal with my issue? They said that my posture wasn't correct, my tone was a little off, I wasn't sensitive to all students, I was "too passionate about the material to present it objectively," and I probably should have been dressed differently. Despite my overconfidence in my teaching abilities, I knew as I left Haliday's exciting and fun-filled class that either teaching wasn't for me or these university professors really had a chip on their shoulders. Or, maybe I was stupid! I should have played the game better!

Despite my internal war and external confrontations with teachers like Haliday, I managed to complete my certification. It took forever. I was even able to trick my student teaching supervisor into thinking that I was a masterful English teacher by doing it the university's way. I was lucky then to have a ninth-grade class that understood the situation and played along with me. Yes, they behaved, acted as if they cared, and made me look great. They appreciated the free time afterwards and the games I had designed for them that, although inclusive of some English lesson, were also fun.

I revisited Tel Aviv University only a month after I had completed my certification program. As I was walking up the stairs, who should I see walking the corridors but Haliday. She was carrying a typewriter. As we approached each other (I would rather have avoided her, but I had no option), she slipped and fell right in front of me. Here was this older woman sprawled across the floor with no one in sight to help her but yours truly. Honestly, the thought crossed my mind. Do I let her get up herself? As I looked down at her, giggling on the inside, serious on the outside, I extended my outstretched hand and commented, "Can I help you, Mrs. Haliday?" Yes, I had finally gotten my revenge! She was at my mercy.

## ME THE TEACHER

I became a teacher for a simple reason: I could use my English language for a profession in a country where Hebrew was the dominant language. I felt that the English language was a rare and usable commodity, and thus I pursued a teaching career using that English tool. Teaching for me was, despite my innate ability to help people, needed to make ends meet.

I want to recount some instances in my public school teaching to capture the themes outlined in prior pages. I taught grades nine through twelve in a fairly well-established high school in a working-class suburb of Tel Aviv. I first entered Gymnasia Realit as a full-time substitute teacher. I took over a tenth-grade class, presumably the worst class on campus. Thirty-eight students stared at me as the principal warned them not to make any trouble. As he left the classroom, students started to talk loudly. I was all of twenty-two years of age. The students were not more than six or seven years younger than me. I taught English language and literature. I distinctly remember handing out a writing assignment. Four well-built males situated themselves at the back and didn't want to work. In fact, they talked more about the upcoming school basketball and handball games than the content I had wanted them to learn. I had a hard time trying to get students to concentrate on their work. However, I also remember that the only way I could connect with these kids (especially the males) was at lunchtime on the basketball court. I learned early in my teaching career that if I could relate to students through their most important experiences, teaching could become enjoyable. Thus, equating teaching to students' personal experiences was the first lesson I learned as a teacher. In short, to reach these jocks, I had to talk the language of the jock. Luckily, that was easy, given my past experiences as a student and sportsman in Australia. Teaching English, then, became much easier after that and far more enjoyable.

My next experience reminds me of my days under the tutelage of Mr. Twomey. I was to teach twenty eleventh-grade girls the next year. Here I was, a rookie teacher, unmarried, with sixteen- and seventeen-year-olds eyeing me—or was I paranoid? Was I eyeing them? This class was the hardest I ever had to teach. There was clear sexual tension in the air. I distinctly recall favoring some girls over others because I was attracted to them. I couldn't admit or implicate myself as a sexist then. Today I can. As a young male, I was vulnerable. Although I never crossed the sexual boundaries as a teacher (i.e., I behaved in what I believed to be a morally correct way), I certainly thought about what would happen if I wasn't morally correct, and I let it go at that. However, today I do realize that sexism reigned supreme then and now. All that the guys spoke about in this school related in large part to sex and sport. Often, the talk about sex was demeaning. I wasn't privy to listen to the girls speak about the opposite gender, but I do recall the unbuttoned blouses, red lipstick, and mascara that they wore. Mr. Twomey would have had a ball. I must say that I was a popular teacher—even though I couldn't discipline the class well. I wonder why!

I fondly remember an eleventh-grade class I taught. Thirty-five students sat in their desks to listen attentively to me read aloud *The Death of a Salesman*. Coby sat at the back and didn't want anything to do with reading or discussing any aspects of the play. In fact, when I assigned an exercise and asked him to complete the required work, he replied, "I don't feel like it." I was offended. Here I was, a young and enthusiastic teacher and there was the student—also young, but totally unenthusiastic. In my eyes, I was the teacher and he the student. He had to listen to me. There was clear hierarchy and authority.

*Barry*: Coby, put away that paper and please start to work.

*Coby*: No, I'm not interested in this.

*Barry*: Put down that paper, now.

At this point other male students next to Coby followed suit. They also began to occupy themselves with things other than the text. Coby had this sly smirk on his face as if to say, "I have you now."

*Barry*: Coby, start to work, now.

*Coby*: Make me!

By this time, all the students in the class were very interested in this exchange. I was an inexperienced teacher. What could I do?

*Barry*: Coby come out here, now.

*Coby*: No!

*Barry*: [tone increase] Now!

Coby came to the front of the class, He was small and thin and I was tall and well built. I recall how I felt. I wanted to physically throw him out of the classroom window. I could have literally done that. Coby approached me with a smirk on his face and stood in front of me. Only inches separated us. I told him that he would work. I was on the verge of getting physical with him. I nearly poked him. He smiled and calmly said, "Just try it, Mr. Kanpol, and you'll be out of this school and out of a job, I'll make sure of that."

This experience still often haunts me. I tell education majors that I fully expected Coby to acquiesce to my authority. More importantly, I realize now that in fact I was being purely authoritarian, demanding Coby (and many like him) to do something he didn't want to do. I never found out about Coby and his personal experiences—his likes or dislikes. I simply wasn't fair to Coby. He didn't disturb anyone until I made an issue out of his lackluster effort to learn English literature. Coby represented a very real, everyday discipline problem, and I handled the problem traditionally. The principal was immediately told of the class happenings. He dealt with Coby in a harsh manner. I can't help but think about the principal I had in my school years (the one who wanted to skin me alive and hang my pieces on the wall). Could I have been equally damaging to Coby as well?

I want to share one other typical incident. I rode a bus to school daily. It dropped me off near school at 7:25 A.M. Class started at 7:30. I usually ran the few meters to school and was in my class with a minute or so to spare. One particular morning, it was raining heavily. I had broken a toe playing rugby, so I hobbled to school and arrived two minutes late, drenched. The principal was standing outside my classroom door looking at his watch and growling, "Why are you late?" There I was, a very wet and extremely frustrated person with a broken toe, feeling misunderstood and underappreciated. I then realized that in school I was accountable for my time as well as my curriculum. Originally, I became a teacher because with my command of the language I thought it would be easy to teach, but also because I believed teachers could be autonomous. This one lesson, among many others, taught me that teachers were accountable for every move they made, rather than really autonomous. I felt like a kid once more, accountable to my principal. I felt as if I had scored 15 on my history exam. My oppressive student experiences were linked to my experiences as a teacher.

With the preceding stories in mind, I want to assure readers that there is a very close relationship between the kinds of stories I told both as a student and as a teacher and the present public discourse on education. I now turn to this public discourse as a way to bridge the gap with my personal stories.

## THE PUBLIC

In probably one of the most startling books written on education over the last twenty years, Jonathan Kozol in *Savage Inequalities* reveals just how devastating an unequal education system can be. One excerpt from Kozol's book will capture that particular spirit:

The problems are systematic. The number of teachers over 60 years of age in the Chicago system is twice that of the teachers under 30. The salary scale, too low to keep exciting, youthful teachers in the system, leads the city to rely on low paid subs, who represent more than a quarter of Chicago's teaching force . . . but even substitute teachers in Chicago are quite frequently in short supply. On an average morning in Chicago, 5,700 children in 190 classrooms come to school to find they have no teacher . . . a student in auto mechanics at Du Sable High School says he'd been in class for 16 weeks before he learned to change a tire. His first teacher quit at the beginning of the year. Another teacher slept through most of the semester. He would come in, the student says, and tell students, "You can talk. Just keep it down." Soon he would be asleep.[6]

The preceding quote and subsequent educational ramifications are symptomatic of a public school system that has been described by many specialists in the government, academics and teachers, as failing or dead zones. Moreover, one must summarize these educational problems as more than just of dropouts or of low incomes. Clearly, there are economic problems that involve monies distribution and tax-related issues. However, there are also the cultural problems of sexual bias that schools reproduce and the curriculum debate of whether to have national testing. In the following sections I outline some of the media presentations of these issues. I have divided the issues into three general themes: economics, teacher accountability, and sexism.

### Economics

We live in harsh and changing economic times. As I write, America is coming out of a deep recession. Like former President Bush who insisted that he was the education president, President Clinton has continued with Bush's education plan. *Yet*, in Pennsylvania, the first budget to suffer is education. Education is not a priority for the U.S. government. All over the United States, teachers have been sarcastic about the Bush plan. The *New York Times* (February 12, 1992 Section A, p. 23) reported that the budget cuts directly impact the classroom. One principal comments on the economic inequities of schools, "Some [school districts] can afford to spend more than other school districts. . . . That's the way the system works." This comment relates to the inequitable economic situation schools find themselves in. In Mount Healthy, Ohio, where teachers complained about the lack of basic necessities such as scissors, out-of-date encyclopedias, no pay raises for three years, and local tax increases; even more state cuts lurk. Says a principal from Mount Healthy, "This is my 24th year in education, and this is the worst I've ever seen it."

Perhaps even worse than the growing endemic district problems are the anomalies of school financing, which are based on property wealth. The *New York Times* (February 12, 1992) reported that there are wealthy school districts, such as Amagansett, Long Island, where classes contain an average of sixteen pupils, and poorer districts, where classes can range up to forty and perhaps more students per class. Within the budget crisis, poorer school districts (especially in the inner cities in the United States) are struggling to cut spending, whereas in more affluent suburbs such as Amagansett, Bridgehampton, and Quoque on Long Island education is personalized and far more is expended per pupil. One doesn't have to look hard in an inner-city school to notice the lack of computers and extracurricular materials as well as see the appalling physical condition of the classrooms. A teacher in the Amagansett school district, who has also taught in two other Suffolk County school districts (on Long Island), comments that in other school districts, "teachers had to scrounge for supplies. They would give you your staples for the month in an envelope. Here, whatever I need for the kids I can pretty much get."

Sadly, the economic crunch has meant a shock treatment to the average teacher in the average middle-class school district. In Montebello, California (*New York Times*, February 19, 1992) the average class ranges from thirty-five to forty students. In part, the reason for this is that the budget cut forced the school district to slash spending by 20 percent. Perhaps even more poignant is that Montebello spends only $4,000 per student (well below the average in the United States, which ranges, depending on the district, from $5,000 to $6,000 per student) and has a highly Hispanic population. In this district as in others, there is an increase in teacher turnover, higher student truancy, and less money per student. All this adds up to growing despair in these kinds of districts. In summary, the inner cities are places where minorities receive an unequal stake in budget decisions, teacher quality, and equipment.[7]

Today it seems that the distribution of wealth has affected profoundly the haves and have nots of the United States in terms of education. With that in mind, it is interesting to note that President Bush compiled the America 2000 plan for all students, generalizable over the whole United States, irrespective of race, class, or gender—certainly a noble project if everyone were equal with respect to finances.

### Teacher Accountability

Current accountability schemes situate teachers to be less creative as instructional leaders than they might otherwise hope to be. For the most part, teachers are responsible for making sure that students get through each grade with predetermined knowledge from a state-mandated curriculum. The public debate on a national curriculum is prevalent today. For example, the *New York Times* February 4, 1992, B5) reports that

an eight-month study by a panel of educators will recommend to the New Jersey Board of Education on Wednesday the uniform testing of fourth, eighth, and eleventh grade students in science, civics, geography and history, as well as the core skills of reading, writing and mathematics. The testing is aimed as establishing a statewide educational assessment and monitoring system . . . under a law passed last year, the authorities are required to devise a uniform system for evaluating performance in New Jersey Schools.

On May 18, 1992 the *Patriot News* (the Harrisburg, Pennsylvania daily) printed an article arguing for the need for a national curriculum which would support a high-tech society. Carol Baer of the *Patriot News* comments as follows:

An article from *Newsweek* recently told how the Lang family moved from Alaska to Colorado to Texas. These moves meant adjusting to three very different schools in three very different districts. When the Langs moved to Texas, the teacher expected every child to know their multiplication tables by heart. In Denver, fourth graders hadn't memorized them yet. This caused their son to have stomachaches and he didn't want to go to school. The Langs eventually hired a tutor so their son would catch up to his classmates, and his stomachaches were over.

It is perhaps sad to think that a student may fare worse in a particular state. But obviously this problem can sometimes be solved without a private tutor. Perhaps even more crucial is the notion that within the national curriculum and teacher accountability model, the notion of restructuring schools appears. Baer comments once more:

Successfully restructuring schools will require states to rethink the nature and mix of accountability mechanisms upon which they rely. States will need to fashion systems that focus on educational outcomes and that provide strong incentives for improved results throughout the system by linking performance with tangible consequences in the form of rewards and sanctions.

This restructuring implies that teachers conform to set standards, goals, and objectives. A national curriculum also imposes on the teacher a performance, outcomes-based model approach to education. This implies that students are all similar—that they all have similar needs and wants and in fact can reach similar academic ends. Interesting to note is that Baer's article did not go without rebuttal. Jay Bodenstein (a former teacher certification student of mine) commented in the *Patriot News* on May 25, 1992 in reply to Baer:

The rich social differences that make up our nation are not addressed by applying national standards to education. The call for national testing and standards completely ignores the social and cultural diversity that make up the nation . . . what national standard can measure the years of dedication and experience that enable a teacher to empower students to think critically and attain self-actualization . . . in searching for common solutions to what appear to be common national problems, it is essential to regard the social, ethnic, cultural, religious and economic differences that make simple solutions likely.

Bodenstein's point is well taken. How, he argues, can a restructuring of schools hold teachers accountable when there are so many diverse cultures, learning styles, socioeconomic and cultural differences? How, I argue, can any curriculum account for all cultural differences? The argument over a national curriculum presupposes a unified school system committed to a curriculum for every student based on equal ability. In my own schooling experiences in Australia, I could never meet the school's rigid requirements for graduation. I was a social outcast in this school. No teacher could help me reach the standards, no matter how good he or she was. I was stereotyped by the principal as a failure. Additionally, in my teacher education training experiences, it was assumed that only one way of teaching was the best. Clearly, no mention of students with different learning styles was dealt with.

Why then, I ask, must teachers be held accountable for areas in schools and the curriculum that they cannot control? The debate over national curricular and teacher accountability models will continue for years to come. Alda Hanna (the *Patriot News*, October 27, 1992), a teacher for twenty-eight years, comments on how a multicultural education may offer us a new perspective on a national curriculum and teacher accountability: "School is boring, so you have to do things to make it interesting. You have to do things that children will be interested in, what they can relate to." Clearly, in a multicultural society, some teachers extend beyond national curriculum boundaries precisely because of student diversity. Thus, teachers become accountable to diversity and not national standards only. Teachers in Hanna's Harrisburg school are not throwing away the traditional curriculum (e.g., about the pilgrims, the Revolutionary War, the presidents, or English literature). It seems that the need arises for teachers to think seriously as to what end are they being held accountable and for what reasons. Teacher accountability is tied inextricably to the national curriculum and national goals. Most prospective and present teachers I meet in university classrooms are adverse to such a curriculum. I personally faltered under such a systematic and (I thought) boring use of curriculum. Presently the high dropout rate in the inner cities climbs rampantly[8] under such a system. Why then do we continue with it? There are no easy answers, although many critical theorists will argue, as I do, that a high dropout rate ensures class division, and this is needed to produce meaningless, low-paid, and exploited labor.

### Sexism

It is extremely difficult for me to talk about sexism. As a white middle-class male, I consider myself socially privileged. Overall I received a solid educational foundation, in spite of initially dropping out of school. I grew up in a society where males were considered number 1. I grew up in a patriarchially based family, where the division of labor was clear cut and role expectations were defined simply; male and females had their structured places in the world. I went to school and observed that males and females were tracked into different subject areas—girls into the humanities and boys into the sciences. Additionally, I was continually observing teachers like Mr. Twomey and his treatment of adolescent girls. Growing up with sexism as a part of my life was bad enough. Yet seeing it in daily operation, in the news and rampant in schools and universities is extremely disturbing.

In an article in the *New York Times* (February 7, 1992), Susan Chira reports that "school is still a place of unequal opportunity, where girls face discrimination from teachers, textbooks, tests and their male classmates." Chira reports that in a recent study,

1. Teachers pay less attention to girls than boys.
2. Girls still lag in mathematics and science scores, and even those who do well in those subjects tend not to choose math and science careers.
3. Reports of sexual harassment of girls by their male classmates are increasing.

4. Some tests remain biased against girls, hurting their chances of scholarships and getting into college.

5. School textbooks still ignore or stereotype women, and girls learn almost nothing in school about many of their most pressing problems, like sexual abuse, discrimination, and depression.

Such reports confirm my view that sexism in schools is not only related to sexual harassment and/or sexual abuse but becomes a national past-time, amplified in many areas of curriculum, teacher-student relationships, and home relationships with mothers, fathers, grandparents, and brothers and sisters. I would go as far as to argue that sexism varies for different cultures, depending on the culture—minority or not!

Not unrelated to the aforementioned issues are abortion concerns. In a recent article in the Harrisburg *Patriot News* (February 24, 1992, section 8, p. 1), Wythe Keever reports on a math teacher who is suing his union "because he opposes the use of his dues to support abortion rights." The math teacher comments, "As a Christian, I believe life begins at conception. . . . I don't believe the union should be involved in supporting something like that . . . unions should just stick to education and leave individuals to make their own decisions on abortion." Underlying these statements are a number of issues. First is the issue of a union's role. Second is the issue of community involvement in issues such as abortion. Sexism raises its ugly head when issues of abortion are not connected to sexism. Third, and perhaps most important, the issue of sexism, abortion rights, or the right of choice is negated in this article by the lengthy discussion that appears later on about where union dues go and what they are used for.

Clearly, our schools are in conflict. As recently as May 16, 1993, the *Patriot News* published an article on what should schools teach. The public was divided, and there were conflictual issues. Thirty-three percent voted not to teach religion, 67 percent voted yes; 43 percent voted not to teach about what homosexuality is, 57 percent voted yes; 43.5 percent voted no to making condoms available to students, 56.5 percent voted yes. The public was divided on how much the federal government should spend on schools. Issues such as drug education, smaller class size, broader curriculum, a safer environment for students, better teaching for minorities, more discipline, better-qualified administrators, better sex education, better-qualified teachers, and more individual attention for students haunt both the schools and public opinion.

The above news items and public conflicts, divided between economics, teacher accountability, and teacher sexism as well as countless other issues, are only the tip of the iceberg in school issues. As we progress in this book, some of these issues become paramount as we begin to understand the theoretical and practical importance of schools in our society.

### Putting Personal Stories into Context in Light of the Public Debate on Education

The personal and public element of these stories must always be scrutinized. That is, I try and glean meaning from them (and others) on a continual basis. I do not own these stories. They are a part of the larger culture in which I was raised and in which I live now. I have no claim to truth regarding their meaning, even though they really happened to me and are happening in public. I set these stories and news items up for scrutiny in a sort of reflexive way, where both students and I can unravel their plot, thicken their meaning, and discuss similar and different occurrences in our personal lives. Of course, open and honest dialogue with students means owning up to one's past and present, race, class, and gender biases, hopefully enough to be both critical of one's biases while building language and thought processes that change the kind of social relations I have described. This book, then, in large part will respond directly to this change issue. I now outline the organizational structure of the book.

### THE CHAPTERS

Chapter 2 will outline the critical theory movement in education. This movement is in many ways a response to the conditions schools find themselves in today—high dropout rates in inner-city and suburban schools, sexism, racial tensions, and class distinctions.

Chapters 3, 4, and 5 describe recently completed studies of teachers in three different grade levels and diversely populated areas of the United States. Each study stands on its own in terms of the similar and different critical elements it brings to us. Rather than analyze each study in depth (although I will do some analysis and interpretation), I describe the dynamics of such things as various curriculum usages, and teacher-principal and teacher-teacher relationships, and I leave the bulk of the analysis to the various teachers and prospective teachers who read this book. To facilitate this, each chapter closes with both discussion questions and exercises for the class to complete.

Chapters 6 and 7 draw on the concepts of Chapter 2. Chapter 6 presents an interdisciplinary curriculum development attempt at some of the critical theory ideas presented earlier in the book. This chapter, it is hoped, will guide teachers to a better understanding on the possibilities of implementing critical pedagogy as a teaching tool. Chapter 7 includes an interview with a noted critical theorist and a student from my educational foundation's class. Again, the material presented in Chapter 7 is related to the earlier chapters and builds on some of those ideas.

## NOTES

1. National Commission on Excellence, "A Nation at Risk: An Imperative for Educational Reform." *Education Week*, April 27, 1983, pp. 12–16.

2. Henry Giroux, *Living Dangerously: Multiculturalism and the Politics of Difference* (New York: Peter Lang Publishers, 1993), pp. 15–16.

3. Jonathan Kozol, *Savage Inequalities* (New York: Crown, 1991).

4. Jean Anyon, "Social class and the hidden curriculum of work." *Journal of Education*, 162(1), 1980.

5. Jeannie Oakes, *Keeping Track: How Schools Structure Inequality* (New Haven, Conn.: Yale University Press, 1985).

6. Kozol, *Savage Inequalities*, pp. 51–52.

7. Kozol, *Savage Inequalities*.

8. Kozol, *Savage Inequalities*.

## CLASSROOM ACTIVITIES

1. a. Break the class into groups of four or five students. Let students (individually at first within the group) discuss their educationally similar and different experiences.

   b. Assign one person from each group to take notes as other groups relate their particular similar and different educational experiences to the class.

   c. Regroup and discuss the commonalities of similarities and differences of educational experiences.

2. Form a circle. Let students respond to what their educational experiences have been by encouraging them to tell stories of their past as related to curriculum, sexism, competition, stereotypes, and so on.

3. Have students collect news items about education. Divide the class into topical news items groups. Discuss current events in education from the standpoint of the news items.

4. Have students write down what their philosophy of education is presently. Have students compare and contrast in groups these responses. Compete the same exercise at the end of the book or of the course.

## QUESTIONS FOR DISCUSSION

1. Why do you want to become a teacher?

2. What is a great teacher?

3. Discuss the kind of environment you grew up in. Was it educationally conducive?

4. What role did your parents play in your education?

5. What values did your parents instill in you regarding education and other issues, such as sex, race, and class?

6. Was there peer pressure to succeed or fail in your school? If so, how did it come about?

7. How have your past school experiences affected your views on education today?

8. Discuss the race, class, and gender relationships in your past educational experiences. That is, how as a female or male can you relate to school experiences?

9. How have the relationships mentioned in question 8 affected your views on race, class, and gender?

10. Discuss what you consider to be a good versus a not-so-good teacher. What values do these teachers promote?

11. What do you consider your primary role as a teacher-to-be?

# 2

# Teachers' Lives in a Period of Crisis: Tensions of Meaning

## INTRODUCTION

We live in times of changing demographies and social upheaval. One doesn't have to search too far in current world events to see this—for example, consider the massive immigration of Hispanics, South East Asians, and now Russians to the United States; Russian immigration to Israel; social upheaval in Germany; prospects of the same in the Middle East; economic recession in the United States and the world; increasing unemployment; and social upheavals such as in Los Angeles following the verdict in the Rodney King case. Despite this, schools in the United States have remained extremely traditional, going about business as usual. Indeed, schools vary little from the social efficiency movement of the 1920s, one whose function was to explore and implement the most efficient ways to increase student achievement (through higher test scores) and which saw teacher output as a form of accountable production. The more one produced, the better. This implied the need for better and/or more efficient teaching and student learning. Teachers in this socially efficient system are judged by how well students achieve, particularly on standardized tests. The higher the student achievement, the better and/or more productive a teacher is judged to be. Schools, it has been argued, in direct relationship with social efficiency ideology, prepare students for the market economy. They do it, argue Bowles and Gintis (1976), in unequal ways. That is, race, class, and gender are distributed unevenly and unequally into the work force in massive ways.

And, in large part, students are tracked into social class divisions (e.g., college-bound chemistry classes in high school versus science classes; those students taking calculus versus those taking shop; students on the dean's list versus the others). The list could go on and on.

Even now, years after the roots of the social efficiency movement were established, schools have installed even stricter teacher accountability models, assertive discipline plans, vastly increased standardized testing (as of today in the United States there are over 100 million standardized tests given per year), as well as a standardized curriculum with its pre-packaged teacher-proof materials.

As I write, deep concerns about the U.S. economy predominate in the White House. Education in the United States can be connected to the economy in at least two traditional ways: funding, and the commonly accepted idea that schools must prepare students for a competitive national and international (global) economy. Nothing could describe this better than the fairly recent national reports (e.g., A Nation at Risk) and former President Bush's insistence that we become the top nation economically. Included in one of the six major objectives in Bush's America 2000 plan is to increase student achievement nationally. Of course, the fallacious assumption here is that if achievement scores increase, there will be a natural tendency to better the economy and, by so doing, help establish equal access to knowledge and equal social relations among student learners. Although President Clinton shows signs of increasing educational funds, the emphasis on the relationship between education and the economy remains a top priority.

As elaborated in the previous chapter, education is in a budget squeeze of great magnitude. In fact, the hardest hit in education are the public institutes of higher education, especially in Pennsylvania and California. How can education departments in higher education function to educate prospective teachers in a qualitatively better way when those professors teaching in- and preservice teachers are under the gun to teach more classes themselves to meet the budget cuts as well as to publish and serve on committees for tenure? The emphasis for education professors, it seems, is on increasing publication rates and higher student/teacher ratios, rather than on dealing qualitatively with issues of in- and preservice teachers and the surrounding cultural milieu (i.e., inner-city schools and their particular cultural, social, and economic realities).

Concurrently, it is worth noting, schools have been variously described as dumping grounds for the economically disadvantaged, in many cases exacerbating the poverty-stricken inner-city school environment. It seems that not a lot is being done to help the disadvantaged, despite some programs like Head Start that attempt to deal with these issues. Less is being done in higher education.

Critical theory, in large part, is both a reaction to and a pragmatic response to the educational problems mentioned above. Within what I shall term the critical theory literature, there is an abundance of relevant information that depicts the unequal social relations of race, class, and gender that public schools reproduce.[1] There is also literature that departs from the notion that schools must be traditional sites only and, rather, shows how teachers' roles may vary and may serve either to reinforce race, class, and gender functions or produce alternative meanings for teachers' lives. Within the realm of critical social theory, and with an understanding that schools are mainly traditional sites, this book offers the reader both a means and a method to "do" critical theory, a very different way of conceiving education despite the traditional limitations (class size, space, official curriculum, policy limitations, old teaching methodologies) that restrict such aspirations. The doing of critical theory has been called in the educational literature critical pedagogy.[2] Critical pedagogy refers to the means and methods that test and hope to change the structures of schools that allow inequalities. Critical pedagogy is a cultural-political tool that takes seriously the notion of human differences, particularly as these differences relate to race, class, and gender. In its most radical sense, critical pedagogy seeks to unoppress the oppressed and unite people in a shared language of critique, struggle, and hope to end various forms of human suffering. Here, the link between university professors and public school teachers is both vital and necessary for social change and transformation and cannot be underestimated. Critical pedagogy incorporates a moral vision of human justice and decency as its common vision. Finally, critical pedagogy also addresses how one's beliefs and faith are embedded in schooling. Under this rubric, a prophetic commitment on the part of the teacher, one that resides on hope, humility, decisions against despair, against permanent consignment to what I will describe as institutional chaos (race, class, and gender inequalities), against oppression, barrenness, and exile from freedom become the guiding light. Justice and compassion for a critical pedagogy tradition reign supreme. Critical pedagogy, then, is indeed a moral enterprise. With this in mind, critical pedagogy is the major concern of this book. Before I outline what I believe to be fundamental concepts within a critical pedagogy theoretical framework, a brief history of critical theory is in order because critical theory and critical pedagogy are bound inextricably.

## CRITICAL THEORY

Critical theory established its roots in Western Marxist philosophy. The interpretative emphasis here was on both mass cultural relations of society (gender, family, aesthetics, popular culture, art, etc.) and on orthodox Marxism, in which the interpretative emphasis was reduced to society's relationship to the economy. Related to schools, an orthodox

Marxist interpretation attributes student failure to lower socioeconomic status. Here, strict Marxist analyses of schools (Bowles and Gintis, 1976) view how low, middle, and upper classes are created as economic divisions in schools. These divisions are supported by parent income and status. Within this interpretation, it becomes predictable as to which students will succeed and fail in the acquisition of cultural capital (knowledge, skills, values, and attitudes) needed for upward mobility.

Other critical theorists (broadly defined as Neo-Marxists) view schools also as a cultural concern. Here schools are seen as encompassing subordinated relationships that are both reproduced and produced through authority, power, and control issues. From a Neo-Marxist perspective, then, one must view schools not only as institutions whose function it is to produce economic inequities but also from a culturally productive perspective. That is, schools also produce different cultures. These cultures, argue educational theorists (Willis, 1977, 1990), produce alternative meanings and symbols to the stagnant stereotypical classical Marxist analysis of schools. Willis argues that groups of students resist institutional logic (individualism in favor of group solidarity), mechanisms of control, and authority structures despite their often failed attempts to rise above their social position.

The above two Marxist views are regarded with great skepticism by critical pedagogists precisely because they are theorists of despair. These theories do not allow education consumers to see how schools can become authentic social and culturally transformative sites.

The roots of critical theory depict how the Industrial Revolution transformed Europe. As a result of the Industrial Revolution, the development of commodity-based societies propelled capitalism to its peak in many countries. Within this capitalistic (economic/political) system, race, class, and gender divisions became increasingly apparent. An example would be the feminization of teaching as women began to work in the 1850s. Many women began to teach. This was viewed as work naturally extending from the domestic side of the home. Women were expected to be nurturers and carers. Ironically it is these values that sometimes demean and/or stereotype both women and the teaching profession. Today, approximately 87 percent of elementary teachers are female (Apple, 1986).

The history of the United States was also structured by the Industrial Revolution. This includes our education system. The critical theory movement rose, at least indirectly, as a result of the Industrial Revolution and especially in response to the World Wars. Events such as the fall of Czarism in Russia, the seizing of power by the Bolshevik Party, the foundations of the German imperial system, the triumphs of the Russian revolutionaries and the resultant economic blockades and economic underdevelopment, the divisions within the German working class, massive inflation, high unemployment and little sign of economic recovery and political stability instigated, at least in part, the rise of the critical theory movement. World War II propelled the Frankfurt School (which included a handful of German intellectuals who viewed the atrocities of the wars with both anger and disdain) to its most critical points of society. In short, the Frankfurt School sought a new moral social order, a social emancipation from the various economic, social, and cultural oppressive qualities, such as social prejudices and economic inequalities.

As an intellectual and practical critical movement, one of the Frankfurt School's mottos was for individuals and groups of people to recollect or recapture a past or history (which is understood particularly from the perspective of human oppression and suffering) that was in danger of falling into obscurity. To recapture history and the alienation, subordination, oppression, and pain suffered by others and ourselves is part of what critical theorists then and now term a struggle for social emancipation.

A major cause for social ills, argue critical theorists, lies in the capitalist relations of production. As an economic system, capitalism forces us to be a commodity-based society bent on competing viciously to gain ascendancy over others. In schools, this translates into the number of stickers children compete for, higher-grade success rates, and awards for sporting and academic accomplishments. My elementary and high school days as described in the previous chapter are typical examples. Social class division is always apparent (typified by different levels of district funding). Real race and gender antagonisms, unequal and stereotypical divisions of labor, and high immigrant populations with problematic inner-city demographies exist in and around schools. Critical theorists and critical pedagogists argue that alternatives to an educational system that on the one hand preaches equal opportunity through values such as hard work, self-discipline, and motivation and on the other hand supports inequality within social, cultural, and economic relations must be realized and changed. According to critical educational and social theorists, this change will result in far less student alienation, subordination, and oppression of peoples. This change will, argue critical theorists and critical pedagogists, bring the education system closer to the democratic ideals that the United States and the Constitution were founded on, which hold morality at a high official but not pragmatic plane.

As a social movement, critical theory caught the imagination of students and intellectuals with full force in the 1960s and 1970s. With the advent of the civil rights, gay, lesbian, environmental, and feminist movements, education critical social theorists have been engaged both inside and outside the United States in a heated debate over the multiple social and cultural relationships schools have with their clientele: students, teachers, and administrators. From a critical theory lens, these theorists have asked, How do schools reproduce inequality? What mechanisms do schools use to reinforce a school system that alienates, oppresses, and subordinates

teachers and students? What alternatives exist for the practitioner to subvert a system and produce an alternative and just vision for schools? Unfortunately, critical theorists have been involved mainly in the first two
questions. They have not been involved as heavily in the last question.

With this in mind, this book will also attempt, at least in part, to answer
this last question. Before I outline how I might do this, a small diversion
to the literature on teachers and critical theory is in order.

### A Review of the Literature

The literature on teachers (and what can be defined broadly as the
launching of a critical social theory of education and its development)
divides itself into earlier empirical works[3] and theoretical works by authors who not only deal with the empirical findings of their own or others, but who also undertake theoretical formulations of education within
a wider critical theory context.[4] The bulk of these works deal with tensions of meaning within educational theory and practice, mainly tensions
that involve the old sociology of education and the new sociology of
education. Tensions of meaning exist around the differing interpretations
of this major question: What is the role of schools in the social order?

In these works, critical theory in education has been established both
to question and act to offset unequal relations between people in the
school (e.g., as related to income spent per student and gender stereotypes). A major tension that a critical theorist has to deal with is between
the meaning of a traditional and a critical lens of education. The traditional school is structured hierarchically, boasts high IQ results, and
tracks students into predetermined work slots. This kind of school often
possesses a stereotypical view of what counts as success, professionalism,
empowerment, effectiveness, excellence, and a clear division of labor,
which gender does what, and in which areas each gender will succeed.
This view differs from those that advocate the critical stance on schools.
These theorists and practitioners believe that schools should challenge
the stereotypical and traditional education platforms. I could go on about
the inequalities that schools, at least in this country, reinforce. My aim in
this chapter, however, is not to summarize tensions of meaning from an
abstract theoretical viewpoint. Rather, I will first analyze conceptually important and key concepts that any teacher can use in the formulation of
a critical theory for classroom practice. A critical pedagogist (one who
undertakes critical theory as a form of practice for teaching) will need to
make distinctions between what I shall term traditional uses of concepts
and their more critical uses. These concepts must be understood and will
be referred to throughout the rest of the chapters. Second, I will outline
the rest of the book.

To understand what a critical pedagogy might look like conceptually and practically, I would like to divide this discussion into two areas: the traditional section and critical responses to the traditional. These traditional and critical components must be viewed under the guiding epistemological (form of knowledge) umbrella of what is commonly known in academia—not only in education but also in schools of philosophy, social sciences, and the humanities—as modernism and postmodernism. After elaborating on this one main distinction, I will outline concepts that fall under their meanings. The division between concepts looks like this:

| TRADITIONAL (Modernism) | CRITICAL THEORY (Modernism and Postmodernism) |
|---|---|
| Hegemony as Cultural Reproduction | Counter Hegemony as Cultural Production (Resistance) |
| Deviancy | Resistance |
| Deskilling | Reskilling |
| Multiculturalism | Similarity within Difference |
| Individualism | Individuality |
| Negative Competition | Positive Competition |
| Authoritarianism | Authority |
| Control | Democracy |
| Traditional Empowerment | Critical Empowerment |
| Traditional Literacy | Critical Literacy |

## Modernism

Modernism (particularly postindustrialism) is divided into two areas. First, modernism is about individuals struggling toward such goals as freedom and universal peace. Within the enlightenment era and beyond, modernism stresses individual free and critical thinking, social responsibility, reason, rationality, and scientific progress and change. Power, it is argued, is placed in the hands of people to control nature through incessant inquiry, discovery, and innovation. Corresponding to this form of modernism is the individual's abiding faith in the capitalistic process, the quest for ultimate achievement, competition, and success, and an assumption that the values that stem from such a view of life represent a truthful existence. Within this form of modernism, reason, reality, truth, and rationality are equated with the free and creative individual. In short, this typifies a fiercely competitive free market just like the quest for grades at the private school I attended, the public school I taught at, and the social efficiency movement in general (which I mentioned earlier in this chapter). In the modern sense, school naturally leads students to competitive and unequal relations of production in what I and others would argue is the false guise of a quality institution. Thus, although tracking may seem necessary in the long run for the economy, it really divides and conquers students and forces them into functional and regulated unequal spaces in the work force (Oakes, 1985).

Second, another form of modernism takes on some very important critical theory elements of social critique. Within this form of modernism, there is hope for personal and public enlightenment. There is a deep-rooted commitment to democracy and community (Habermas, 1981). Through individual reason and ongoing reflection, there evolves a unity of the individual and society in an ongoing vision of human development, emancipation, and possibility for individual and communal betterment. Liberty and justice become the emancipatory modernistic guiding principles. These utopian dreams, it must be said, are not unworthy. It could be argued that these dreams are for an idealized democracy, one that the first form of modernism discussed earlier cannot achieve fully because of its inherent contradictions (for our purposes, the school's ability to divide students unequally, despite rhetoric of equal opportunity of education for all members of the educational community).

In part, it could be argued that schools equate very well with the first form of modernism as evidenced by ongoing achievement tests, rating scales, stereotypes, and the like, although these may speak concurrently of schools as producing forms of community, nurture, compassion, and care. Indeed, these two forms of modernism do exist in schools. Certainly, a function of schools is to produce good, upstanding, moral citizens who are part of a democratic community. However, with the emphasis on the school's relation to the economy as more vital, schools take on more of the first part of modernism at the expense of schools as sites of democratic possibility.

*Postmodernism*

Contrasted to modernism, postmodernism negates world views that are held together by absolutes. In a postmodern world view, there can be no universal truth or universal reason (Lyotard, 1984; Lyotard, 1993). Often, questions arising out of postmodernism are as follows: Whose world view is it we are trying to understand? How is singular and group cultural identity constructed? How is knowledge transmitted? How many ways do people learn? Can there be any form of knowledge? How many realities are there? In its most conservative sense, postmodernism only tries to understand multiple forms of difference, multiple interpretations, multiple ways of knowing or constructing knowledge. This postmodernism could be called the phenomonology or hermeneutics of knowledge.

Critical postmodernism, a more advanced form of postmodernism (at least for the purpose of this book and as related to teachers and critical pedagogy in particular), aligns more closely with the second form of modernism discussed previously. Critical postmodernism, just like other forms of modernism, shares a similar quest for human emancipation and liberation. Yet, apart from modernism, postmodernism (as well as critical postmodernism) relies on deconstructing (unraveling) social, cultural, and human differences. With differences in mind, the critical postmodern political project shifts the locus of power to the underprivileged, the marginalized, and the oppressed. This may include any form of minorities. Regarding teachers, the struggle to overcome oppressive teacher conditions such as dehumanizing rating scales, accountability schemes, standardized curricula, and authoritarian administrators and their guiding bureaucracies becomes a central focus for the critical pedagogue within a critical postmodern condition.

In addition, critical postmodernism is about real people struggling in the everyday world within their multishaped identities and subjectivities. Simply put, what the relations of race, class, and gender may be to any individual will always be different and changing, always in flux. For example, today I am not only a father, ex-husband, son, lover, colleague, writer, professor, actor, sportsman, or friend. I am all of these in shifting moments, all mixed at various times during the day. As a student and teacher, my past history in institutions taught me to wear only one hat at a time. This proved to be fateful and oppressive to me and probably had something to do with my dropping out of high school. Additionally, the America 2000 plan or the outcomes-based education plan proposed in Pennsylvania presuppose that all students can reach certain areas of knowledge with similar accuracy. From a critical postmodern platform, what is not considered is human differences—not everyone can know the same because of different human experiences and life perspectives and, of course, different learning styles and habits. From a critical postmodern perspective, what is at stake is change: from a narrow, privatized market logic of school choice for the privileged to a primacy of the moral, ethical, and civic within the public arena every day. It is not enough, for instance, simply to understand and/or deconstruct differences. Within a critical postmodern frame of reference, the critical pedagogue always seeks just and fair ways to alter a system which, by and large, and despite seemingly good intentions, has effectively oppressed many of its members. Critical postmodernism, then, is not only about passive judgment but also about active engagement in change and reform issues that seek to sever inequalities and other forms of social and cultural injustices. With this in mind, I turn to other important concepts needed for understanding these points.

## Hegemony versus Counterhegemony

*Hegemony*

In a typically traditional school setting, the reproduction of school inequalities is paramount.[5] This reproduction, or what we shall term hegemony, occurs when administrative, teacher, and student experience is unquestioned and when values and actions are lived as commonsensical despite, it could be argued, the best intentions for modernism's quest for community and enlightenment. Within hegemonic formations lies what is commonly called in the education literature the hidden curriculum—those unspoken values, norms, and ideologies that are passed on to students as common sense (competition, success, discipline, stereotype, gender division, etc.). As a clear example of hegemony, schools, like many other social institutions, contain people who stereotype. The teacher and student construct about what counts as a nerd, jock, brain, bright, capable, or average student presupposes unquestioned and dominant values and meanings. Often, these meanings subordinate and alienate others. Additionally, these socially constructed meanings are often shared and accepted by a social group or collectivity, as evidenced in the media that promote these stereotypes (e.g., Alex P. Keaton in "Family Ties" as the brain, or Arvard in "Head of the Class" as the nerd).

Hegemony acts to exert control over groups of people and their accepted, common-sense interpretations. Thus, a general adoption of ideas, values, images, and feeling structures occurs. Nothing could describe this better than the division of administrator, teacher, and student labor at school. It has been argued that schools divide labor by gender. That is, because women occupy the major teaching roles and males the major administrative roles, this difference in gender provided an important form of social control[6] and/or hidden curriculum in which teaching was viewed both as women's work and socially inferior. This is just one slice of hegemony. Mr. Twomey's treatment of females in my math class became a form of hegemonic hidden curriculum. It did so because of this actions, which were subordinative to female students and were supported by males (in our adoption of similar responses to females as convenient objects) in my class.

Studies on the hidden curriculum show how schools reproduce inequalities based on socioeconomic status[7] reinforced by a cumbersome tracking system. As you will note in Chapter 4, even one principal whom I interviewed in an elementary school stereotyped Hispanic students to be "vocationally bound, even though they are hard workers." The common-sense acceptance of such stagnant views, the research on inequities that the aforementioned studies depict, plus the stereotypes on what counts as success (the highest grade necessarily implying who might succeed in life, the best basketball player necessarily implying who might be the most popular and better person, and the girls who parade in their cheerleading outfits necessarily implying both popularity and sexiness as another form of female gender control or male domination) make for the hegemonic acceptance of dominant values as unquestioned, *fait accompli*, or taken for granted. This acceptance not only oppresses those who are subjected to such dogma but just as equally oppresses those who create these social injustices.

It seems that there is a general willingness in schools to embrace the symbols of cultural reproduction (i.e., the language, rules, norms, and symbols). Hegemony, then, accepts social relations as natural, normal, unquestioned, and necessarily right—a sort of passive accepted logic of domination and social control. In the prior chapter, a slice of hegemony in my life was the natural acceptance of the value of competition at the expense of others' welfare.

### Counterhegemony

Within the critical theory tradition, the literature calls counterhegemony or cultural production a source of struggle, hope, affirmation, and a possibility for teacher and student meaning making (and possibly hidden curriculum) that is rooted in social transformation or resistance to the hegemonic controls. Counterhegemony takes on two forms. First, it can be viewed as a form of meaning making and/or alternative knowledge that moves away from hegemonic forms of control. Second, counterhegemony merges resistant groups (those groups that challenge dominant assumptions, like hippies, rock groups, and other subcultures) into subordinate relations as well. For example, just because a student challenges a school system by seeing through structural weaknesses like not studying for what the student considers a meaningless test or by challenging various school authorities, this student is not transforming himself or herself or society. That student is not placing himself or herself well for the job market and is preparing for a life of meaningless labor—which the economy needs to succeed because it requires unskilled labor to carry out meaningless work tasks. What seems like a form of alternative knowledge backfires on the student. For instance, the movie *Dead Poets Society* depicts the liberal teacher (Robin Williams as Keating) challenging a very traditional, conservative school. He revamps the curriculum. He challenges students to question their lives. In short, this teacher provides options for his students with an alternative view to the stagnant one depicted by the private, bourgeois white school. The teacher is eventually fired. The school replaces him with an older and conservative teacher, the principal. Lessons once more become predictable. In short, this school system tolerated and incorporated the teacher and some students' reactions until the powers decided they had to reinforce old systems and traditional values. Some students in this movie were left with an alternative view of the world (despite their privileged class position of whiteness) initiated by Keating (as evidenced in some students standing on their chairs and applauding Keating, the departing and never to be forgotten radical teacher). Indeed, some of these students may remain critical forever. Yet clearly the double view of hegemony is accomplished. It is at once a form of resistance (alternative views of knowledge) and accommodation of the status quo (conformity through the firing of the teacher and reestablishment of older values, power bases of the privileged students, and sexist assumptions by some students, such as the objectification of females and the uncriticality of one's own race or class). A form of counterhegemony in my life was seeing through the school's structural weaknesses such as meaningless tests. Concurrently, this worked against me in the long run. I left school in the eleventh grade because I didn't conform to competitive academic values.

From a critical postmodern perspective, we must try to fathom that indeed there are multiple forms of possibilities for counterhegemony. Hegemonic resistance can rear its head both consciously and unconsciously. A critical pedagogue using critical postmodernism will not only attempt to understand forms of hegemony but act to counter forms of oppressive values, learning that counterhegemony is multiple, possible, and never final. For a teacher to see through structural weaknesses of tests (i.e., their obvious biases) is not enough for transformational change. Critical postmodernism begs the teacher to ask questions like, Who constructed the tests? Whose knowledge is represented? How can evaluation be conducted besides using stagnant, objective multiple-choice tests? How is each individual represented on tests? Which culture is the test representing? Whose reality is the test constructed for? Moreover, critical postmodernism seeks to answer these questions and necessarily begins to change oppressive relations that these questions and answers are addressing.

### Deviance versus Resistance

#### Deviance

There is often much confusion in the critical theory educational literature about what counts as deviance or what composes deviant and/or resistant acts. Deviance occurs when rules, boundaries, and various sorts of moral classification system lines are crossed. When things don't fit they are usually labeled as deviant. For instance, putting shoes on the table or having incestuous sex are deviant acts, and the latter is punishable by law. Both acts involve out-of-place behavior and are threats to original social structures (Wuthnow et al. 1984). At best, deviance accommodates rule breakers through a change of rules (e.g., teachers coming late to meetings may be classified as deviant but may argue that the meeting time is poor and has to be changed). At worst, deviance involves moral irregularities (crime is the typical example). Here ritual ceremonies (court trials, prisons, death penalty) draw attention to the moral imperfections.

In schools, teachers and administrators often view student behavior as deviant. Thus, students are labeled as discipline problems, hard-core cases, or simply bad kids. As a result, schools have consequences in order to reestablish the moral order—after-school and Saturday detention, and so on. In my school days I could have been classified as mildly deviant— coming to class late, not standing in line correctly, chewing gum when that was against the rules, and so on. These acts of deviance are far different from acts of resistance.

*Resistance*

Resistance involves the conscious and unconscious attempt by anyone (but, for our case, particularly teachers and students) to challenge the dominant and/or hegemonic values in our society. As distinct from deviance, critical theorists look at resistance as possible acts of social and cultural transformation.

Like counterhegemony, resistance entails acts that counter the oppressive race, class, and gender stereotypes as well as challenges to other dominant structural values such as individualism, rampant competition, success-only orientations, and authoritarianism. Resistance is both a theoretical and practical endeavor. Importantly, it is also an intellectual enterprise. That is, as part of resistance, reflecting about one's own subjectivity and multiple identities within the borders of race, class, gender, parent, teacher, husband, lover, and so on is a necessary condition before action can take place to undo oppressive social relations.

The critical pedagogue often confuses acts of opposition such as deviance as resistance. Aronowitz and Giroux (1985) argue correctly that not all oppositional behaviors have radical intentions. That is, not all oppositional behavior is a statement about or a reply to forces of domination. What might be viewed as an act of resistance might simply be a deviant act. The task of the critical pedagogue is to explore the radical and resistant possibilities of student and teacher actions that undertake the possibilities of altering oppressive social structures.

## Deskilling verus Reskilling

### Deskilling

Within a traditional school setting, teachers are deskilled. Empirical work[8] shows, through detailed description, how teacher work is reduced mainly to its technical aspects, as in the application of rules and, for the most part, the exclusion of teachers from curriculum-making processes. Here, teachers lose control over their own labor, allowing outside forces to control their work. Deskilling has to do with teachers executing someone else's goals and plans. In industry, this is referred to as the separation of conception from execution. In school this appears as well. Teachers in teacher education departments, for instance, are taught the skills to teach—to execute tasks, manage the classroom, develop discipline procedures, create assignments, make tests, evaluate tests, disseminate the curriculum, build unit plans, and vary teaching methodologies. Ironically, this teaching works in ways to deskill teachers. This happens when the skills teachers are taught in teacher education departments across the country are unusable in practice, such as in highly populated, minority-dominated inner-city schools.[9] For instance, certain techniques taught by some teacher education departments simply don't work in the heart of inner-city schools. Schools traditionally and continually expect teachers to conform to a single form of discipline. Teachers who adhere to these discipline policies without question are not the conceivers over alternative discipline procedures that may, in fact, work for other cultures. They are deskilled despite their acquisition of the so-called technical expertise in their certification programs. The whole concept of discipline can and has been scrutinized (Chambers, 1983) and in a true postmodern sense encompasses many realities and meanings for different people.

Deskilling is at its peak when teachers are denied or have much less autonomy and less control over the teaching process than they think they have. By making teachers accountable for state-mandated curriculum (such as basal reading materials) and by promoting competency-based education, system management, and employing rigid and dehumanizing forms of evaluation along with numerical rating scales, teachers are controlled and simply march to the tune of the state. Nothing could better amplify state control than the incessant bombardment of reports, such as the now much publicized *A Nation at Risk*. It has been argued cogently by Shapiro[10] and a host of others that the carrying out of these proposed reforms (including extra homework, longer school days, and more teaching hours), under the state's claim for increased evaluation and closer scrutiny of teachers, merely exacerbates the alienation, oppression, and subordination of teachers. Even regarding the use of technology, teachers' skills are being eroded. Apple (1986) comments,

The reliance on pre-packaged software can have a number of long-term effects. First, it can cause a decided loss of important skills and dispositions on the part of teachers. When the skill of the local curriculum planning, individual evaluation, and so on are not used, they atrophy. The tendency to look outside of one's own or one's colleagues' historical experiences about curriculum and teaching is lessened as considerably more of the curriculum, and teaching and evaluative practices that surround it, is viewed as something one purchases—the school itself is turned into a lucrative market.[11]

To recapitulate, in a traditional school, deskilling is at its peak when teachers have no control over decisions made that directly or indirectly affect their lives, such as the very important issue of choice of curriculum materials. Such was the case in my own teaching experiences in Israel. The curriculum went simply untested. Personally, I never questioned its validity. Nor did the teachers with whom I worked.

With the notion that teachers are deskilled when they lose control over schoolwide matters (such as curriculum and policy concerns), other issues related to the deskilling process come to mind. For example, teacher and administrative tasks are both clearly and authoritatively defined. Harris's[12] notion of the proletarianization of teachers is also of relevance here. Teachers' jobs are salaried, activities are shared, clientele cannot be selected, and there is extremely little occupational independence. Additionally, gender biases in school predominate,[13] which subject both female and male teachers to the dominant value of patriarchy. Teacher deskilling, in this case, occurs precisely when teachers have no control over gender, race, or class bias. Hegemony, then, in its multiple and at times hard-to-decipher forms, becomes the deskilling of the teacher. Within a modernistic framework (the first distinction of modernism made earlier), the intent of schools is to empower teachers formally with curriculum guidelines, easy evaluation procedures, and a clear division of subject matter (college bound, vocational education, etc.). This is all done with efficiency and mastery of content in mind without considering vast human differences (particularly as related to different ethnicities).

### Reskilling

Within the critical theory process (and in schools), a move away from deskilling occurs when teachers are better able to intellectualize the role that the state plays in hegemonic constructions. The notion of reskilling occurs, then, when teachers become first aware of and then critical of the multiple forms of deskilling—issues of technical control, such as who makes and decides on curriculum issues; stagnant forms of teaching methodologies; and the reproduction of values that oppress, alienate, and subordinate people (especially, for our concerns, students and teachers as related to race, class, and gender configurations). Within this reskilling mode, critical pedagogic teachers challenge stereotyping, find ways to subvert tracking through alternative teaching methodologies, build curriculum with open and critical spirits, become involved in the policy-oriented decisions of the state and local school district site, and form group solidarity over issues of value-laden importance. To do this would propel teachers to become not only critical pedagogues but also what Aronowitz and Giroux term "transformative intellectuals."[14]

In short, reskilling occurs not only when teachers take control over their work and personal lives. This is a first step in the reskilling process. Within the more enlightened modernistic view, teachers work for the betterment of the community because they are a part of it. Having control over their labor is one way to help ensure that students also are reskilled. From a critical postmodern perspective and as a critical pedagogue, to reskill oneself is not only an issue of control of curriculum content or working for the betterment of the community, but also an act of reflection on the subject matter in the curriculum and its relationship to the dominant values, with the short- and long-range goals of transforming those values that oppress, alienate, and subordinate others. This includes serious scrutiny of any curricular materials, particularly as related to race, class, and gender differences. All this must be attempted within the confines of the traditional institution. As the reader will note throughout this book, reskilling issues are multiple and at times confusing. This book, in large part, is about teachers as critical pedagogues (or potential teacher pedagogues) who consciously or unconsciously attempt to walk the path of the reskilled practitioner.

## Multiculturalism versus Similarity within Difference

### Multiculturalism

The multicultural movement has historically been (since the civil rights movement and the influx of so many immigrants into the United States beginning in the mid-1960s) a modernistic attempt at equalizing educational opportunity. In most school districts, a multicultural emphasis is added into official curricular documents at some point. Usually, this takes the form of a policy statement within a vision or mission statement paragraph. One school district that I have recently been in contact with writes the following in its vision statement:

We envision a caring and supportive educational system, one in which creativity and individual differences are welcomed as opportunities for learning . . . where we prepare students to become caring and responsible citizens able to work cooperatively, think critically, and communicate effectively in a changing global society.[15]

Typically, multicultural education in schools involves, at first, the extrinsic acceptance of others. That is, different cultures' holidays and special events may be given some voice and/or credence in schools. There may be a specially designated food day, in which a school devotes its time once a year to experiencing the tastes of different ethnic foods, thus alerting the school population to some cultural differences. Additionally, various curricular divisions, such as social studies, art, and/or English, may devote a part of their curriculum concerns to understanding different cultures. Clearly, the intent of this form of multiculturalism within traditional school settings is both noble and good. However, such viewpoints on multiculturalism are purely extrinsic. Learning about cultural differences and their attending values doesn't necessarily imply acceptance of these values as being equal or better than Western cultural norms and values. Perhaps this point is best substantiated by Darder (1991) in her analysis of multicultural education:

Multicultural materials and activities do not, in and of themselves, ensure that a culturally democratic process is at work . . . and many situations exist in which students are presented with games, food, stories, language, music, and other cultural forms in such a way as to strip these expressions of intent by reducing them to mere objects disembodied from their cultural meaning.[16]

Clearly, Darder argues, educators must be more critical of a multicultural process, in particular the personal and philosophical platforms that teachers enter class with. In a modernistic sense, having some form of multicultural education clearly fits neatly and compactly into the curriculum. Multiculturalism in this form is part of a structure (curriculum) that fits into the whole curriculum and child's learning experience. On another level, multiculturalism meets modernism's quest for striving to understand and attain unity within a diverse community. As such, there are even attempts to instill required course work on diversity throughout U.S. colleges and universities at the undergraduate level. On one minute level, I argue, this meets the structural need for understanding the need for diversity. However, I do feel that multicultural education (multiculturalism) has far more critical components to it as well. With this in mind, I turn to the more critical appraisal of multicultural education.

### Similarities within Differences

Within what I have termed traditional school settings, a critical theory of multiculturalism (let us call this critical postmodern multiculturalism) has been advocated by many writers.[17] This approach to multicultural education will seriously consider race, class, and gender relations of minority cultures. Within this approach, a critical pedagogue will attempt to change stagnant or stereotypical views about ethnic groups. To do this, a critical pedagogue must first view ethnic minority family, social, value-oriented, and economic relations as different from (extrinsic to) Western culture in their multiple formations. Second, a critical postmodern theory of multiculturalism will require the critical pedagogue to critique the present cultural situation that doesn't allow for extrinsic acceptance of another culture or cultures. This critique will be geared to finding ways for school clientele (students and teachers in particular) to accept others intrinsically (be they minorities, as in this case, or anyone else) as equal based on the simple fact that we are all human and are all different. The second approach within a traditional setting becomes the utopian view of a critical postmodern theory of multiculturalism, a struggle to undo the morally reprehensible acceptance of the dominant culture (white-Anglo-American) as pure truth, the best or only living culture in this country (this is a blatant form of ethnocentrism).

At various times in this book, particularly Chapter 5, I will argue that a teacher who considers himself or herself a critical pedagogue within a critical theory of multiculturalism must seriously appraise the concept of similarity within difference as connected to a view of empathy.

At the base of individual differences lie the commonalities or similarities of oppression, pain, and feelings, albeit in different forms. For example, although all immigrants may share similar feelings of frustration with forms of acculturation, which may include personal insecurities, low self-esteem, literacy problems, certain paranoia, and possibly a low socioeconomic status, within their personal history and various experiences most immigrants would differ. This is evidenced by various immigrants who are hegemonized by a patriarchal father and subservient mother, or by a matriarchal mother. Some immigrants may assimilate into their new culture better than others. A similarities-within-differences theme can clearly represent all groups, not only immigrant groups. For instance, some inner-city and even some suburban schools are technically racially divided. All races have their particular cultural forms, histories, and experiences—what critical theorists call voice (I will deal with this concept at greater depth throughout this book). But for now, as a teacher, I bring my personal cultural baggage (history, experiences, likes and dislikes) into the classroom. This baggage will be clearly different (in many ways) from the multiple cultural representations in any one classroom. Such was the case with my teaching in the Israeli culture.

Within a critical postmodern theory view of multiculturalism, teachers will seek similarities within differences as a starting point empathetically and intrinsically to accept other cultures. Given my life experiences, as an educator I will identify with those who have felt alienation and certain forms of suffering and oppression, even though our respective particular circumstances may have differed. In part, I am calling for the teacher critical pedagogue to recover his or her history and experiences that will allow meeting points with other cultures, despite the many differences that exist between them. As a critical pedagogue, it becomes a teacher's responsibility to understand his or her actions and feelings that are similar to and different from other cultures. For example, although I can never physically be black, Puerto Rican, Hispanic, Asian, or a woman, the challenge within a critical postmodern multicultural education is for me to seek an understanding through similarities of mine and other cultures as well as to understand and accept differences. Empathy can only be created when this type of reflection occurs. Only then can a change of stagnant and stereotypic viewpoints over cultures take place and the move to a critical postmodern theory of multicultural education be an option to traditional multicultural uses. One example may help clarify this point. I taught Hispanic students as a substitute teacher while researching Chapter 5. My whiteness was pitted against me and represented a different ethnicity. Our histories and experiences, family make-up, and class structure were different. What brought us together were our respective similarities of being immigrants, lost in a new country, not speaking the dominant language, and having values different from the dominant culture. A critical postmodern multiculturalism seeks to understand these differences and similarities with the intent of engaging students in democratic classroom relations in an ultimate effort to sever inequities.

### Individualism versus Individuality

#### Individualism

The way that individualism and individuality appears in schools is quite simple. Conceptually, individualism is intrinsically related to a modernistic view of Western civilization. Values such as hard labor, self-discipline, and self-motivation carry overtones of a general quest for human individual supremacy, critical mindedness, and self-achievement. These values are reinforced by self-gratification, instant gratification, and narcissism[18] within the culture—striving for one's own in the guise of community welfare. Egocentricity, the belief that the individual is the central unit of life, becomes the central motif of American living. Darwin's survival of the fittest theme fits in well here. Resultantly, individual separateness and the quest for individual material goods (commodities and wealth) becomes a form of hegemony that schools both live and revive daily.

As a form of hegemony, schools transmit this view of life as the correct one—as commonsensical. Individual success and high achievement are emphasized (who made the honor role today?, who was the MVP in last night's game?, who received the most stickers?, who's on the college-bound track?, who's in the gifted program?, what was your S.A.T. score?, who's the brain, nerd, or jock?, what school or university did you get into?, who made the cheerleading team?, what car do you drive?, did you get merit pay this year?). Simply put, individualism in schools leads to teacher and student worth being judged by individual achievement—a modernistic triumph. Purpel (1989) is worth quoting here:

Achievement becomes the basic condition for acceptance. Students learn very quickly that the rewards that the schools provide—grades, honors, recognitions, affections—are conditioned upon achievement and certain behaviors of respect, obedience and docility.[19]

At its worst, individualism breeds various forms of unhealthy competition. The notion of student cheating, for instance, is one outcome of extreme forms of individualism. Readers will recall that as part of my past experiences as a middle school and high school student, I was so ashamed at scoring poorly on exams that I sometimes changed my report cards' grades. Moreover, I was scared of the reactions my parents would have to my poor performances, let alone the shame I felt in front of my friends when my grade was read aloud in class for public scrutiny. I do not want to blame my parents here. They were only a part of the problem. The principal of my high school had certain expectations as well. My fear of him, I'm sure, had something to do with cheating. However, the culture surrounding the home, which stressed individual achievement at all costs, and my school, which reinforced a do-or-die attitude (military mentality) about learning and test taking, made me act in such an extreme way. It is common knowledge that in schools teachers lead isolated lives. For example, they have separate classrooms, teach different subject matter, have different lunch hours, and often have different teaching styles and approaches to problem solving. In short, these differences lead to separateness within the school community. The isolation doesn't lend itself to teachers working together as a community of professionals and intellectuals to further develop curriculum and other matters that concern the entire school community. This structural division breeds separate ideas, separate ways of doing things, and little interactive dialogue. This may simply, but not necessarily, lead to forms of individualism, as in, "My students scored higher than yours," or "I got merit pay this year."

Traditional school sites also offer the praising of individuality. I now want to distinguish between traditional individuality and a postmodern critical theory view of individuality.

### Individuality

Traditional individuality (the second form of modernity) assumes that achievement is always relative. One's worth is based on genuine effort (as opposed to grades or points scored during a game, or the mean of a class's performance in a subject area). Purpel (1989) comments again:

The mark of a so-called progressive school is not necessarily that it rejects achievement but that it extends the realms of areas worthy of recognition—for example, the hardest working, the student who has made the most progress, or the most congenial.[20]

Within the traditional school, individuality goes hand in hand with respect for the individual's accomplishments no matter the level at which they are achieved. Respect becomes part of establishing good community relations.

Critical individuality (critical postmodernism) will go further than merely acknowledging individual accomplishments and traits. A critical pedagogue will adopt critical individuality by always listening to the students' (and teachers', if the case may be) cultural and social heritage as a method to learn more about the individual's particular historical, cultural, social, and economic circumstances and differences. For instance, critical individuality involves understanding the student's home life (for instance, if the home is patriarchally or matriarchially dominated) and understanding the child's social life in and out of school and how this affects student learning. In short, critical postmodern individuality will allow the critical pedagogue to hear student voices. McLaren (1989) comments, "A student's voice is shaped by its owner's particular cultural history and prior experience."[21] A critical pedagogue will be able to apply critical individuality to everyday school activities so an understanding of the social and cultural picture of the student is far clearer. For example, in an inner-city school situation with an all African-American student body, I might change from a more traditional teaching technique of standing up in front of the room and lecturing, to a more co-operative style if I understand that some cultures communicate better in groups. Understanding how cultures form will allow me to change teaching techniques. Some individuals may simply flourish better in groups rather than being stranded and opposed individually. Another example of critical individuality may be understanding that in various cultures, some households are so male dominant that to impose myself (as a male) on female students by inviting them to speak up in class (because they don't in their culture), although noble and liberal in intent, may simply be an invasion of their private cultural codes. Such was the experience I had while teaching in an inner-city school in California in a predominantly Hispanic community (see Chapter 5). As a critical pedagogue who is concerned with critical individuality, I will begin to hear the other culture by not authoritatively imposing my values, even though I may believe my values to be better than and/or more noble in intent than other cultures'. Thus, I respect the other cultures' values, both extrinsically and intrinsically. Clearly, the critical postmodernist will be able to move between his or her own values and others' values, opening dialogue that allows students to question their own values and to transform inequities that may exist between themselves and others. In summary, critical individuality is about changing the individual, opening him or her to seeing, understanding, and helping to transform unequal social relationships.

## Negative Competition versus Positive Competition

### Negative Competition

In all schools (given their traditional bent), competition as a part of the drive to succeed is apparent in multiple forms. There are challenges to be the best student with the highest grades, or to be the captain of the cheerleading squad or the debate team, or to be a member of an athletic team. There is a great deal of status accompanying these roles. Students are taught that to be the best you can be is a norm that is most highly valued, and if it is not lived up to, one must suffer the social and academic consequences.

The emphasis on this form of competition is called negative competition (this ideal was taught in my school, especially concerning sports and grades). It is negative because it reminds us of Darwin's theory of the survival of the fittest. Only the best can and will succeed, but the only way to succeed is at the expense of another person who is trying to succeed at your expense; this is clearly a catch-22 situation. The obsession of individuals to succeed is so high in our society that "personal achievement and success includes an erosion of our traditional commitment to equality."[22] Competition of this type is also negative because it brings about negative feelings between people and lowers the self-esteem of individuals. An example may help. When I reflect on my own schooling, I recall that I was always picked as captain of my football team. I was also charged with the responsibility to choose those players who would not only play all-out to win, but who *would* win. Winning was the issue, not playing for enjoyment's sake. Winning was enjoyment. I also recall the students whom I constantly picked last. They were the nerds, those people who I thought couldn't help me attain my ultimate goal of winning, even though, at heart, they may have possessed the winning spirit. There was no thought on my part of social justice and equality or compassion for the nonsport achievers. My only concern was for supremacy over the next person or team, the want and need for one-upmanship, for individualism at its worst because it negatively affected the self-esteem of others.

I am not the only one to blame for my insistence on competition. Hegemony has its fine-tuned ways. I was receiving multiple messages about this form of competition everywhere—at home, within peer groups (particularly in classrooms, where the rewards for high grades were always evident), on the street with my friends, in extracurricular activities, and in the media. Upon reflection, this negative form of competition, which eroded the rights of individuals to be treated for whom they were, became a form of social control that surrounded me at every turn. I was under some spell (unknown to me at the time) and quite frankly, as a form of hegemony, I felt rather good about myself. A part of modernism's success has been to make us feel good about the quest for achievement and competition. That is, without competition, there could not be a society that functioned to assure that certain people had particular jobs and different statuses. In schools, this form of competition raises its ugly head in all corners and exacerbates the individualistic logic—the struggle to be number 1 at all cost.

I don't want the reader of this text to feel that competition is always negative. In a postmodern sense, if we continue the argument that schools can foster critical individuality, a teacher critical pedagogue can actively create meaningful moments in classroom activities that both undermine and negate negative forms of competition. From a critical postmodern stance, they seek competition that can be explored in a positive light.

### Positive Competition

Rich[23] comments that this positive competition implies conforming to rules, where the goals for everyone are just. I want to take this argument just a little further. Positive competition for a critical pedagogue means directing the students to see multiple aspects of competition. To do so allows students to discriminate between various forms of competition. For instance, positive competition can involve the student performing to his or her maximum creativity in a subject area rather than only against someone else. I may, for instance, be competitive in the mile run by running to improve my personal best time, even if I finish last in a race against others, or I may strive to do better on an exam as a personal goal rather than as a goal to overtake others.

Contrary to Rich, I argue that one can only understand positive competition when one actively makes critical choices such as when to be competitive against oneself. A critical pedagogue will alert students to negative forms of competition and steer them to search for alternatives. Additionally, the critical pedagogue will make sure that other areas in the school that support negative competition will be challenged actively. Within the practice of teaching, a conscious effort not to stereotype, varying one's grading procedures (and telling students why), mixing cooperative learning groups with various student ability levels, and applauding individuality in all students (which requires the teacher to both understand and search out each student's strengths) are just a few ways one can foster positive competition.

To reiterate, in a traditional school setting, a critical pedagogue cannot simply walk into class and wipe out hegemony. There will always be negative forms of competition that undermine equal social relations. This is the nature of the capitalist society in which we live. However, the task of the critical pedagogue in this postmodern era is to at least plant the seeds of critical thought in students, which allows them to imagine, feel, and act on the conflicting forms of competition. To do so would allow for an alternative critical postmodern approach that can both challenge and negate negative competition and create an atmosphere of what I have termed positive competition.

### Control versus Democracy

#### Control

Within the modern world, democracy has become the guiding force in social relations. The United States, with all its positive and negative qualities, has become the international benchmark for democracy. It has been argued by some that true democracy in America is merely an illusion (McLaren, 1989), that schools do more to harm democracy than promote it. Given the appalling statistics on school dropout rates[24] and the savage inequalities in our schools (Kozol, 1991), modernism's quest for equality can only be described as having failed, or at least as flawed in many areas.

Rather than promote equality, traditional (modern) schools, like the workplace and home environments, rely on "control mechanisms" (Purpel, 1989) to assert themselves. On many levels this contradicts forms of democracy. In the first chapter, we talked about the issue of teacher accountability. I now connect accountability to the control issue. Purpel (1989) comments,

Schools have been captured by the concept of accountability, which has been transformed from a notion that schools need to be responsive and responsible to community concerns to one in which numbers are used to demonstrate that schools have met their minimal requirements—a reductionism which has given higher priority to the need to control than to educational considerations. The need to control produces control mechanisms, and for schools this has meant a proliferation of tests—a kind of quality control mechanism borrowed crudely and inappropriately from certain industrial settings. We control the curriculum, teachers and staff by insisting on predefined minimal performances on specified tests . . . in this case it means metaphors like efficiency, cost-effectiveness, quality control, production . . . obsession with control also gets expressed in school policy on "discipline," an interesting term which transfers to gain control over behavior.[25]

I want to take this notion of control that Purpel offers just one step further. Schools control the way we act, feel, and think. If we continue the argument that hegemony saturates individuals with control mechanisms (like the media and commodity culture), control of ideas and values simply dumps itself in school arenas. Control occurs when there are no conscious options to challenge ideas and feeling structures. When I view a beer commercial on TV, I learn that macho behavior is rewarded in society, just as jock behavior is rewarded. When I view the TV comedy "Head of the Class," I learn how to laugh at a nerd. When I view the TV game show "Family Feud," a question is asked: Name five groups of students that hang out together in schools. The first answer is jocks, the second is nerds, and the third is cheerleaders. The commonsensical acceptance or social construction of what these terms mean becomes the control mechanism that stifles creativity and hampers alternative forms of teacher, student, administrator, and public construction of meaning.

To summarize, traditional schools exert control through the external pressures of government (the federal government report *A Nation at Risk* supports more homework, longer hours, more testing, etc.), parental expectations, teacher expectancy, and a values orientation that constructs our reality for us, all in the guise of creating democracy.

### Democracy

It could be argued that in large part, public schools are charged with the responsibility of both sustaining and promoting democratic principles. Such school curricula as social studies, citizenship classes, and government and history classes are the critical outlet for these democratic principles. However, critical pedagogy holds that democratic principles must govern school experience in all subject areas and in all extracurricular activities. There must be not only student governance but teacher governance as well, especially concerning curricular and other policy matters that will directly or indirectly affect the classroom or teachers' lives in the school building.

Within a critical postmodern condition, a critical pedagogue will seek ways to challenge control mechanisms. Teacher authority will be negotiated with students. That is, within the confines of their bureaucratically granted authority, teachers will create a classroom climate that allows open deliberation of teacher-student relationships. Teacher-student relationships will become dialogical and not remain distant and aloof. Decision making will be shared. Examples include teachers and students who create the limits for behavior control by writing class rules cooperatively, and teachers and students who negotiate various forms of testing and exams (I call them intellectual jamborees to lower student stress levels). In my experience as a student, democracy was not part of the school system. As students, we had no choice in curricular issues (just like teachers, for the most part) and no say in the construction of class rules. We were totally controlled.

Critical postmodernism seeks to create and foster a democratic class-room environment. In doing so, critical pedagogical teachers will attempt to undercut the negative aspects of individualism and competition—two principles that brush against the grain of equal and fair civic participation—as well as other forms of hegemonic control. More cooperative learning (which implies far less lecturing and student regurgitation of facts on exams, forever to be forgotten), less stress on the value of success as the major reason for coming to schools in the first place, and more individual student participation in written, verbal, or math projects will allow for the possibility of student voices to be heard. In a democratic environment, a critical pedagogue teacher must attempt to hear that student voice. Not to do so implies that the teacher (both automatically and possibly without being aware of it) denies the student democratic participation.

Within a traditional school environment, a critical pedagogue teacher must be aware of control mechanisms and work within their boundaries to create democratic environments. For example, a critical pedagogue teacher seeks to test democratically, negotiates curriculum with administrators and students, and works within school rules to create a just and fair system that all can live with. For instance, there will not be just one or two captains or leaders of sports teams (as in my school years). To be a captain or leader of a group will be an option for anyone who desires to be one. In short, critical postmodernism is about viewing how multiple forms of control seek to undercut the democratic environment. The critical pedagogue is committed to exploring avenues that allow for what I will describe as democratic control. This is not a contradiction in terms. Democratic control assumes that the critical pedagogue is both willing and able to control one's life in order to find democratic ways in and out of the classroom. To do this, any teacher must assume both the modernistic quest for creative individual thinking and combine this with the postmodern notion of incessant deconstruction, especially of taken-for-granted daily activities that undermine individual thinking. To combine these two traditions, I argue, allows for critical postmodernism to flourish and the critical pedagogue to explore ways to build democratic relations in the classroom and to move away from undemocratic control mechanisms.

## Authoritarianism versus Authority

### Authoritarianism

A critical pedagogist understands that schools (as described traditionally) are authoritarian in nature. That is, control mechanisms (standardized curricula, a rigid rule structure, top-down hierarchy, and time constraints) guide the modern authoritarian nature of school. Indirectly (as evidenced by Mr. Twomey, for example, or my British history teacher), particular stereotypical values having to do with race, class, and gender distinctions become another avenue for authoritarian control.

These control mechanisms rear their heads in a bureaucratic system. Clearly defined structural leaders and their subordinates form a hierarchical ladder of control and division of labor (teacher tasks, various male- or female-related student tasks, division of principal and vice-principal tasks, predominant male principals and female vice-principals). From the superintendent, to the principal and vice-principal, to the counselor, to the teacher, to the secretary, to the custodian (somewhere in there lies the student), schools have become a place where authority becomes a dominant value. My high school principal and teachers were authoritarian and used their power and/or locus of control to lower my self-esteem—either intentionally or unintentionally, either through exams or stereotypes.

*Authority*

Within a critical theory tradition, the notion of authority has many meanings. First, the teacher is an authority over his or her subject knowledge area. Second, the teacher is not the only authority in the classroom. Teachers and students share each other's knowledge. Learning becomes reciprocal and dialogical. That is, teachers learn as well—in particular about student cultures. In other words, students become authorities over their own cultures. For instance, for a white male or female to teach successfully in the inner city, he or she would have to understand and respect the cultural diversity of the students. Third, teachers can use their traditional authority to create relationships of caring and nurturing that challenge oppressive gender, race, and class stereotypes. Teachers can be in charge of how students relate to race, class, and gender, seating arrangements, language construction in the class, and the abolition of stereotypes. These are just a few examples of what the teacher must look into within the context of a critical authority.

In short, a critical postmodern use of authority will also open avenues for teachers and students to discuss differences. This notion of authority, then, supersedes the structural aspects of authoritarianism that are so pervasive in American schools (as was also the case in my own schooling in Australia and my teaching in Israel). A critical postmodern notion of authority would allow teachers and students to explore multiple avenues, where authority can be redefined in the name of establishing social relationships that are not only critical but are also a lens for creating critical spaces for redefining what authority can be, both in personal and public lives. A critical postmodern notion of authority first allows for multiple uses and users of authority. Teachers and students will discuss language use, stereotypes, and seating arrangements. Dialogue on multiple levels will take place. Achieving this will allow for changing the destiny of those authoritarian ways in which teachers' lives are constructed.

### Traditional Empowerment versus Critical Empowerment

#### Traditional Empowerment

Like most concepts that float around schools (e.g., what is an effective teacher or an excellent teacher and/or school), the concept of empowerment has joined the bandwagon of jargon words in education. In my dealings with teachers in schools, with master- and doctoral-level students, and with in- and preservice students in educational foundations classes, the word *empowerment* has entered the teacher lexicon in full force. Additionally, numerous authors (including myself) have written on empowerment and its multiple uses. A short distinction between traditional and critical uses of such a term is in order because it will allow the reader to understand how I will be using it throughout this book.

Traditional empowerment typically refers to school personnel (administrators, teachers, and students in particular) who are either granted, grant others, or possess the institutional power to make decisions. I call this form of empowerment institutional empowerment. For example, the principal is granted the power by the local district to lead his or her staff, make decisions, and delegate authority. Such decisions could include the principal institutionally empowering the staff to make school schedules, write policy, or employ site-based management tactics to distribute power among teachers. This would include the creation of a dialogical rather than an authoritarian approach to supervision.

Regarding teachers, institutional empowerment grants the teacher some authority, autonomy, and control over his or her labor.[26] Institutional empowerment includes the teachers' ability to make decisions (both policy and personal), choose various forms of specific curricula for their students, and be a master at their profession (possess a variety of pedagogical tools, such as multiple teaching styles). An institutionally empowered teacher will act as the stereotypical professional.[27] In a traditional setting, this typically involves adhering to policy, conforming to dress code, and establishing distance with others on a hierarchy (principals, students, and staff).

In the modern tradition, what is assumed within traditional empowerment is fair play for all. That is, teachers are presupposed to have power and use that power in equal terms within the context of their workday and habits. Unfortunately, an inherent contradiction exists. Although the notion of traditional empowerment is a good and noble one, it exists within a hierarchical tradition. Power in this mode is unequal. In other words, teachers are empowered into unequal social relations where it is decided for them who will be empowered. For an example of this I return to my teaching days in high school. The principal empowered teachers (myself included) to be active curriculum decision makers. It was great to feel autonomous over the ability to choose curriculum. Empowerment seemed in place. I felt equal to others, had a sense of control over my professional life, and a sense of freedom. I was hegemonized to feel good. I didn't realize, however, that a hidden curriculum existed. I couldn't grasp then that to be given the power to make a curriculum decision meant nothing in terms of empowerment if I didn't question the type of curriculum knowledge I was transmitting to students both within the curriculum and outside of it. For the most part, teachers in my high school in Israel never questioned the validity of a book chosen. There was never a question raised, for instance, about race, class, or gender within the curriculum in our discussions.

*Critical Empowerment*

The leap from traditional empowerment to critical empowerment can be confusing. However, to simplify matters I want to argue that critical empowerment necessarily involves a conscious reflection on the part of the principal and teacher (and because this book concerns teachers, I will refer mainly to teachers) on the activities completed within the school day (decisions and policy agreed on, curriculum used, etc). I have called this cultural empowerment. This cultural (critical) empowerment necessarily includes informed decision making as related to the various cultures in the school. For whom and why is the decision made? Why would I need an alternative teaching methodology? How are my decisions affected by the traditional setting I am in? Am I reinforcing stereotypes? Am I reproducing inequities? How can I undercut inequities? How can I challenge alienating accountability measures set by the school? What forms of alternative testing (other than grades) exist that do not track students? How does my teaching affect race, class, and gender? These types of questions become the stuff of critically (or culturally) empowered teachers. Within a critical postmodernism, the teacher must seriously investigate multiple forms of knowledge as related to race, class, and gender with the intent to modify and/or change curricular usage to alleviate alienation, subordination, and oppression of others. A critical pedagogue will seek both questions that will allow for such an investigation and answers to help ameliorate inequalities.

In short, institutional empowerment is functional. It allows teachers the room to make decisions and feel a small measure of autonomy and control over their labor. Institutional empowerment is a granted right. Granted rights are lawlike and institutionally bound. For example, a child has the right to go to school until sixteen years of age. Institutional empowerment is thus only granted by the local authorities (i.e., teachers

have certain institutional powers such as the right to decide some discipline measures and decide on grades). Cultural (critical) empowerment,
however, involves more teacher reflection and teacher action to instill
change within a school system teachers are employed under. As critical
postmodern change agents, teacher critical pedagogues are culturally and
critically empowered when they begin to transform culture at the
school—for example, challenge stereotypes and various forms of tracking. A culturally and critically empowered critical pedagogical teacher
differs greatly from an institutionally empowered teacher.

### Traditional Literacy versus Critical Literacy

#### Traditional Literacy

Traditionally, in the modernistic sense, it is the moral obligation of
schools in a social efficiency environment to create a literate student for
the sake of equal opportunity or access to society's goods and services.
That translates into employment after the completion of school years. I
refer here to functional literacy or "the technical mastery of particular
skills necessary for students to decode simple texts such as street signs,
instruction manuals or the front page of a daily newspaper."[28] Functional
literacy includes mathematics computation and basic reading and writing
skills. Some will argue that functional literacy occurs when all students
reach tenth- or twelfth-grade competency. Others will argue that functional literacy equals a fourth- or fifth-grade level of competence. It has
been argued (and proven) that 60 million Americans are functionally illiterate, and "twenty-five million Americans cannot read the poison warn-
ings of a can of pesticide, a letter from the child's teacher, or the front
page of a daily paper and an additional thirty-five million read only at a
level which is less than equal to the full survival needs of our society."[29]
The point here is not only to embrace despair but to realize that traditional American schools in modernistic America are cultural sites (students learn differently, no matter what race, class, or gender) as well as
functional sites and must stress increasing the number of critically and
culturally literate and functionally literate students.

#### Critical Literacy

Critical literacy is distinct from functional literacy. Critical literacy em-
powers, in the postmodern sense, individuals to analyze and synthesize
the culture of the school and their own particular cultural circumstances
(race, class, and gender relations as connected to policy making, curricular concerns, teacher-student and teacher-teacher relationship). Within
this postmodern critical literacy, a critical pedagogue makes decisions
that are consciously moral and political. Issues such as gender and race

sensitivity become paramount. For example, critical literacy implies that the teacher consciously divides (with the democratic negotiation of the students) cooperative learning groups into equal race, class, and gender sets. Critical literacy allows the teacher to connect curriculum texts to student experience—making curriculum knowledge both meaningful and relevant as well as introspective for both the teacher and student. Critical literacy informs teachers who are transformative agents in and out of the classroom. Change is formulated from a critical stance. That is, what counts as change is not so much the level of functional attainment of school knowledge (although this is, of course, important as well and must not be negated) but the ability for teachers and students to be both better consumers and competent of understanding the cultural reasons that cause functional illiteracy and socioeconomic conditions, in particular.

## CONCLUSION

One very important point must be made clear. The move within a traditional setting (as most teachers will start their careers) to a critical pedagogical stance will not be easy. My personal experiences as a student, teacher, and professor suggest that to question the status quo, even if for the ultimate good of students and teachers, is always problematic, especially within the confines of a traditional setting. Thus, moves of this sort must be viewed cautiously.

I have tried to portray how schools can be seen through binary oppositions. Within this context, it is too simple a matter to say that a teacher who undertakes a traditional or nontraditional stance is a good or bad modernist or postmodernist. Schools combine and mix both these traditions in their often ambiguous formations within their binary oppositions outlined in their chapter. In a postmodern sense, no oppositions are ever stagnant. For example, I can be both traditionally and/or critically empowered at once, or I can be an authority and an authoritarian simultaneously. It seems to me that the beauty of being a teacher is that no one educator is either black or white, deskilled or reskilled, and so on. In the best postmodern sense, teachers and schools are multifarious subjects and objects made up of infinite parts that are never so clearly definable that any single person can say "I am this or that." Even though I can say that I am a critical pedagogue, I must realize that I have many identities. I am also a product of a modernistic environment in the traditional and critical senses. I am also a male who grew up in a male-dominated society and in an authoritarian school system. I may classify myself a critical pedagogue, but in doing so I must work within more than one particular postmodern tradition. In a postmodern sense, then, I realize that I am much more than a critical pedagogue. I am a product of a traditional system that creates inequities, trying to survive it, having sustained it, yet wanting to change its oppressive forms.

The following chapters will present more subtle and intricate strategies that teachers can use in their classrooms as both a critical and political platform, an arena for both hegemonic resistance as well as conformity (accommodation) to unequal relations of race, class, and gender. This book will provide, if only in part, a vision and methodology within the framework of a traditional school setting that is an alternative to the often stultifying vision that the more traditional school framework espouses. It will, I hope, provide students with a lens to view schools as social institutions and cultural sites where multiple interpretations of events can occur. The interpretation of these events, however, revolves around who you are as teachers, what you believe in, what you are committed to, and what vision you see yourself partaking in over the next decades in American education.

## NOTES

1. Paul Willis, *Learning to Labor: How Working Class Kids Get Working Class Jobs* (Lexington, Mass.: D. C. Heath, 1977); Jean Anyon, "Social Class and the Hidden Curriculum of Work." *Journal of Education*, 162 (1), 1980, pp. 66–92; Jean Anyon, "Social Class and Social Knowledge." *Journal of Curriculum Inquiry*, 11 (1), 1981, pp. 3–42; Jeannie Oakes, *Keeping Track: How Schools Structure Inequality* (New Haven, Conn.: Yale University Press, 1985).

2. Henry Giroux and Roger Simon, *Popular Culture: Schooling and Everyday Life* (South Hadley, Mass.: Bergin & Garvey, 1989); Barry Kanpol, *Towards a Theory and Practice of Teacher Cultural Politics: Continuing the Postmodern Debate* (Norwood, N.J.: Ablex, 1992); Peter McLaren and Rhonda Hammer, "Critical Pedagogy and the Postmodern Challenge." *Educational Foundations*, 3 (3), 1989, pp. 29–62; Elizabeth Ellsworth, "Why Doesn't This Feel Empowering: Working through the Repressive Myths of Critical Pedagogy." *Harvard Educational Review*, 59 (3), 1989, pp. 297–324.

3. Philip Jackson, *Life in Classrooms* (New York: Holt, Rinehart and Winston, 1968); Andrew Gitlin, "Understanding Teachers Dialogically." *Teachers College Record*, 91 (4), 1990, pp. 537–563; Kathleen Weiler, *Women Teaching for Change* (South Hadley, Mass.: Bergin & Garvey, 1987).

4. Henry Giroux, *Border Crossings* (New York: Routledge, 1992), pp. 39–88; 161–179; Peter McLaren, *Life in Schools* (New York: Longman, 1989); Kevin Harris, *Teachers and Classes: A Marxist Analysis* (London: Routledge & Kegan Paul, 1982); Hank Bromley, "Identity Politics and Critical Pedagogy." *Educational Theory*, 39 (3), 1989, pp. 207–223.

5. Jonathan Kozol, *Savage Inequalities* (New York: Crown, 1991), pp. 83–132.

6. Michael Apple, *Teachers and Texts* (New York: Routledge & Kegan Paul, 1986), pp. 31–80.

7. Oakes, *Keeping Track*, pp. 1–14; Samuel Bowles and Herbert Gintis, *Schooling in Capitalist America* (New York: Basic Books, 1976), pp. 53–101.

8. Robert Bullough, Andrew Gitlin, and Alan Goldstein, "Ideology, Teacher Role, and Resistance." *Teachers College Record*, 87, (1984), pp. 219–237; Michael Apple and Keith Teitlebaum, "Are Teachers Losing Control of Their Skills and Curriculum?" *Journal of Curriculum Studies*, 18 (3), 1986, pp. 177–184.

9. Barry Kanpol and Fred Yeo, "Teacher Education and the Inner City School Gap." *NASSP Bulletin*, December, 1990, pp. 83–87.

10. Svi Shapiro, "Capitalism at Risk: The Political Economy of the Educational Reports of 1983." *Educational Theory*, 35 (1), 1985, pp. 77–79; "Reply to Stedman." *Educational Theory*, 37 (1), 1987, pp. 77–79.

11. Apple, *Teachers and Texts*, p. 163.

12. Harris, *Teachers and Classes*, pp. 65–67.

13. Apple, *Teachers and Texts*, pp. 54–80; M. Strober and David Tyack, "Why Do Women Teach and Men Manage? A Report on Research in Schools." *Signs*, 5 (31), 1980, pp. 19–27; David Tyack and E. Hansot, "Silence and Policy Talk: Historical Puzzles about Gender and Education." *Educational Researcher*, 17 (3), 1988, pp. 33–41.

14. Stanley Aronowitz and Henry Giroux, *Education under Siege* (South Hadley, Mass.: Bergin & Garvey, 1985). The transformative intellectual is related to teachers committed to understanding the oppressive social structures (race, class, and gender) surrounding and part of the school. The transformative intellectual also tries to change these structures.

15. Derry Township School District, Pennsylvania, October 1991: 3. Vision Statement of English/Reading Curriculum Review and Planning Process, and all other curricular materials including Business Education and Science.

16. Antonia Darder. *Culture and Power in the Classroom* (New York: Bergin & Garvey, 1991).

17. Carl Grant and Christine Sleeter, *Turning on Learning: Five Approaches for Multicultural Teaching Plans for Race, Class, Gender and Disability* (New York: Macmillan, 1989); James A. Banks, *Multiethnic Education* (Boston, Mass.: Allyn and Bacon, 1994).

18. R. Bellah et al., *Habits of the Heart* (New York: Harper & Row, 1985); Christopher Lasch, *The Culture of Narcissism* (New York: Norton, 1978); Christopher Lasch, *The Minimal Self* (New York: Norton, 1984).

19. David Purpel, *The Moral and Spiritual Crisis in Public Education* (South Hadley, Mass.: Bergin & Garvey, 1989), p. 35.

20. Ibid., p. 37.

21. McLaren, *Life in Schools* (New York: Longman, 1989), p. 230.

22. Purpel, *Crisis*, p. 37.

23. J. M. Rich, "Competition in Education." *Education Theory*, 38 (2) 1988, pp. 183–189.

24. Kozol, *Savage Inequalities*, pp. 7–39.

25. Purpel, *Crisis*, pp. 48, 49.

26. Harris, *Education and Classes*, pp. 35–37.

27. Barry Kanpol, "A Contradiction in Teacher Professionalism: A Gender Critique." *Critical Pedagogy Networker*, 2 (4), 1990, pp. 1–5.

28. McLaren, *Life in Schools*, p. 196.

29. Jonathan Kozol, *Illiterate America* (New York: Doubleday & Company, 1985).

## CLASSROOM ACTIVITIES

1.  a. Divide the class into groups of four or five students. Let the individual students in the groups discuss their similar and different personal and educational experiences.

    b. Assign one person in each group to take notes as the groups relate their similar and different experiences.

    c. Regroup as a class and discuss the commonalities of similarities and differences among the groups.

2. In groups, summarize the meaning of the concepts outlined in this chapter as pertaining to students' prior experiences. The groups can discuss the same concept, or each group can decide to discuss its own concept. In this case, let the groups decide democratically which concept they prefer to discuss.

3. Divide the students into two debating teams. Each team will form a group and will justify either a traditional and/or critical position (e.g., on empowerment, deskilling or reskilling). This task should last fifteen minutes or so. Each group (with individuals making various contributions) will outline its preferred position on a concept and that position's practical applications. Allow five to ten minutes for this activity. Each side will be allowed to rebut for two to three minutes. Two students can be chosen arbitrarily by the teacher to act as judges on the strengths and weaknesses of each side's argument.

4. Divide the class into democratic and conservative constituencies. Have them build what they believe to be a modernistic and/or critical postmodern platform as related to everyday school issues such as curriculum choice, tracking, social clubs, and so on.

## QUESTIONS FOR DISCUSSION

1. What are the main aims of critical theory?

2. Based on the following movies about schools (and any others), discuss how there are forms of hegemony and counterhegemony in the schools depicted: *Dead Poets Society, To Sir, with Love, The Breakfast Club, Pump up the Volume,* and *Stand and Deliver.*

3. Discuss the acts of deviance and/or resistance that you experienced as a student.

4. Name the areas in schools where teachers can be deskilled and/or reskilled.

5. Is multiculturalism possible from a critical standpoint? Describe how one may go about creating empathy with other cultures.

6. How can you as a teacher foster more individuality than individualism?

Clarify your response with specific examples from your past and/or present school experiences.

7. As a teacher, relate how you may operate within a system that at once controls, yet concurrently espouses democracy as a central motif. How do your past experiences amplify this?

8. If you claim to be empowered, what does this mean in terms of your contributions to the teaching profession?

9. What is your role as a teacher concerning the literacy issue?

10. What are the different and/or similar aims of the modernistic and critical postmodern agenda?

11. After reading this chapter, discuss what your role is as a teacher. How differently can this role be conceived than you traditionally thought?

12. How has your philosophy of education changed as you continue to discuss and think about the issues of Chapters 1 and 2?

# 3

# Tensions of and between Cultures

## INTRODUCTION

This chapter presents a general description of Hillview Middle School, the setting for this particular case study.[1] What follows is first an overview of the students, staff, and administration. Second, the official routines and breaks of those official routines (pragmatic routines) that portray the thoughts, perceptions, and actions of teachers will be examined. This chapter is the first of three case studies about teachers. Its origin goes back nearly ten years (to 1985 when I was in graduate school). In subsequent case studies, I had further developed my theoretical knowledge. So the reader will witness a natural progression of the types of questions I ask and the theoretical formulations I develop. Moreover, this chapter provides a background for the final chapters, which discuss critical pedagogues and schools, possible curriculum considerations, and other practical and theoretical considerations within a critical pedagogy platform.

## AN OVERVIEW OF THE SCHOOL

If the school in this study (Hillview) were located in a suburban upper-middle-class area, one would not be surprised. A peacefulness of sorts surrounds it. As I turn right onto the street where the school is situated, I pass an overpriced Lawsons food store. Often on my way to school, I stop off for a quick cup of coffee, always astounded at the price of cookies, milk, and, on one occasion, a cassette I needed. The placement of

Lawsons at this juncture, with its cleanliness, bright lights, and its friendly, "have a nice day" attitude presents a major contrast to the atmosphere at the middle school I have named Hillview.

As I drive away from Lawsons, I pass the Y.M.C.A. and some open grassland used for recreational activities. Whenever I pass the Y.M.C.A. and arrive at Hillview, there are never many people outside. At this early time of day it is quiet, peaceful, and serene. The grass of the Y.M.C.A. is green or covered with snow during some parts of my stay at the school, and the road leading to school is the primary route to a highway leading to town. Thus, there is never a shortage of cars passing by on this narrow road. There are usually five or six school busses outside the school. They contain students who are bussed in from the near east side of town. A number of teachers' and administrators' cars arrive either before or after my arrival, which is at about 7:15 A.M. As I make the turn from Lawsons, I can't help but notice the police station—situated on the left side of Lawsons, not more than a few yards from the local community swimming pool. The drive to school, the stop-off at Lawsons, and the preparations for my morning in the field are always pleasurable.

There is a feeling of a factory atmosphere as I leave my car. This is, however, personal due to past experiences of rising early and going to work both as a factory worker and as a teacher. It is still dark outside, as it is the middle of winter.

There is no official school time clock, yet the principal stands outside at 7:20 A.M. or so to welcome the incoming students. I enter the building quickly after paying my morning respects to the principal.

As I open the teachers' room door, I hear the teachers, most with either a newspaper or coffee in hand, chitchatting about one student or another or some other personal issue. They sit at two round tables; next to the tables are three worn-out red sofas. It is here also that the school custodians and bus drivers sit. The cooks arrive at 6:00 A.M. to do their duties and are already working busily.

As I sit to have coffee and reflect on my upcoming day and present research, I can't help but feel that after a short stay at this school, I am almost one of the teachers at this site. I feel good being at Hillview. "Oh, he's one of us," comments the librarian to a visiting resource person from downtown. "He lives here," the librarian comments. It is no wonder, then, that I feel at home here in the teachers' room, a home away from home, in the working atmosphere that other teachers, cooks, and custodians are involved in.

Hillview is one of the larger middle schools in the city district. There are thirty-three teachers with an average of thirteen years of teaching experience. Most teachers have a Master's degree. A few have only a Bachelor's degree.

There are varying sorts of student cultures in this school. Most notably for this study, though, there are students who defy authority in countless ways and students who adhere to the written and unspoken rules of a teacher-student exchange. This exchange means that in return for the teacher's knowledge, skills, and values, the student will behave well and adhere to the authority of the teacher. To break rules, not respect the teacher, and so on is to withdraw one's consent to this exchange. Dressed in jeans, I play basketball with one of the school's best, talk informally to the students, and learn about their perspectives on the teachers, school, and their lives in general.

Students' color, race, and gender are evenly distributed, with 60 percent white, 35 percent black, and 5 percent Cambodian refugees. The principal prides himself in the English as a Second Language Program (E.S.L.). He is also well aware of the working-class nature of the school. He says that this is the type of school where research ought to be conducted but isn't. "We are like a virgin school," he comments to me in an interview.

Free or partially paid for meals are distributed to over 70 percent of the students. In general, the students are from either poor or broken homes and do not come from an atmosphere that initiates academic interest. There is always a rhythm in the hallways—a special tone to the students' talk that originates with the "hoods." There are the preps, too, who don't have a collective sound. These are two of the stereotypes of students at this school.

Hillview was set up as a middle school many years ago. Its large auditorium is gloomy and not well lit. Before the official start of the day the hallways are usually empty and spacious. Gray lockers line the school's one story in every direction. There are bells, fire drills, and assemblies at designated times. The sports facilities are at the furthermost end of the building, away from the administrative offices. As students fill the halls one always hears the noise of whistling, teachers yelling across the hall to other students to stop them from either running or creating havoc. The look on some teachers' faces expresses the feeling, "Oh, another day with these kids." There are old rest room facilities for both teachers and students and a shabby teachers' room. This is quite a contrast to the brightly lit, well heated, and clean principal and vice-principal's offices, where the carpets, clean shelves, fresh coffee brewing in clean coffee pots, and up-to-date reading materials are noticed immediately. This obvious distinction between working quarters defines why teachers in this study feel that there is a difference between them and administrators. This status difference exists.

For the purposes of this study, I will define certain teachers by a letter X, A, W, or Y. I will refer to other teachers on the eighth-grade staff as "another teacher." It is imperative to differentiate between teachers, given their different views on schooling and teaching. Both in thought and in deed, teachers X, A, W, and Y share a common bond—they are part of the eighth-grade team of teachers at this school.

## Mr. X

Mr. X is tall, erect, and always well dressed. He wears a tie, and his hair is always combed back neatly. His well-kept beard gives him a distinctive look. He is an imposing figure outside his door (which is situated opposite the school office) as he observes students, teachers, and administrators who pass by. Mr. X is opinionated about life at Hillview and the people in the building, including students, other teachers, and administrators.

He is hard working and always busy. As he stands in class looking down at students, one judges that Mr. X has things under control. He is quick to hand out both assignments and punishments. He is at times sarcastic to students and rarely smiles in class. Says Mr. X to a student, jokingly, "I know you are up to no good as usual." "You guys don't know where you are going," says Mr. X, commenting to the class on the schedule change, taking for granted that his class will be disoriented because of the change in schedule and because they do not approve of the change. He is the epitome of the taskmaster, standing physically and organizationally high above the students sitting in front of him.

He executes health and science assignments methodically, going over the student requirements, answering questions, and relaying the answers in an almost nonstop pace. He varies his work activities in the form of movies and guest lectures. His students don't dare talk, for if they do, a punishment is immediately forthcoming. In his classroom, work is the order of the day—task activities, regurgitation exercises, or copying notes from books or the overhead projector. Mr. X says that he wants to instill some responsibility in his students, and it is from this stance that he does his work.

He is always occupied. He is always carrying his gradebooks and curriculum materials, looking for suitable places to put them, arranging materials in a certain order, being responsible for a clean, neat, and ordered class.

Yet Mr. X is frustrated. He wants out of the middle school, into a high school setting, or possibly out of public education altogether. He stays, however, continuously smirking at the issues of the school that he believes result from a poor administration.

## Ms. A

As with Mr. X, Ms. A is always neatly dressed, with slacks and her hair combed back. She is short, but this is not too noticeable because Ms. A stands erect, with an authoritative tone to her voice. Ms. A is always doing busy work, both in and out of the classroom, preparing student academic exercises or using the computer to record grades and prepare exercises, or even doing administrative kinds of things such as reminding teachers about certain extracurricular activities like intramural sports. She calls this work the real hard work of school, something the administration doesn't want to do.

Ms. A is forceful yet friendly in her teaching approach. She tries to be innovative in her assignments by allowing students freedom to choose reading materials on their level instead of having them read the designated curriculum, which she believes is beyond their reading level.

Ms. A can best be described as into or deeply involved in Hillview life. She cares about all administrative decisions, not only those that affect her personally. She often voices her opinion about school issues in front of the principal.

On the one hand, Ms. A is reserved. But when the issues of school policy (that obviously bother her) become topics of discussion, Ms. A is in the thick of things, voicing her opinions and always ready to dialogue.

She is not sarcastic to students. Ms. A tries to learn more about their home backgrounds. She is caring, always softspoken to students, and she listens sympathetically to their problems. She is admittedly frustrated and would rather teach a different subject than English. She says she enjoys teaching math more. On the whole, Ms. A tries to understand students and their plights. She is constantly on the go, with time a major factor in her day, always in a rush to accomplish things in a quick, effective, and efficient manner.

### Ms. Y

As with Ms. A, Ms. Y is also short. She dresses differently from the rest. Dressed in jeans, she comes closer to looking like one of the students than the other teachers.

Ms. Y is an innovator, the idea person for the eighth-grade students. Both Ms. Y and her students are involved in classroom issues involving racism and prejudice. She is, as I have come to learn over the years, the feminist of this school. She is deeply concerned, caring, and compassionate about social issues. She is presently a social studies teacher, and in her career to date she has taught grades 6 through 8.

A look as Ms. Y's classroom reveals a student sitting on Ms. Y's chair and other students milling around her table. Ms. Y is easygoing; she is not perturbed by a student speaking out of turn or a class with seats that are not ordered in the traditional classroom setting. She realizes the job that has to be done and is an efficient worker. She prefers to experiment for most of the time to achieve results. Thus, every Friday morning she has what she calls a "quest" period, which is a group discussion on problematic issues such as prejudice. Ms. Y's students write poetry about these issues and the class is responsive. She even has the students collectively build a portfolio of their poems on prejudice, which is disseminated to other teachers for reading. Ms. Y can also be forceful in her teaching approach and is extremely task oriented. Time is not an issue when hard work is at the forefront. The class work simply has to get done.

Both Ms. A and Ms. Y are involved in intramural activities. Ms. Y joins in the fun of playing basketball on Thursday mornings (part of the club activities) as well as organizing the girls' volleyball team. She is, as the principal describes her, "a great part of the school" and it would be a "shame to lose her." Ms. Y has mentioned that she wants to transfer because she is exasperated with the tension at the school. She is, on the one hand, quiet and youthful, and on the other hand she is able to push an opinion forcefully before the administration and students, through letters (administration) or debates (students). She cares about her students and is prepared to spend endless hours after school aiding them in their studies or problems with their personal lives.

The tasks she sets for her students are usually either simple rote tasks or more creative ones such as poetry writing. Overall, she combines a variety of teaching approaches, and her easy attitude is offset by a task attitude of getting on with the job at hand.

### Ms. W

Ms. W is heavier set than both Ms. A and Ms. Y. Her hair is also longer. It is combed neatly back. Unlike Ms. A and Ms. Y, she usually dresses in a skirt.

Ms. W is the language teacher for the eighth grade. She is a combination of jolliness and sarcasm, always smiling yet putting students down. When a student jokingly comments on a television comedy, Ms. W returns the comment frustratedly and sarcastically, "What an expanse on your brain. I'm going to grease that mouth of yours." Ms. W can be perfectly delightful one minute, and yet for various reasons she can be upset with a student the next minute. Moreover, Ms. W is not afraid to talk about her feelings to students.

She possesses the uncanny ability to forget a bad moment concerning a student or a remark she has made about a student and/or the administration with the jolliness of her humor. Students like Ms. W. She is friendly. She talks with them about issues that they are concerned with, like new car models and their personal likes and dislikes. She is involved in school activities such as the school dance and the candy sale. She not only collects money, which in itself is time consuming, but she is also responsible for moving the candy boxes and storing them in certain corners of the classroom.

Ms. W is different from the other teachers. She readily admits that she is "not the most structured person in the world," and this results in lesson plans made up in her head at the last minute and a desk cluttered with books, pens, and papers, making it hard to find things. She is able to cope with all this and the problem classes with her sense of humor and empathy for each child's life and present situation. She exhibits the dichotomy of caring for students but also being extremely critical of them. She also wants to move on to secondary school because she feels stuck in the middle school—stuck between caring and criticizing.

### Overview of the Teachers

The casual observer may look on these four teachers as people just doing a simple but important job, smiling to each other in the corridors, chitchatting to each other in the teachers' lounge about topics unrelated to school life, babysitting their students—having an easy life in general, being the typical public servant. In this case, the casual observer would be wrong.

As for having an easy job, it is evident that this is not true. These teachers work hard. There is rarely time off from the duties of the classroom, and they are extremely task oriented. They assume administrative duties that are not officially their designated duties. They worry constantly about their students' performances. They are always on the move, and they are constantly involved both individually and as a group in getting things accomplished. On the whole, their work is often physical—carrying boxes of computer handouts, organizing storage space for candy, moving bleachers in the basketball gymnasium, carting boxes upon boxes of soda to the soda machine, or trotting to the office during class time to accomplish tasks these teachers literally have no time for. In short, life for these teachers involves more than a casual observer might see on the outside.

Overall, the teachers whom I followed are disillusioned and always complaining: "Oh, we haven't got an efficient administration here." They are frustrated with students, but particularly with the administration. More importantly, despite the obvious talent that each teacher possesses individually, they are frustrated at their individual positions and plight within the school system, frustrated with what Ms. Y has called the tension at this particular school. How are these frustrations accommodated or disguised? What actions do these teachers take in their daily routine to make them feel more adequate, worthwhile, and needed during a day so that teaching may hold more meaning for them?

## TEACHER-ADMINISTRATOR EXCHANGE

Basic to our society is the capitalist exchange. Here, the worker exchanges labor for a wage. In school, as has been discussed previously, there is another kind of exchange: the teacher-learner exchange. The teacher passes knowledge to students. In return, students are expected to respect the teacher and behave well and, for the most part, passively accept the knowledge handed down as truth. There is yet another exchange in school. This exchange has to do with teachers and administrators (principal/vice-principal and a counselor, for instance). Importantly, on an official basis, the principal and vice-principal have control of the school in the immediate sense (i.e., on school grounds). They possess the authority and control over decisions about private policies in a public sector.

The exchange between administrators and teachers arises because of the distance between them in their defining roles. Because the principal/vice-principal has the legal and professional authority to be in charge, certain teacher behavior is expected. This behavior entails the teacher providing certain knowledge, skills, values, and attitudes that will promote his or her good work in and out of class. Respect is desired by administrators and is part of this exchange. In return, the teacher may receive a good evaluation, a possible letter of recommendation, and an understanding that may involve the principal being lenient in some cases to teachers who buy into this exchange. Importantly, one must ask, what happens when the exchange doesn't occur? Why doesn't it occur? What happens when teachers don't buy into all aspects of the exchange? This is a vital issue at Hillview and can be viewed as forming the tension between cultures at the school. These questions can be answered by noting the tension between the official and pragmatic routines at Hillview.

### Tensions between Cultures

To recapitulate briefly, the instances of official routines and the breaks of those routines form the tension between two types of teacher cultures. One of them is the official version of what a teacher's day is supposed to look like as delineated in official documents such as the *Basic Components of Middle Schools*, the *Teacher's Handbook*, teacher contracts, and the *Official Graded Course of Study for Middle Schools*.[2] The other is the actual day a teacher goes through that either meets the official requirements laid out by the written documents or is altered in ways to allow the teacher to survive his or her day at school. What we are looking at is the dichotomy between what is supposed to happen at schools at the official level (standardized curriculum, contracts, and other official policies) as opposed to teacher action, which could be called the pragmatic level.

Because of the tension of these two cultures, there exists a teacher counter culture—that is, a culture that differentiates itself from the official aspects of what a teacher is supposed to be and doing exists on the practical level. This differentiation manifests itself in numerous ways and can be described as a break of supposed official policy teacher routines.

## The Official versus the Actual

When trying to define what official means in the Hillview School setting—a middle school consisting of grades 6, 7, and 8—certain assumptions about the administration (including the principal, vice-principal, and counseling positions) define what an administrator should be. It is important for teachers to know what an administrator is officially supposed to be and what he or she is perceived to be. In some part, administrators form a different culture from teachers that is defined simply by their differing bureaucratic roles.

There are some major issues that fall under the guise of administrative positions. One could refer to the literature on leadership and simply pick leadership-type qualities. I choose not to do this, however, as this is not in the bounds of this particular study. Instead, I will stay within the boundaries of the *Basic Components of Middle Schools*, which lays out certain desired characteristics of administrators.

Certainly, a necessary quality is a distinct preference for working at a middle school as opposed to an elementary or high school. From a teacher's standpoint, the most important quality is for the administrator effectively to lead all staff members. This would entail close evaluation, reflective strategies to aid the teacher in his or her class, the ability to create harmony among teachers, and the ability to set an example for teachers by not only listening to teacher grievances but acting on them when necessary. Officially, as described by the *Basic Components of Middle Schools*, an administrator should be able to capitalize on the strengths of teachers. This would mean knowing the details of a teacher's weaker teaching traits, the stronger ones, and nourishing their strengths (i.e., classroom management, humor, and clarity). This would eventually aid in placing students who may work better with the particular strengths of a teacher and using a teacher's weaker traits as a point of further strengthening and development. An administrator should demonstrate the ability to be flexible and be able to facilitate change. This entails understanding teachers' grievances, being able to judge their merit or worth, and implementing change that would not only benefit teachers but students as well.

A good leader is one who is a jack of all trades and can serve as a resource to the staff (e.g., he or she provides research information about teaching or different types of students). A good leader should be able to take over a class when necessary and gain the respect of students. He or she would lead or direct staff meetings positively by using the time not only for relaying information about the upcoming school dance, for instance, but rather using the time for teacher, curricula, and student development. Finally, the administrator must be task oriented—be able to develop the school schedule efficiently, visit classes frequently, and show a personal interest in what is going on in the various teachers' classes.

Some actions I describe as of the teacher counterculture arise because of what teachers perceive as an inadequate administration. Thus, what an administration is supposed to be as an ideal versus how teachers perceive the administration justifies certain acts of resistance by teachers.

### Consent: The Assent to Authority[3]

The aforementioned qualities broadly define the role of an effective administrator. A teacher withdrawal of consent may arise due to the teacher's perceived notions that the administration is weak and inept.

Basic to the exchange of teachers and administrators is the giving of consent by teachers to administrators to lead in their way, without any or much interference. This notion is met with resistance by some teachers at Hillview, as seen in smirking faces and ongoing disagreements over discipline procedures during staff meetings of the principal and teachers. This tension results in teachers and administrators avoiding each other.

I sensed that teachers wish to do their own thing, quietly going about completing their tasks and also taking administrative tasks into their own hands, such as building the schedule for the school year. The administration's ineptitude confirms to teachers that actions taken to defy official aspects of the school are justified.

Basic to teacher withdrawal of consent is oppositional talk. Eighth-grade teacher interviews and responses to questionnaires indicate that teachers judge the administration as lacking strong leadership skills. The teachers agree that little good leadership exists. The judgment of weak leadership is not only expressed behind the principal's and vice-principal's back, but also directly to them. Mr. X commented about the administration, "My relationship with the administration is not very good. Lack of respect on my part. I don't take them to be professional or to be here for the kids. A general lack of respect as there's no leadership." This teacher approached me one day and commented that he was physically sick. Part of the reason for being sick, he said, was that "I dreamed about him [the principal] last night and this morning I was just laying on my back in pure disgust thinking of him. I felt like vomiting."

The concern of Mrs. A is that the principal is not doing his job. This is a major element of her daily thoughts. On occasion she leaves her students to go about their business so that she can use the time to meet the principal on an issue concerning money the principal was supposed to have kept for her class field trip. The meeting takes place during the first period, when students are supposedly doing their silent reading. Although the teacher's misgivings about a weak administration are not shared with the class, they are with other teachers. As the second period ends on the same day, Ms. Y enters another class and both teachers begin to talk about the principal, about how it is "his responsibility to take care of things" and how "he isn't doing his job well." Apparently, the principal lost or misplaced the class trip money and would have to replace it from his own pocket. In an interview, Ms. A expresses concern: "He's ready to retire, he's just putting in his years now." Ms. A is upset because the principal doesn't make the time or have the patience to ask what is being done in class. In fact, this teacher admits that she hardly ever talks with the principal "unless she needs something."

This oppositional talk about the leadership of the administration occurs daily. In another incident, an inspector from the state who is at the school to inspect the physical facilities, the number of computers, and the teachers' written behavioral objectives as part of the lesson plans, addresses the eighth-grade team and the principal. The teachers, desiring to get in their word about the administration to someone outside the school, voice their opinions under their breath so no one can actually hear them. Mrs. A says to a colleague in the meeting, almost in front of the principal, "I hope that we can get a chance to speak to her [the state inspector]. Hope we can throw him [the principal] out. I want to speak to the inspector about him." Eventually, the principal leaves the room, allowing the inspector to speak to the eighth-grade team alone. Immediately, Ms. A pounces on the state inspector with these comments about teacher evaluation:

When he said he was going to get out more often into the classrooms, I just about fell out of my chair. He's out in the halls. He rarely handles any discipline problems. He doesn't tell teachers who aren't doing their job to do it. There's a big staff morale problem. That's why it's so low. . . . I don't think there is anyone in control here, or any strong leadership . . . kids do what they want around here . . . doing things here like with discipline problems and getting things done is like butting heads all the time.

Ms. A is so concerned about the inability of the principal to be a good leader that in a subsequent meeting with the school district area supervisor she makes clear her feelings about his leadership. She is upset that nothing is being done at the school with regard to dealing quickly with discipline problems. When the area supervisor talks about how there must be "open communication" lines, Ms. A openly confronts the area supervisor about the principal:

Everything you told us here, we already know that stuff you know. We're just talking around the whole central issue, that I personally, I can't speak for the rest of the team on this, I just don't think we have a whole lot of leadership. I'm sorry to say, but he's very inconsistent.

These judgments of Ms. A are confirmed constantly and reinforced through specific actions of the principal. For instance, on one day Ms. A's students for the S.O.A.R. period (an acronym for Special Opportunities to Achieve Results Program) don't come to class, and at 8:05 A.M. Ms. A is told by one of her students that everyone is in the auditorium for a special assembly involving a West Point graduate. This situation is judged by Ms. A and other teachers as representing the administration's lack of ability to get things under control and relate messages efficiently. Thus, the administration is usually judged by these teachers as inept.

On the first day back from winter vacation, Mr. X comments to me and his class that no one was told of the change from the S.O.A.R. period on Monday morning to a Unified Arts period: "The principal has screwed this up; everything switches. I hope they understand what a screw-up they've done in this office." In another incident, Mr. X is visibly upset when he notices that nothing is accomplished in his meeting with the vice-principal about the issue of a female student who is an ongoing discipline problem:

Well, I went to the office and got a discipline [I-90] form back, and it says, "talked to her." This girl plays games and knows how to work the offices—another reason for my being infuriated . . . my opinion was that she should be suspended. Well, I went to see her [the vice-principal] this morning, and she said that this girl agreed with me that she was wrong. I thought that she'd get at least a Saturday school detention, and she [the vice-principal] told me that even if she gave one, she wouldn't show up for it. So I said, "you mean to tell me that because I get a speeding ticket I don't have to show up to court?"

Mr. X is deeply concerned that little gets changed or done at the school. In fact, he blames the administration in large part for these failings, especially the principal. Of a proposed meeting with the area supervisor, Mr. X comments,

The principal covered up what we talked to him about in the meeting. He lied to him on the phone. He was covering his ass. He's got a power struggle here. He doesn't like the way he is being mellowed. He's like everyone else in their own little world, and nobody wants to make waves. He is concerned with the fact that there is much miscommunication, and therefore no one knows what the rules are . . . we can't follow rules . . . we have no administration support.

Mr. X's perceptions of the administration's falterings is evident in a meeting with a State Inspector. Mr. X tells the Inspector that he would like

to be able to have some authority and to have complete back-up from the administrative personnel. There's too much miscommunication, a lot of secrecy, and the fact that the communication between us and the people downtown is so sporadic nobody knows what anybody is doing.

Another eighth-grade teacher comments that "the eighth-grade team should run the school." Although we share some laughter about this, there is a seriousness in her voice and she comments, "Each one of us has different expertise, and we could run the school without the principal." She also says that they (the eighth-grade team of teachers) "do run the school, but aren't given credit for it." I sense as I talk to this teacher some sarcasm and strength. I also sense feelings of despair and hopelessness.

On the same issue, another eighth-grade teacher comments that "we had to change the kids' schedule ourselves and it's the administration's responsibility, and they didn't end up doing it, so we ended up doing it in our spare time." These actions by the administration, whether by the principal or vice-principal, confirm the teachers' judgments about weak administrative leadership and a lack of control of immediate and long-term discipline situations. This prompts the eight-grade team to take certain actions, individually and as a team, to get things accomplished.

The teachers also comment that they haven't been evaluated in any consistent fashion in years. Even though there was some form of evaluation recently, it was done so sporadically, say teachers, that they can't call it evaluation. One teacher complains, "He doesn't know what's going on in our classes . . . usually, when I shut the door I do whatever I want as far as some of the rules . . . they say you're supposed to be following the course of study, but they never come in to know whatever you are doing." It's little wonder, then, that particular strengths or weaknesses of teachers aren't really known. These actions, or rather non-actions, by the administration only confirm to teachers that they must take leadership into their own hands. Such was the case with the school discipline plan and with scheduling.

In another incident involving three eighth-grade boys and two girls, one of the boys was officially accused of sexually assaulting one of the girls off the school grounds. The teachers were upset that they weren't told about the incident until two months after its occurrence and that nothing was done about the boy except that he was put on probation. In fact, he was still in school, roaming about and confronting the girl daily. This situation was explained by the principal as not being in his jurisdiction—yet the eighth-grade team feels otherwise. Even though the principal seems to have covered his nonactions (as perceived by the eight-grade staff) legitimately, a letter of compliant with the signatures of each member of the team is sent to the principal and the area supervisor. The letter reads as follows:

It is hard for us to understand two items: (1) why we were not informed of the incident and (2) why there was not school disciplinary action against those in-volved . . . from this unfortunate incident we would like to see several policy changes. First, we feel it necessary that we are informed of such events when they occur—not two months later. Second, the school needs to respond to such in-cidents in a swift, effective, and visible manner.[4]

In a team meeting over this issue, Ms. Y and Ms. A sit slumped in their chairs. An African American teacher sits behind the table, and the principal and other teachers sit around the table. Immediately following the principal's claim that what happened was not in his jurisdiction, the African American teacher comments, "He's right, you know, there are rules." Ms. Y immediately retorted, "You mean to say you've never felt any oppression and/or harassment in your life?" The exchange continues as follows:

*African American teacher*: Why, yes, of course.
*Ms. Y*: Then if you have, can't you understand that this oppressive experience might equate with some of your own? Can't you or any of us here show compassion because maybe we can feel what happened?
*African American teacher*: I guess I can.

In part, this incident led Ms. Y to help her students prepare poems on the topic of prejudice and observe how in the movie *Mask* lives can be affected by ignorance. Clearly, there is a connection between Ms. Y's ac-tivities outside of the classroom with the administration and her prag-matic curriculum content. Whatever the reasons for things not getting done, the aforementioned incidents confirm a number of things to teach-ers: The principal and vice-principal do not have the ability to lead staff members or capitalize on their strengths or deal with such strong cultural issues as sexism. Another eighth-grade teacher comments, "They never come in with any resources; they don't know what I'm ever teaching." According to members of the eighth-grade team, there really is no coun-seling. Ms. Y comments that "the kids just don't get the counseling they need; we don't know what the counselor is even here for." There are 750 kids and one counselor. This prompts Ms. Y to do her own counseling, taking matters into her own hands by either phoning parents or grandparents of students who have personal problems, or just talking with students about the problems that counselors are expected to take care of, spending extra hours after school doing this.

Additionally, the administration is not flexible, according to the eighth-grade staff. This is apparent in administrative non-action concerning student incidents like the sexual assault issue. The schedule, which is the official responsibility of the administration, is completed by the eighth-grade staff and is unappreciated by the administration, according to the eighth-grade team.

Hence, weak leadership is a key issue that the eighth-grade teachers talk about. There is little or none, in their eyes. One reason that some eighth-grade teachers want to move away from Hillview is because of the administration's inability to lead effectively. The lack of leadership is confirmed to these teachers in countless ways, thereby nullifying the teacher-administration exchange. Teachers take matters into their own hands. To illustrate this, I will first lay out official components of schooling and then describe teacher counterculture or informal groups, in which teachers as individuals and as a group confront the weaknesses of the structure of schooling.

## Official versus Pragmatic Routines

### Middle School Philosophy

The Middle School philosophy is officially written up in the *Basic Components of Middle Schools*. The entire school staff is asked to function as a team, along with parents and students. Teachers need a special attitude so they can work with the social, physical, emotional, and intellectual changes of this age group. Because of the unique problems that middle school students have, teachers are asked to develop programs to meet their students' needs. The philosophy calls for students to develop independent learning skills, and delve into abstract concepts. It introduces the notion of exploration as part of what the students should be experiencing. One would expect, then, for teachers not only to follow but also to believe in the middle school philosophy.

Certain components of the day are written up within the time schedule set up in the *Teacher's Handbook*. Officially, teachers are supposed to be in their classrooms at 7:35 A.M., a full ten minutes before homeroom period begins at 7:45 A.M. They are to remain in the school building until 3:00 P.M., fifteen minutes after the students have been dismissed. If leaving early, the principal or vice-principal must be notified so that arrangements can be made for a replacement teacher. Concerning discipline, teachers have strict procedures they must follow and corrective measures they must adhere to. Three procedures of the six that involve discipline are the prerogative of teachers. They are to (1) reprimand, (2) issue after-school detentions, and (3) send students to the time-out room (a room where students can think about what they did wrong). The other three measures—Saturday school, in-school suspension (not attending classes, but doing jobs in the school), and out-of-school suspension—are acted on by the administration only. Basically, after the first three conditions are met by teachers, their hands are tied and they can do no more within the official policy.

### The Move from Official to Pragmatic: Routinization

The *Basic Components of Middle Schools* specifies that teachers are expected to (1) maintain a close daily contact with students, (2) meet individual needs of the students, and (3) as individuals and as a staff exhibit characteristics of warmth, security, consistency, and predictability. However, this is not always the case.

### Actual Attitude toward Students

One of the reasons that the eighth-grade teachers I followed want to move out of Hillview is because of what is perceived as a weak administration. Another reason is the impossibility of teachers to reach the ideal goals set forth by official outlines. This is due to certain limitations of the students as perceived by teachers at Hillview. Whereas Mr. X looks upon matters as "we can't help a lot of these students at Hillview," other eighth-grade teachers are not of the same opinion. Ms. A comments about a fourteen-year-old girl who has already had a baby and comes to school often smelling of liquor: "I want to reach out to her. I feel we both have things in common . . . but it's like she doesn't want to." Ms. A and Ms. Y are often involved in preparing incentive field trips for the eighth-grade students. The details of organization—when and where to meet, which teachers will replace those going—is an intricate, time-consuming, and bureaucratic task. Ms. W works hard on the candy sale and all teachers are involved in the selling of candy for the school dance, obtaining parental permission slips, and following up with students who don't have permission slips. The teachers in this study work overtime for their students.

One thing is certain. All but one of the teachers I followed have had enough of working at Hillview. Two want to move to a secondary school, and another is thinking of a transfer to a different middle school. In a team meeting, the principal explains that next year's lower number of students will mean that one eighth-grade teacher will be without a job. Ms. Y says to the team, in front of the principal with the area supervisor sitting nearby, "I've been thinking of a transfer—I hate the tension at this school anyway." The eighth-grade staff often say that they are frustrated by the tensions of the school. One teacher says that "we are frustrated high school teachers teaching in middle school." Yet, through it all, the teachers have one thing in common. Frustrated or not, tired of the tension or not, they agree that they are basically at the school to "help students." To understand this better, let's take a peek at what goes on in their classrooms.

The four teachers socialize with their students by talking about personal issues of the students or about the activities of the weekend. Some teachers socialize more, others less. But it is obvious that talking about students' personal lives is a daily practical routine. It is time consuming but vitally important to the eighth-grade students, as I suspect it would be to a lot of students. This talk often involves activities done at school, like the science fair project, the selling of candy for the upcoming eighth-grade dance, an upcoming field trip, or even the kind of car a teacher may own as compared to other teachers' cars. As I follow the teachers, I can see that each teacher has a good rapport with the students. Obviously, each teacher has a different style and personality, but students in general like these teachers, even though one student comments that "Mr. X makes me work, work, work, copy notes all the time. He's a hard man, but he's still good." This student says that Ms. A "lets us talk quietly instead of reading silently," and although Ms. W. "comes late all the time," it's allright. Students are generally appreciative of their teachers.

However, one must take a closer look at the type of talk that goes on in class to picture what other attitudes teachers hold toward their students. It may be that these attitudes differ from the supposed, official guidelines set up for teachers. Until now, these attitudes have been depicted as falling into the guidelines of the officially expected, making for a positive classroom climate for all concerned. This, however, is not always the case. Mr. X says to students who don't pay attention, "Part of the problem is that you don't pay attention. Are you sure I haven't been transported to another planet?" Mr. X is at times perplexed not only by the attitudes but also by the standards of his students:

I know that most of you guys have forgotten your names. You guys don't know where you are going. . . . I'm to get your brains started again and the only excuse for you not doing your assignment is if you are in a coma, not your dog pissing on a paper. Tell your parents how you didn't do this assignment, and you know what they'll do after they beat you up.

At this point the class bursts out in general laughter at the apparent joke make by Mr. X. It is obvious, though, that although Mr. X was being sarcastic, his words had a serious bite. In a talk with another teacher, Mr. X comments about his attitude regarding the students: "My attitude is to help the kids who want to learn, and those screwing up and getting suspended—to hell with them, because we don't have the time or facility, and there's nothing we can do to change board policy." Whereas Mr. X is both perplexed and frustrated by the attitude of students and aware of the controlling factor of board policy over him, Ms. W is mostly concerned with establishing a semblance of order in her classes. As she enters class, usually late, coffee in one hand, books in another, she says to students, "Ssh, quiet, shut up, can't you keep your mouths shut?" at the top of her voice. Most students don't really pay attention to her attempt to obtain order. Finally, when some semblance of order is established, it lasts for only a few seconds. She socializes with students on the one hand, but on the other Ms. W is quick to comment to me that if one of her students "would get a grade for attitude, it would be below F, that bastard. This girl couldn't pass an orange." This type of talk is part of the everyday talk that Ms. W uses to describe her students. Very rarely is a positive comment about a student's progress related. In fact, more often than not, Ms. W can be heard talking about the students in a negative manner. She often says, "I don't feel like being here with these brats again."

Often, teachers will threaten their students to get some work done. Ms. Y says to her students, "It would be wise to do your homework, or don't bother coming to school, and if your task is not completed in ten minutes, you'll be in the time-out room for two hours." Ms. Y also comments to students "to get on with the job and stop talking or else there will be an after-school detention. And if that doesn't work an I-90 will be written up." Talk like this to students becomes pervasive within class time.

Out-of-class talk also relates attitudes of teachers to their students. On his way to grading a test given to all his classes, Mr. X says,

It's a pity that I have to give them these objective tests, but I wouldn't do it any other way. It's the easiest, especially when there's 120 people to grade; besides, they haven't got the skills to write comprehensively, which is in great part due to the State Department, federal policy, and this school here that doesn't want to hear about distinctions over individuals. We're not organizing the problem that we have over class differences. The principal's big bitch is not to have ability groups. Therefore, this school is not recognizing the problem of illiteracy.

Again, on his way to the teachers' room for the third period common planning sessions (which is really used as a break time), Mr. X comments on a student's hygiene: "It is unbelievable . . . he used to make me sick . . . I used to say 'stay right there, no closer' . . . probably didn't change his underwear for a month." Mr. X's concern is that his last "normal" eighth-grade class was over three years ago. He comments to me in the teachers' room, "Some kids will make a career out of lying . . . it's like pulling teeth doing work with them, because they can't do it, they don't have the skills, the background, they don't care . . . there's nothing we can do for them here." At this point Ms. W storms into the teachers' room and comments that she'd like to "walk out that door and not walk back, it's depressing . . . I want that little son of a bitch out, I'm so tired, those little bastards, they piss me off."

Talking about the students is a large part of the daily activities of teachers at Hillview. It is not only evident in class, but out of class as well, especially in the teachers' room. Types of talk portray, on the one hand, total devotion to students and, on the other hand, the frustration of being an eighth-grade teacher at Hillview. The talk exhibits also a negative attitude about the students that these teachers teach. Ultimately, routinized activities stem from this attitude.

A very important question is whether the administration inadvertently or directly has anything to do with teacher attitudes regarding students. According to the eighth-grade team, "If the administration would change its policies, so would we." This, they believe, would change the sometimes morbid atmosphere at the school. One must ask, then, if attitudes toward students in this school are developed because of a weak administration or if students are used by teachers to fight the tension they feel with upper-level management? Answering this question, of course, is always site specific but generalizable to some of the issues and discussions of Chapter 2 such as empowerment, hegemony, deskilling, and reskilling.

The tension between what is the official policy—the supposed-to-be attitudes toward students—as opposed to what actually is leads to a specific teacher counter-culture. This claim is argued in the ensuing sections.

## S.O.A.R. AND COMMON PLANNING TIME: OFFICIAL AND PRAGMATIC

Period 0 or the S.O.A.R. (Special Opportunities to Achieve Results) period is an officially set aside block of time to provide students with individual assistance, sustained silent reading, extracurricular activities, student council meetings, assemblies, and music practice sessions. This period is commonly known as flex time, an official component of the day in which students and teachers are supposed to share similar activities, be it sustained silent reading for the whole school, clubs, or independent studies. In addition to the 0 period, third period is also a common planning time period. These periods, 0 and 3, are noninstructional periods. The third period is a supposed official session for the eighth-grade team. Teachers in the eighth grade are supposed to attend what is called a common planning time. The key to this team approach, as advocated in the *Basic Components of Middle Schools*, is for teachers to interact and exchange ideas continually, improving and changing the curriculum—

whatever that may mean. Ideally, the talent and skills of the team should be capitalized on by a sharing of instructional and innovative ideas.

This period is officially used for counseling students, if need be. Teachers are assigned various duties designated by the school, such as hall duty, academic assistance, or being in the time-out room. It is also a time when parents can meet with teachers to talk about students. Also, once a week, on Tuesdays, the principal holds what he calls a team meeting during this third period. Because I was only in the school building until the end of the fourth period—or time-off period—I was not able to view the playground or lunch period.

### Actual Activities

Usually Mr. X sits behind his desk and grades papers during the S.O.A.R. period, enters grades in his grading book, and puts students papers in order. He also is frequently out of class during the S.O.A.R. period, at times for a fifteen- or twenty-minute duration. He completes discipline forms by writing out I-90s or follows up on a discipline problem with the vice-principal. During one S.O.A.R. period, Mr. X handed out four punishments to different students for tardiness. The amount of time spent handing out the punishments, talking about discipline to students, and running to the office during S.O.A.R. period sometimes takes more than one third of the period. This becomes part of the daily routine that Mr. X undergoes. It is sometimes overdone, according to Mr. X, "on purpose, just to get the principal angry." Mr. X has a way of turning the discipline cases into a routine to "get at" the administration, whom he has come to distrust on the matter of what he feels should be proper discipline procedures.

Not only does Mr. X use S.O.A.R. for acting on discipline problems, but he also uses it for teaching preparation. During one S.O.A.R. period, Mr. X raises his voice and comments to his students, "Find something to do or write sentences." With one student folding paper, another tearing paper, and another scribbling, Mr. X continues to complete his tasks regardless of the activity going on in the class. It takes Mr. X only a few minutes to leave his post and continue with his daily routine, including raising discipline issues with the administration. These actions have become the daily routine for Mr. X. Although Mr. X is well aware that S.O.A.R. officially exists as a middle school concept to assist students, the problem, says Mr. X, is that "None of the students like it, me neither. I don't think it is effective. The kids don't know how to study. Most of it is a waste of time; there is no study. There is no academic achievement." When asked why he accepts the official purpose, Mr. X comments that "teachers still bitch about it, but there's not much we can do about it unless we have an entire uprising of the staff, and we're not going to do that." The underlying point is that, at least individually, Mr. X does something about it within his daily activities. Although he does not like or agree with the official purpose of S.O.A.R., he utilizes his time not to "babysit," as another eighth-grade teacher puts it, but to his own advantage. Getting through the day will be far easier doing it Mr. X's way. The underlying notion is that Mr. X grasps the way the school system works, or in this case, the uselessness of S.O.A.R. With this understanding, Mr. X manages his affairs and gets through the school day.

In contrast, Ms. A tends to socialize at the beginning of the S.O.A.R. period. On one occasion she compliments some of her students on their science fair projects: "Did you get an award? You guys should be proud of yourselves for going to all the trouble." Although twice a week S.O.A.R. is supposed to be used as a silent reading period, this is not always the case in Ms. A's classes. Some students take the liberty to either read or talk quietly to neighbors, others move around the class slowly, talking to other students. One student tells me that Ms. A lets students choose between "talking quietly" or following the set, official routine, which is sustained silent reading for that particular period.

Clearly, Ms. A uses the S.O.A.R. period for a number of purposes. On one occasion, students who hadn't taken the vocabulary test the previous day were tested on the words during the S.O.A.R. period. Ms. A asked one of the students to conduct the test for the eight students who missed the test, and while this was going on Ms. A was either preparing for the next class or involved in some administrative duties, like organizing the candy slips for the upcoming school dance. It seems, then, that S.O.A.R. is a period used not only for individual studies, but also for various teacher activities. Twice in my observations of Ms. A's class the eighth grade was summoned to the assembly hall. On one occasion, a graduate from West Point came to visit the school to talk about his success story and the $43,000 he makes a year. More importantly, though, the eighth-grade teachers are told either very late about new arrangements for the S.O.A.R. period or are not told when the S.O.A.R. period has officially started, and therefore they have to rush to the auditorium where everyone else is already seated in the auditorium.

On other days, Ms. A uses the S.O.A.R. period to leave class for up to ten minutes for what she describes as "administrative duties," which may involve talking to the principal or just reading the literature book assigned for the two periods directly following the S.O.A.R. period. Ms. A permits her students to speak quietly while she relaxes or involves herself in tasks that prepare her for the day. She calls this time period a "period for not doing things" or "playing hooky." In an interview with Ms. A, she comments that there are a number of problems with S.O.A.R. The first is administrative: "The principal wants to look good downtown, and what is intended is not achieved . . . teachers use S.O.A.R. as a period of wast-

ing time, where kids socialize." Sustained silent reading, or study hall, is
not always the case in Ms. A's class. Understanding S.O.A.R.'s limitations,
Ms. A is able to arrange her school day by making S.O.A.R. her own free-
time period. More significantly, Ms. A comprehends S.O.A.R.'s official de-
ficiencies, thus enabling her to manipulate this official component of the
day into a pragmatic routine.

Such is also the case with Ms. W. Asked for her impressions on S.O.
A.R., she comments that "it's a waste of time, everybody's time, my time,
their time." Yet for Ms. W, S.O.A.R. is more than just a waste of time. As
with other teachers, Ms. W uses S.O.A.R. to her personal advantage by
"running dittos some days, grading papers some other days, or reading
the newspaper or a book during the silent reading period." Socializing
with students is a major aspect of Ms. W's period. As with Ms. A, time is
taken to talk to students about affairs that are not academic. When the
bell rings at 8:00 A.M. for the start of the S.O.A.R. period, Ms. W talks to
students about personal matters and about the sale of candy for the upcoming dance:

*Ms. W*: What will we do if we sell so much candy that there will be money left
over? Maybe we'll go to Wyandotte Lake.

*Student*: No, there's no roller coasters, man, no fun.

Because of teacher-student interaction, the official purpose of independent sustained silent reading is not accomplished. Of the eighteen
students who are attending Ms. W's S.O.A.R. period, the majority do not
complete the designated activity. Ms. W does not run after them to check
if they are busy. Some students sleep, others draw pictures, stare into
open space, or chatter quietly. If not socializing, Ms. W tidies her desk,
organizes her storage closet for the candy to be stored, leaves the class
for up to ten minutes and returns with coffee in hand, or admittedly goes
to the office to run some dittos for the following periods. It is no wonder,
then, that Ms. W believes that S.O.A.R. is "wasted time." Yet on the other
hand, this structured time period gives her a chance to accomplish teaching tasks and other bureaucratic activities that otherwise would have to
be accomplished at other times during the day—for example, her time-
off period.

As with other teachers, Ms. Y uses the S.O.A.R. period "for preparing
for the whole day." This, however, is not the official use as defined in
the *Teacher's Handbook*. Officially, teachers must supervise students; instead, Ms. Y concerns herself with other issues such as the sexual assault
charge brought by a student in the school. She is concerned about how
the young women in the school will be affected and with the fact that
teachers were notified so late about the sexual assault charge. She writes
a letter of complaint to the superintendent about this.

Whether it be socializing or leaving the room for whatever reason—administrative matters or preparing class lessons for the following periods—it is obvious that the S.O.A.R. period is not only a designated supervision or babysitting service, as a casual observer may perceive, or a supposed individual assistance period. It is a period in which teachers adjust their time to suit their own needs. They catch up on other work to be done during the day. Teachers understand that if they can manipulate the official aspects of S.O.A.R. into pragmatic routines, such as "getting at the principal," writing letters of complaint, or doing administrative duties, the day becomes that much more bearable for them.

## OFFICIAL ASPECTS OF TEACHING

In the *Basic Components of Middle Schools*, teaching strategies are delineated under such headings as "Planning for Teaching," "Lecture," "Lecture Recitation," "Discussion Groups," "Simulation," "Independent Study," "Performance Contracting," "Inquiry Programmed Learning," and "Interest Centers." My aim is not to determine whether a teacher falls under one of these categories and then judge if what is achieved in class is good or bad, but to look at what is actually taught. This will be done to establish a tension between the official and pragmatic aspects of teaching.

The *Course of Study* from kindergarten through grade 12 is a pamphlet designed solely for the public schools. Thus, it supposedly contains the instructional curriculum which teachers follow. It is what the superintendent of schools calls "a significant curriculum document."[5] Each subject area outlines general areas of study, which are followed by lists of desired outcomes. For example, the subject of health for eighth graders includes such topics as nutrition, mental health, and alcohol and drugs. Under these main headings are two or more points under subheadings, which are supposedly able to guide the teacher about what content should be taught. These outlines are brief, with no follow-up suggestions or activities to aid the teacher in choice of materials. Materials such as booklets on alcoholism or other story books are generally assigned and are the property of the school, loaned by the State Department of Education, and cannot be taken off school grounds by students.

### Pragmatic Curriculum Activities

Ms. A is deeply concerned that her class, which contains a number of Cambodian refugees who now speak English rather well, do not talk much in class, and are extremely difficult to motivate. As I observe the English lessons, each student is given a reading turn, and it becomes obvious that upon questioning students after a story is read, many students do not understand it. The literature book being used has been recommended by teachers at the high school that these youngsters will be attending the following year. It represents the official part of the curriculum.

It is clear to Ms. A that she cannot use the curriculum guidelines, and as a result, for practical purposes, she must deviate from the given curriculum. Often during the literature lesson, Ms. A will tell her students to forget about the present curriculum while they do something else: "What I'm going to do is let you relax and read different types of easier literature using the characterization, time and place, thoughts and feelings. Before we start doing anything else, I want to read to you *Sylvester and the Magic Pebble.*" While reading the simpler story, students begin to show great interest and follow it in greater depth than the discussion of the regular curriculum choice. By giving the third-grade reading material to her class, Ms. A has succeeded in meeting the class's standards. At the same time, she is able to keep close to the curriculum by using the same themes for discussion that she would have for the more difficult literature. Originally, Ms. A was supposed to team teach with another eighth-grade teacher next door. Once dependent on the official curriculum and the task-oriented exercises prepared by the other teacher, Ms. A now believes that she must take things into her own hands and do more creative, pragmatic activities with her students than the official curriculum suggests or the teacher next door designates for her own class.

Even though the official curriculum is used at times, the end for which it is used is questioned. Teachers tend to use the curriculum for their own personal needs, which may or may not be useful for student learning. Let us see how this works.

Mr. X gives students an activity to complete by the end of class. The activity involves reading about a topic such as alcoholism, disease, or drugs. Students are expected to read and answer questions prepared by Mr. X on the topic. The students in Mr. X's class are used to working hard for him, and thus exercises on the whole are accepted and done quietly. Many students comment that the tasks are "boring, too many words, we copy notes most of the time in class." Students are always busy, as is Mr. X. It is not uncommon for Mr. X to leave the class for a short duration and return with a cup of coffee while students are completing an exercise. At other times, Mr. X utilizes this time to record grades, file materials, prepare overhead transparencies with answers to a particular exercise, and deal with I-90 discipline forms to "get at the principal," as during the S.O.A.R. period. Mr. X admits that he doesn't want to work after he leaves school. In some ways, then, he must organize and manage his affairs so that everything gets done within the school day. Thus, although the official curriculum is adhered to constantly so students complete exercises, it seems that it is also adhered to so Mr. X can gain control over his daily routines.

All teachers whom I follow admit that this behavior is commonly the case. For instance, the movie *Mask* is shown in Ms. Y's class, both as a reward and as supplementary curriculum material to the current issues of discussion in class on prejudice. While the movie is playing, Ms. Y's concern is with having some free time and organizing the day by preparing other content curriculum materials. She also concerns herself with the sexual assault issue that has the eighth-grade team buzzing. She writes letters to the principal and the area supervisor that will eventually be signed by the eighth-grade team.

These are only a few of many instances of how teachers at Hillview adjust the official curriculum to suit their own purposes, be it "to delete things that don't interest me" or to deviate from the handed-down curriculum. These actions become pragmatic routines and make the day more manageable and meaningful for the teachers. The adjustment from the official curriculum to a more pragmatic curriculum and other teacher-controlled activities becomes a major part of the day for these teachers at Hillview. After all, "life is better doing it my way," suggests one of the teachers.

The commonality across the board, then, is the actual activity teachers routinely engage in when students are doing classwork. Some of these activities involve testing the administrative authority over discipline issues. It is within the testing of authority that these teachers are able to probe the weaknesses of the administration. Teachers exploit these weaknesses to their advantage in order to make their lives easier at school. The knowledge that the teachers can complain, fight the system, at least "make it work for us," or "get at the principal" suggests a daily existence that is ultimately tied to the informal pragmatic level of teacher routines.

### Other Official Routines of the Teacher's Day versus Pragmatic Routines

All teachers are required to prepare lesson plans. According to Ohio's State Department of Education's *Revised Minimum Standards*, "There should be a lesson plan for each class in order to meet the advanced needs of students . . . and they should be available on a daily basis in an obvious place, preferably on the teacher's desk, for the administrative review." It is also stated in the *Basic Components of Middle Schools* that desired characteristics of teachers should entail the distinct preference for working in the middle school as opposed to, say, the elementary or secondary school level.

One would expect, then, that teachers preferring a certain grade level would be committed to the philosophy and objectives of the middle school, as shown by a positive attitude toward students, a willingness to understand the educational and personal needs of the students, and a willingness to respond to those needs. Cooperative teacher planning is desired as well. This includes some sort of group curriculum development and/or other classroom projects that a group of teachers would decide on. These matters may include attention to discipline problems, policy, curricular agreements and implementations, and teaching plans that are group based and worked out cooperatively. Moreover, it is expected that teachers will follow school policy and rules, such as being in class before students arrive, informing the administration of leaving school early so a replacement can be found, and not eating in class, thus setting a positive example for students. To follow rules, then, is a designated official activity.

### Actual Lesson Plans

Not all teachers at Hillview Middle School comply with state-mandated lesson plans. Ms. Y comments, "I do what I want in class. Nobody sits on us and tells us what to do. I haven't had my lesson plans checked in twelve years." While I am sitting in the teachers' room with Ms. Y and talking to her about the upcoming visit of the State Department of Education representative, Ms. Y says that she "will make a month's lesson plans on Sunday evening." She laughs mockingly at the idea that lesson plans are taken even remotely seriously by teachers.

Ms. Y isn't the only one not to prepare lesson plans. Ms. W openly admits that she "just thinks about lesson plans and rarely writes down stuff. I rarely write objectives, mostly in my mind. I know that I have to by official guidelines, but I do. Usually it's a mental thought process." Most teachers who prepare lesson plans do so during the day. In an interview with me, Ms. A holds a small piece of paper with five or six scribbled and crossed-out words. I ask her if that is her lesson plan, and she replies, "that's it." She comments, "You know, we don't even hand in lesson plans here . . . at some schools we had to hand them in every week."

### Rules and Rule Breaking

Besides arriving late to faculty team meetings, teachers admit that there are breaches of other school rules. It is interesting to note that one teacher I followed was ten to fifteen minutes tardy to school on ten occasions during one month. This ultimately drew an official warning in a letter from the principal. On other occasions, teachers were at their posts at the official starting time of 7:35 A.M. However, on other occasions I sat in class, and students had already entered and the teacher followed four to five minutes later.

Tardiness plays a role in teacher group actions. Mr. X comments, "We all agreed that standing outside the door at 7:35 was useless, so we just do not do it all the time. This is a kind of group unspoken agreement." One teacher admits that she is "rarely at the door at 7:35," and as I observe the four teachers, rarely do they follow the rule about standing outside their doors at 7:35 A.M. In class, patrolling the halls, or during lunch, rules are broken by teachers. That is not to say that teachers are never found standing outside their doors at the designated, official time, but only that the rules are often broken, both on an individual level and on a group level. Teachers, in this school, do either drink coffee or eat in class in front of their students, although officially they are not permitted to do so. Ms. A readily admits that she eats in the classroom and is quick to mention that other rules get broken: "I have parties when I shouldn't, for instance." Indeed, as I partake in a party involving other eighth-grade classes, another eighth-grade teacher joins who has left her class unattended. I eat donuts and drink orange juice with as much enjoyment as the students and the three eighth-grade teachers. The party, however, is conducted without consent given by higher authority, with a group of three eighth-grade teachers who don't even consider asking permission to have it. Ms. A also admits that she leaves school early and has done so on more than one occasion. On the topic of why she doesn't report leaving school early, she says, "I know Monday I had a doctor's appointment. I left and I didn't tell him [the principal]. I arranged someone else to take my class. We help each other when it comes to these matters." Ms. A admits that this is all "a challenge to his authority" (the principal's). The same could be said about her reflecting on the student sustained silent reading in the S.O.A.R. period. She believes this is also, to some extent, a "challenge to his authority," and she admits, on the other hand, that her students like to "chatter or read easier material."

Most teachers admit that they overuse the teacher-allotted quota of photocopies. Ms. A says she does this for practical purposes because sometimes she needs a quick amount of copies for the next class if she is "running short of time." Ms. W says that she is "Miss Ditto Queen," and although she realizes that there are limitations on the use of the copying machine, she admits that "I occasionally break the rules. We all do."

## CONCLUSION

On the whole, it is the notion of the individual and we (the group) that justifies actual teacher routines as opposed to official routines. The former include intentional teacher resistance to authority and defiance of the structural imitations. Resistance and accommodation allow teachers to suit their own personal needs and alleviate their occupational frustrations. There is also a sense of accomplishment and pride in Mr. X's tone of voice when he succeeds in "getting at the principal." The same can be said when Ms. A breaks a school rule. This sense of accomplishment is part of a larger picture. A different culture is created by these eighth-grade teachers, first as separate individuals and then as the teacher group forms. This group runs counter to the official routines and expectations of the school. It is an informal counterculture that typifies this new order in this particular school. Ultimately, the question remains, so what? Caught between two realms, official and pragmatic, with certain routines, where do teachers go from here? What does this all mean?

These questions propelled me into the next study. I was concerned with my extreme emotional investment in this study, but I learned that in this type of research, the affective domain was paramount to understanding teacher realities. Additionally, I was more concerned than ever before in writing about an agenda that would allow possibilities to see through oppressive values. I saw critical theory both as a movement and its underlying basic assumptions as one avenue for portraying schools as sites of emancipatory possibility.

The study of these four teachers had its limitations (as do all case studies), particularly as it dealt with deep structural concerns (rules, policies, relationships, etc.) and not as much with how teachers altered oppressive cultural values such as sexism, racism, individualism, and competitiveness. As I proceeded to my next study, I began to feel and look for what the literature in education (and particularly outside of education) called difference. Within this concept, I began to view my work in a new and different emancipatory light.

## NOTES

1. This study was conducted in Columbus, Ohio, in the 1985–1986 academic year.

2. *Basic Components of Middle Schools*, Columbus Public Schools, Columbus, Ohio, 1984; *Teachers Handbook*, 1984, in-house teacher handbook; *Official Graded Course of Study for Middle Schools*, Columbus Public Schools, Columbus, Ohio, 1983; State Department Revised Minimum Standards, Ohio State Department of Education, Columbus, Ohio, 1983.

3. Willis (1977), *Learning to Labor*, p. 64, talks about the notion of consent in terms of teacher-student exchange as follows: The "teacher's authority must therefore be won and maintained on moral, not coercive, grounds. There must be consent from the taught." In the same way, within the teacher-administration paradigm there must be consent given to the administration by teachers on a moral basis for an exchange is to take place.

4. This is part of the eighth-grade team letter sent to the superintendent and the principal.

5. For the sake of anonymity, the name of the superintendent who describes the curriculum document will not be mentioned.

## CLASSROOM ACTIVITIES

1. Groups of students will describe the perfect administration. In addition, they will discuss their expectations as teachers and how they think such expectations can be met realistically.
2. Groups of students will describe their projected official and pragmatic goals for teaching, particularly regarding curriculum matters.

## QUESTIONS FOR DISCUSSION

1. Of the four teachers on the eighth-grade team, which teacher would you identify with? Why?
2. Do teachers act individually; if not, how is their group manifested?
3. Discuss these teachers as related to the reskilling and deskilling process; relate this to curriculum issues and the structural aspects of schools.
4. How are these teachers hegemonized?
5. Is there a sense of autonomy and/or control in the teachers' lives at the school?
6. How does teacher resistance manifest itself here? What would deviance look like in this chapter?
7. If you were in these teachers' situations, what tools would you use to help alleviate the conflicts these teachers face?
8. Are there teacher critical pedagogues in this chapter? Do they challenge taken-for-granted views? Is interpretation challenged?
9. Could you see yourself working in such a school? Why or why not?
10. What causes tensions for these teachers besides mere administration ineptness?
11. What would a positive critical theory environment over the administration look like?
12. How are teachers empowered in this study?
13. In what ways is the hidden curriculum manifested in this study?

# 4

---

# Coming to Terms with Difference

## INTRODUCTION

If there are some students reading this text who feel that in the last chapter there was too much emphasis on the relationship between the administration and teachers or vice-versa, there would be some justification for these thoughts. With that in mind, I want to again remind readers of my past history. I was schooled in a rigid system in which I viewed the administration, particularly the principal and even the vice-principal, as extreme authoritarian figures. As a teacher I was extremely aware of administration control and of teachers as deskilled workers, especially through standardized curriculum and accountability procedures. It is of no surprise, then, that looking back on Chapter 3 and on the time that the data for that chapter were collected I can say that a lot of what was seen through my eyes was, in some part at least, a reflection of my own student and teaching life. Thus, it must be argued that we as educational researchers and teachers cannot be value free or objective in our assumptions. Just as I will always argue that there is no objective curriculum, I will as strongly point out to my pre- and in-service students in university classes that there is no teacher who doesn't instill his or her values into teaching at some point. We are the product of history, ours and others. This subjectivity is conveyed consciously and/or unconsciously through what I described in Chapter 2 as the hidden curriculum.

Thus, values such as success and competition (carried to extremes), conformity, and sexist and racist attitudes are all transmitted at various times and in different forms throughout the school day and year. I tell my students that for all their good and bad qualities, I was a combination of the teachers at Hillview. I was lazy, disorganized, a social activist, and, at times, an authoritarian. I did instill both meaningless activities as well as meaningful exercises about social issues. These social issues, were, however, passed on with far less frequency. I was an intimidating teacher as well, in large part because I demanded a lot from my students. But I also cared deeply about my students and invited them to my home. I was, I believe, a good teacher. It is clear to me now that I possessed the capacity to think critically despite the hegemonic (hidden and accepted dominant values) and material and structural constraints (class size, handed-down-from-above curriculum, authoritarian figures) set upon me. Although I was never exposed to alternative ideas about education (such as those espoused by critical pedagogy and postmodernism), I would argue that a great many teachers already possess a lot of similar social qualities of incessant inquiry, social agitation, and a desire to change the world. When I ask students today why they want to become teachers, they usually say, "to make a difference and cause change." I then ask them what they mean by difference and change. These students' replies are limited to comments like "helping kids" or to "teach students to achieve better." In other words, although the responses seem to be both noble and moral, they are empty of deep meaning and/or understanding of the school system they are entering. Yet it must also be argued that these responses are the best of democratic ideals and should be explored critically. That is, the cause that drives people to be teachers inherently consists of noble and compassionate qualities about teaching—qualities that run against the grain of a socially efficient school system that slowly drains teachers of such qualities.

It became clear to me that the kinds of questions I was asking as a graduate student, and what I was seeing as a researcher and social theorist, were very limited, as were my students' initial responses to my question about why they wanted to become teachers. Yet the ingredients were there to further my curiosity about teachers. If anything, I had learned in the cast study in Chapter 3, as I had from my life experiences, that conflict could be a way of life. But conflict runs much deeper than I could have ever imagined. Conflict is more than just teacher frustration over administration weaknesses (although this is important, too). Conflict for me (as I was now reading the more theoretical parts of social and educational literature) and the teachers I was observing had a great deal to do with understanding how difference operates in social surroundings.

Clearly, I had grown up as a product of difference. In Australia I was viewed through my Jewish identity. Often, I heard myself referred to as a "dirty Jew" or "Jew boy" by my non-Jewish football teammates. I was treated differently by my classmates. Our food was different. Our values were also different. I was both afraid and ashamed to bring non-Jews to my home. Moreover, I was not encouraged to do so. In Israel I didn't speak, read or write Hebrew very well and felt illiterate in the language. And although I knew I had an advantage in being a white foreigner in Israel, it didn't always work in my favor. I was constantly misunderstood. My nonverbal gestures, gregarious personality (a product, I believe, of my Australian background), and views on middle-class life were distorted in Israel. I was faced with military imposition and by not joining the army I was viewed as less worthy than the average Israeli and was generally looked down on—at least I felt so. I often had to repeat my needs or wants in the simplest of places (like grocery stores or banks) at least three times to make myself understood in this new and foreign language. Even though I have been in the United States for eleven years now, my accent and pronunciation continues to be different. I am still asked to repeat myself more than once. I always wondered, is this my fault? Possibly it is no-one's fault! Is there a proper way of speaking? Who defines that way?

Arriving in California in July of 1988 on professorial assignment at a small college, I was struck by the multiple cultures that walked the streets. On these streets of Orange, California, English was a rare commodity. I felt more at home here than in the previous places I had visited and lived in in the United States. There was no doubt in my mind that walking the streets of difference, and having felt different all my life, California would be a haven for personal intellectual growth and exploration. With that in mind and the contents of Chapter 3 behind me, I arrived in California full of anticipation, excitement, and motivation. Similarly, I entered Parkview Elementary with the same fervor. Importantly, the questions I was asking differed from the ones that I explored in Chapter 3. Yet, on some level, they were all connected. What differences meant, how community in the classroom was established, how competition played itself out, how individualism was downplayed, and so on became focal questions, concerns, and inquiries as I entered my next research agenda. I want to remind students that I had come to these questions not only through the cast study in Chapter 3. If I am a product of my own history, then the same questions I had as a boy in Australia, as a youth in Israel, and as a young academic in the United States, are still the focal point of my life.

At the time of the study discussed in this chapter, there was little doubt about the extraordinary importance of the new theories of education that had abounded since 1970. And the onslaught of critical social theory in the education literature (and explored in Chapter 2) can be seen, in part, as a reply to the certainty in which schools were viewed, such as what counted for truth in student evaluation construction, or stereotypical responses about who was going to succeed.

It has been increasingly disappointing to me (even today) that little within critical pedagogy had linked schools to a growing emancipatory agenda, one that had as its core some form of practical purpose and/or platform. In my mind, the complexity of educational social theory thought had moved to more modern and postmodern analyses that acknowledged the moments in which students and teachers sought desperately both to undermine and humanize the process of cultural transmission.[1] It seems to me that little theoretical and practical work on the nature of the construction of self, difference, identity, and community was available for in- and pre-service educators seeking a language to use for social activists in the field.

With the preceding caveat in mind, one aim in this chapter is to provide empirical support for the concepts of self, difference, and community. I want to start this exploration by first elaborating on G. H. Mead's ideas on self and community. I feel that this is imperative to a better understanding of difference. I will then present data to support these concepts. In some ways, these concepts are intimately connected to the dominant ideological constructs of individualism and competition, concepts that, although lived out in the real world, have been ingrained into our consciousness. As a final thought for this chapter, I want readers to think about the ramifications of self and community as related to a counterhegemonic framework for educational theorists and practitioners as well as the uncertainty that faces critical social theorists in the construction of resistance as a tool used in response to dominant ideological mainstream consciousness.

## SELF AND COMMUNITY

I now turn to Herbert Mead's social theory. I relate how the self and community are constructed. I suggest that Mead has something important to offer critical pedagogists and teachers regarding an emancipatory agenda in schools. Understanding Mead will allow us to challenge the meaning of dominant values, such as community, individualism, and negative competition. Placing Mead into a critical context necessarily involves understanding the meaning and role that the process of reflection may play on the constructs of self and community.

In *Mind, Self and Society*, Mead[2] describes at length the process, construction, and internalization of the social being or person as the self. That is, the self and society are entwined. They are both intimately related. They both emerge from an ongoing social experience and social symbols—meanings that are shared by people engaged in social interaction and an understanding of the intentions of others (being able to assume another's point of view or taking the role of the other). Empathy becomes paramount in this construction. That is, Mead at least implies that self and community are constructed around empathy—the ability to assume the role of the *other*, to feel the other's position in life, including pain, oppression, and subordination.

Mead describes the self as composed of two parts: The *I* and *me*. Mead called the subjective element of the self the I. Here, all spontaneous action is understood as the operation of the I. That is, any action we render, such as egotistic thoughts (I must buy a car today, get a haircut today, sunbathe today, visit my friend today, etc.), is a part of the I. Second, the self is also an object because it is seen from the perspective of others. That is, others see your I as you operate (I am a professor, father, teacher, ex-husband, etc.). While the self initiates interaction with others (as I), it becomes an object to itself (me) by assuming the role of the other. That is, you as the actor complete actions similar to those actions of others. Your actions, although they may be momentarily different from mine, may, at some point, assume some similarities. For example, when I was in high school I was a part of a cheating system. My I was in operation. I desired a good grade, for selfish reasons. Others may have viewed this with disdain. Yet friends of mine had similar experiences. These similarities make possible the connection between the I and me due to what I shall term empathic connection. We all shared the common element of cheating for various individual (I) egotistic purposes. In all social interaction the I and the me are evolving through an ongoing process that continues through the life of the individual and the community. The self becomes social and responds to its actions based on the responses of others.

For Mead, the organized community or social group which gives the individual a unity of self is called the generalized other. This generalized other is part of every self. An inner dialogue occurs between the I and the attitudes of others, unifying the self and others within a community. Consequently, individual acts and thoughts contain internalized cultural norms, behaviors, values, attitudes, symbols, gestures, and language that are embedded in and are a part of a community. Thus, what is conformity, deviance, and/or resistance take on particular social significance demarcated by law and the norms of society. The ability of the self to understand, empathize, and take the role of the other is accomplished through this shared communication. Typically in schools, gender issues are constructed around these concerns. Male bonding, despite its patriarchal and often demeaning bent, assumes shared communication. Female bonding is also shared communication around social concerns. Friendship at early ages is often based around shared social meanings. In my math class, for example, I recall Mr. Twomey's sexist attitudes. I also recall how a lot of the males used this sexism as an I and a me to develop shared communication and a sense of their male community (which is connected to the larger male culture) and common bond.

The emergence of the self does not end here. Changing social experi-

ences such as that which critical pedagogy advocates, combined with reflection on an old self, can reshape each individual and produce a new
thinking, feeling, and acting subject. Furthermore, Mead's social reconstruction presupposes a basis of common social interests by individuals
whose combined minds both participate in and bring about that reconstruction. This reconstruction, critical pedagogues would argue, must involve certain changes in ourselves. For critical pedagogy, change
necessarily starts with reflection on Mead's I and me construction.
Change can only start by understanding the make-up of self and other.
It is this non-deterministic and deconstructive view of the construction
of the self and the other which furnishes a further interpretation of the
construction of what I shall term the critical pedagogy self: the self that
both reflects on and critiques the I and me as it relates to social relationships that affect alienation, oppression, and subordination within the
context of social relationships.

Another illustration of self and community is in the offing. Mead drew
two constructs of children's activities: play and game. In play, the child
interacts with an imaginary partner and through this activity anticipates
the behaviors of the other. This stage is followed by the child's ability to
engage in group play. It could be argued that what is expected of this
generalized other is conformity or nonconformity to the rules of the game
and to the values, attitudes, and norms of the group. This illustration
supports the relationship between the development of self in a personal
dialectic of self and generalized other as it connects to the group or
community into which one attempts entrance. Within this personal dialectic, the critical pedagogy self seeks to understand the self construction
in an ongoing dialectic with oppressive social structures. How I, me, and
other can work dialectically both to oppress and emancipate us becomes
of increasing importance to critical pedagogists. With this in mind, a description of a fourth-grade teacher and her students will help depict this
dialectical self and community.

### Parkview Elementary

Parkview[3] is an urban, elementary school situated off a main street in
an industrial neighborhood in southern California. The street is lined
with small houses. At best, the school could be described as a school in
a working-class, blue-collar neighborhood. According to my fellow
teacher education colleagues involved in educational research, the school
could also be described as conservative. *Change* is not a pleasant word.
Many teachers have settled into their careers at this school. Status quo
best describes their overall attitude. Follow the official curriculum—no
questions asked! Some school classrooms are large and clean; others are
large and dirty. For the most part, however, all classes are equipped with

TVs and enough chairs for students. Unlike a lot of typical inner-city schools, this school is not exactly of that ilk. There is no graffiti. There is heating in the classrooms in the winter. Some classes even have ceiling fans. The library is neat. As in most elementary schools, the playground noise level is high. On the whole, students seem to enjoy themselves at Parkview.

Parkview is described by the principal as being very involved in meeting the goals of the California Aptitude and Proficiency Test (CAP) with the thrust in math, science, and language arts and with less emphasis on social science, art, and music. Stereotypically, then, science and math reign supreme and the humanities (as has historically been the case) take a back seat. Teachers have been at Parkview for ten to thirty-five years. There is one new teacher and another who has been there for five years.

The principal described the school as "blue-collar intellectual, where parents are blue-collar workers and their children strive to do better." The majority of the student body is minority, mostly Hispanic. These students, commented the principal, are "vocationally bound, and I don't know if we give them what they want." I was struck by the principal's eagerness to have me at the school. I was impressed with her enthusiasm for running a smooth, productive, efficiently organized machine. I was angered, however, at her social ignorance. How, I said to myself, can you assume that certain students are determined to be vocationally bound? Having read many books on tracking,[4] I found the principal to be symbolic of this sorting-machine device.

The students at Parkview, it seemed, were caught in the stereotypical trap of low parent education with low-paid occupations and a district and teacher inability to provide these working-class students with the equal opportunity for cultural capital (knowledge, skills, values, and attitudes) for mobility out of their predetermined economic and social class. After observing some teachers, I began to see that teacher attitudes, boring classroom activities (sometimes I fell asleep while observing teachers in this school who use the standardized curriculum excessively), and meaningless exams helped formulate these predetermined student social identities. After observing one particular class for one year, however, it seems to me that the notions of self and community have great effects on students rising above a predetermined, stereotypical view of what it is that they can or cannot achieve in this school, at least as perceived by the principal and some teachers. I now turn to a teacher who, for the most part, challenged stereotypical views.

*Betty*

For this particular case study in the 1988/1989 academic year, a fourth-grade teacher named Betty (name changed) was chosen for observation primarily because of her involvement and my interest in a funded global education project (the connection and interconnection of America to other parts of the world). I observed Betty on and off for a year. There were times when I was in her class for three hours every morning for weeks on end, particularly at the beginning of the school year and toward the end of the school year.

Over time, I became what the educational and social research literature describes as a classic participant-observer. I participated in class activities and observed how students learned and how Betty taught. Students in Betty's class were extremely responsive to me. Gaining their trust as well as Betty's was gradual and was enhanced when I taught lessons on the Jewish festival of Hanukkah and made presentations on Israel and Australia—two countries where, as readers know, I had lived previously. My ongoing presence in the classes allowed me to move between the roles of researcher, teacher, and friend to both Betty and her students. With this in mind, and able to determine how Betty acted individually and with her students, I began to zero in on my research concerns. What effect global education had for curriculum, self, and community was an important issue for me. How students responded to global education as a critical tool for understanding the terms *difference* and *empathy* became another major concern.

I chose to observe Betty because she seemed to infuse her curriculum with different cultural perspectives, particularly as it related to difference. She also seemed affectionate, devoted, and caring about what happened to her pupils and her school district. Betty had twenty-nine students in her class. This was her first year as a fourth-grade teacher. She was a first-grade teacher for many years and is skeptical if not worried about how her first fourth-grade teaching experience will turn out. Betty is a very committed teacher. Her students are her life. A high percentage of Betty's students are Hispanic. Betty is also Hispanic and speaks fluent English and Spanish.

As I walk into school I am greeted by Betty's smile and general warmth. She hands me the key to her class and says that I can open the classroom door. On the way to her class I pass happy children in the playground, benches where teachers sit, an old basketball court, and a long patch of green grass called the playground. As I enter Betty's class, I am overwhelmed by the largeness of the room. Chairs are placed neatly on her tables. There is a television, organized library, calendar, and various pictures hanging on the walls. There is a saying that hangs in the classroom, and it strikes my eye immediately. It reads, "Creative imagination is the seed to greatness." The overarching classroom message hangs above the chalkboard in large letters. It reads, "The limits we have are those that we set for ourselves." These expressions at once surprise me because they seem, at least at first glance, to counter the principal's perception of student abilities in this school. Rules are also noticeable in the classroom—"respect your neighbor, listen to others talk, and share with others." These kinds of rule constructions organized dialogically and democratically by Betty and her students, are different from traditional class rules that revolve around leaving-the-room policies, talking policies, and so on.

Students' Indian tepees are set neatly on one table, a library is at the back of the room, and one side wall is covered with student work from the previous day—math problems and drawings. Students are, for the most part, attentive to Betty. Even when a student falls out of line, Betty singles out an attentive student and comments, "Look how well Manual is behaving. He's so good today." Students look to Manual for support, and the misbehaving students, for the most part, shape up. Betty thus has an uncanny way of attaining order without denigrating, punishing, or reprimanding anyone.

Betty builds self-esteem into her students. She accomplishes this in part through a continual appraisal of a student's worth. She comments at the beginning of each class, "Close your eyes, feel yourselves getting close to each other, pass your energy and support yourselves." At approximately 8:15 every morning, after Betty's initial prior comments, students shout "My Creed" at the top of their lungs: "Today is a new day. Today I believe in myself. I respect others and I care about my friends. Today I will work hard to learn all I can learn. I am intelligent. I am wonderful. I know I am very special. I'm glad I'm here and I'm going to make today a great day." Betty's class usually undergoes an energy circle ritual. After the creed is repeated, Betty often calls the class to the front of the room, again in support of feeling empathically for each other. Betty comments to her students, "First we must have everyone supporting each other. Let's again hold hands and give each other energy. Close your eyes. Now, pass the energy around, feel the energy go through you. We are now connected, we now have energy. Now I want people who read yesterday to say something about your friend's story." Immediately, each student praises the next for his or her story telling:

*Betty*: Everyone needs to support each other.

*Student 1*: David read well.

*Student 2*: I liked Manual's story. It was interesting.

*Student 3*: Lupe had an interesting story.

*Betty*: Everyone give Lupe and Manual a big hand.

Through these exercises, an atmosphere of building self-esteem, confidence, and respect for one's peers became the dominant themes. Self was affirmed in Betty's class. Students' I's were acknowledged. Me's were, if not understood, at least eventually negotiated or strived for. Around these issues, themes became central to this particular study.

## TEACHER THEMES

### *The Building of Self and Community: Official versus Pragmatic Curriculum*

As in the case study in Chapter 3, the distinction between official and pragmatic duties, rules, and curriculum continues. Most in-service teachers who take my courses confirm that the only sense of autonomy they seem to have lies in a pragmatic curriculum—especially when they close their doors and teach what they like to. This closing of doors is both an act of resistance to authority as well as a teacher cry to leave me alone and let me do my thing without continual surveillance. It was of no surprise then, that teachers in this elementary school were officially supposed to follow and be accountable for the ITV (Instructional Television Program) for social studies purposes. Heavy reliance on the ITV for art, music, and social studies, combined with a top-down authoritarian decision structure in the district, suggests that teachers are deskilled through the loss of curriculum decision-making power in these curricular areas as well as the loss of creativity to adjust their particular curriculum.

Betty, however, pragmatically does what she wants to, or at least attempts to. For the most part, Betty moves between official and pragmatic curriculum. Having been involved in a global education project for four years and being a firm believer in teaching about different countries, Betty decided (after I probed her about her views and after she received permission from the principal) to create a three-week unit on different countries. In fact, Parkview Elementary had not officially accepted the global education project as a schoolwide implementation program. Global education to most teachers was a radical concept. In my naive way, I couldn't understand why this was the case. Slowly I began to understand why many teachers and administrators believed that anything that moves teachers away from the set curriculum, or anything that may sound weird or different, should not be taught. In fact, the rumor around the school was that anyone who thought seriously of using global education was considered radical. Asked why she used this form of curriculum, Betty comments,

Some prejudice that I experienced made me want to know what others were like and why there's discrimination and so on. Our regular curriculum doesn't go into that stuff. So I do what I have to to incorporate curriculum we aren't told about. Besides, they trust me here. I can use global education in reading and social studies and still promote self-esteem.

It seems that using this form of curriculum ties in with Betty's personal history (or subjectivity) regarding the prejudices she had faced previously in her life. In my mind this is hardly a radical view but a very pragmatic one. Not discounting the ITV, Betty commented about this pragmatic curriculum (again, not officially designated, but thought by her to be the most practical curriculum for her students):

The ITV is just the tip of the iceberg. The real teaching comes when I connect peoples of the world with the ecology movement, for example. I will do more simulations that could also be political. For instance, we will learn about some countries' hunger problems, and why we must do away with that. At the same time, while we work on these ideas, we do them in groups, for the purpose of working together and sharing ideas, accepting and understanding different points of view, just being a community.

In general, Betty's dominant class theme of working together, "just being a community," permeates her day with her students. For instance, in one group project with her students, these daily themes of community and cooperation are often highlighted:

*Betty*: We are now going to talk about things we did well together.
*Student 1*: Sharing stories.
*Student 2*: Listening.
*Student 3*: Team work.
*Betty*: That's great. That's wonderful. What can we do even better tomorrow?
*Student 4*: Finish our work.
*Student 5*: Do your own job better.
*Betty*: What skills can we work at together?
*Student 1*: Looking for information.
*Student 6*: Active listening.
*Student 7*: Use quieter voices.
*Student 8*: Be even more cooperative.
*Betty*: Name one thing groups can do better.
*Student 6*: Encourage each other more.

Thus, the preparation for any group work with Betty is advantageous in that it leads directly to a notion of community, sharing, and empathy. Indeed, the three-week project becomes a shared group activity. There are five members to a group. Each group is delegated a different country to study and then report on to the class after two weeks of research. Each student is assigned multiple roles: There is the scribe, the geography or map person, the stories and games person, the video person, and the reader/materials person. Each student is responsible for research in the library and checking if others in the group are supportive and helpful. A research station is set up at the back of the class. The countries to be researched are Kenya, Russia, Indonesia, Sri Lanka, and Zimbabwe.

It is through this teacher-created pragmatic curriculum that themes concerning (1) different points of view (the building of empathy) and (2) community and competition arose.

### Different Points of View: The Building of Empathy

In my mind, Betty was a master at extracting student feelings about their views concerning themselves, other people in class, and different countries. She allowed students to feel their I and understand the me. In one exercise, for instance, Betty placed different items on a round table at the front of the class. Students listed everything they saw from where they were seated. After five minutes studying the table, the class then met on the floor.

*Betty*: What did you discover?

*Student 1*: I can't see from a distance.

*Student 2*: That nobody's perfect.

*Betty*: Would you like to have had a perfect list? How would you feel about not seeing everything; good about it; upset?

*Student 1*: Upset. Cheated because some people saw different things and we were all sitting at different places.

*Betty*: What would you wished you'd have done?

*Student 3*: I felt mistreated.

*Betty*: How could you get all the information?

*Student 4*: Look differently.

*Student 5*: Look for different points of view.

*Betty*: How many points of view are there?

*Student 6*: Many, at least two. You can see different things if you stand in different places.

*Betty*: Can you see everything when you are really close?

*Students*: Yeah.

*Betty*: What can you tell me about your point of view? What can change your point of view?

*Student 1*: When you look different?

*Betty*: If I put more make-up on or dress differently, does that change my point of view? What can you do to change your point of view?

*Student 7*: Use your imagination.

*Betty*: Can you learn to like someone and accept their point of view?

*Student 8*: Yes, by sharing with them your ideas, to take them as your partners.

*Student 1*: Yes, by working with them.

*Betty*: How do you feel about different points of view?

*Students*: Good.

Betty placed a white sheet on the board and immediately asked her students for similarities and differences between people. After this exercise was completed and numerous similarities and differences were mentioned, the conversation continued:

*Betty*: Are we the same?

*Student 9*: We all work.

*Student 10*: Poor people don't.

*Student 5*: We all have some money.

*Betty*: Do all people have some money? I want to know similar things. Not that all people have money.

Overall, Betty teaches that members of the group will have different points of view and that different countries have different customs and habits. All this happens around the themes of community and sharing. Additionally, Betty allows for individual expression of thought and shared group sentiments. In closing, she comments warmly,

You need to pat yourselves on the back, support and encourage everyone, and say "you're doing a good job." Remember in this exercise we learn about different points of view, different countries. We don't just memorize the different facts about the countries. We must be on task and check our feelings, that everyone is feeling good about themselves. You all have important jobs to do. Let's get to work and do our research on the different countries.

### Community and Competition

The sometimes contradictory traits of community and competition are emphasized continuously in Betty's class. We must remind ourselves that in America in general, these themes are pervasive in all walks of life; community functions and struggles for one-upmanship in the job market are examples of this. Betty comments, "I always break the class into groups in order to learn that we can work together. Many times, though, groups don't work well together and often I have to sit down with individuals and talk with them about why they aren't working well together." It becomes difficult for students to stick together as a unit. This is in part due to some of their individual competitive spirit to be selfish or better than the next person. Many times differences of opinion arise.

Joshua is continually upset that he can't do things his own way. He often looks disgruntled:

*Betty*: We need to cooperate. If your material is not ready, please help each other. You need to share.

*Joshua*: Cathy wants my folder.

*Betty*: [Sternly] Look, Cathy's the scribe, she needs it now.

*Joshua*: I want to do this my way and she says I can't.

*Betty*: Can't you work this out together?

When the situation gets out of hand, Betty motions to Joshua on more than one occasion, Finally Joshua and Betty get together at the side of the classroom where there are no students. They perform a role-reversal ritual. Joshua assumes the role of the other student and is asked to feel for the other person. Over the following two days and during more role-reversal situations, Joshua becomes a more cooperative working member of the group.

Groups begin to compete with each other. Many times a group member from Kenya or Sri Lanka will wander to another "country" and check who has "the better project." Betty's main concern, one that involves establishing community, sharing, and cooperation at the beginning of the global education project, is expressed in her journal that she prepares daily for me: "The groups are not yet bonded. These groups compete with each other and within themselves as well. To get bonded will be a challenge that will help us all." By the end of the first week of research, Betty comments, "I am a nervous wreck. I want this to work out so much. I can see the groups beginning to settle down and bond nicely. I want so much for each child to feel successful and to do their part for their group." By the end of the global education project, Betty comments, "I feel really good today. All the groups are really making progress and supporting each other. Of course, some groups are ahead of others and some children need to be directed daily." Clearly, Betty had achieved one of her major objectives. Students built community and developed a sense of trust and mutual respect for each other and their individual differences.

## STUDENT THEMES

### Response to Journal Questions

I had read with great care the much-quoted Jean Anyon (1980, 1981) articles about social class and school knowledge. Much criticism of Anyon's work in the education journals centered around what I shall describe as a deterministic analysis of class location. All seemed to fit neatly into place. Students and teachers responded to questions, as if they were in lower, middle, upper, or executive elite classes. One typical example is when Anyon asked students and teachers of lower- to middle-class schools what the term *knowledge* meant. Most responses were "to get the right answer." In the upper-class schools, responses were to "be creative, to think." Student, as well as teacher expectations, fell neatly into their predictor of social mobility. Working-class kids would end up with boring, stereotypical, blue-collar pen and paper work (if they were lucky), and the upper-class school would eventually occupy creative professional positions. Their school work includes creating art projects, participating in more dialogue in class, and, in general, doing more creative activities.

In response to these issues, and with the idea that Betty did believe in student creativity, cooperation, and pushing students to their limits, I was convinced that on some levels, if I were to ask questions similar to those Anyon asked, the responses I would receive might be different from the study she conducted. What I was looking for, then, were not predetermined responses (there were obviously some) but student responses that would contradict students' stereotypical class location, as portrayed by the principal's comments earlier in the study.

Within the three-week unit on global education, I asked students to define *knowledge* in the journals they prepared daily for me. There were three dominant responses: (1) "being smart," (2) "to learn," and (3) "to have an open mind." Asked to define *smart*, the major response was to "stretch, grow, or get a good education," "be helpful," and "listen to others." Asked to define *learn*, major responses were "to learn new stuff about people," "to get a lot of information in your mind," and "expand your brain."

I asked students to define the term *think*. Major responses included, "to wonder," "to sort things out," "to create." Asked what it means to *create*, dominant student responses included "to do something new" and to "have an open mind." It seemed that these students were more than just being creative in responding to these questions. In many senses students were, through their open, creative, and thought-provoking responses, combating and/or resisting a deterministic stereotype. Thus, the potential within this contradiction is for conflict and a challenge to stagnant views and eventual liberation from stereotypes.

## Development of Conscience

Within the aforementioned contradiction, Betty probed students' collective conscience. In short, Betty didn't advocate individualism but stressed support and community. Another class discussion was as follows:

*Betty*: Are we being supportive?

*Class*: No!

*Betty*: Have you all worked hard? Nick is feeling really bad, you're not supporting him. Now what do you do to get support?

*Student 1*: Give support.

*Betty*: How do you give support?

*Student 2*: Not to talk.

*Student 3*: Sing when we are asked to.

*Student 4*: Listen to each other.

*Student 5*: Active listening.

*Betty*: OK, our guests are coming to see our projects. Let's show them our support!

This form of support and community led students to a sense of what it meant to be a moral human being. After the Hanukkah lesson students were asked, If you were told to do something you knew was not right for you, how would you react? Student responses included "get people together to fight for what we believe in," "ignore him," "just keep on doing what I've been doing," "turn your back and walk away," and "understand the other people." Throughout the year, and especially during the global education project, students expressed a sense of group solidarity, rightness and justice, and an attempt to understand the other.

In particular, Betty tried to develop a sense of conscience with her students. Major efforts came in the formation of groups; group decision-making was of paramount importance. Interactive dialogue between teachers, students, and among students themselves was paramount. Many times groups would get rowdy. To create a sense of order, Betty commented to the "Kenyan" group, "I think it is better if we work together rather than disagree all the time. Look at how Sri Lanka is working together. Come on, we can do it." This coaxing was often needed for the group to become cohesive. Eventually, groups did cooperate and work as a unit. This is typified by student responses in journals to the question, "What is it like to work as groups?"

It's fun to work in groups . . . I like what David is doing, it's neat to work together . . . I understand what my group's doing because we share stuff . . . I don't like Josh sometimes, because he won't help me . . . It's fun to learn like this.

## Teacher Participation

Often during my time at Parkview, Betty commented on the desperate need for teachers to involve themselves in something like global education, particularly to understand difference. Betty also realized that many teachers viewed her as a threat. Betty was always willing to try new things, whereas most teachers at Parkview are, as Betty describes, "afraid of global education." Global education was not the status quo. Teachers, she once commented, are "very conservative and status-quo-type people." Despite all this, Betty was and is revered by her principal. During the student presentations on different countries, I see the principal entering the classroom to view two different groups make their presentations. Betty also has an influence on new teachers. At various times during my stay at the school, Betty commented to me more elaborately about other teachers. Among her other remarks are two striking examples: "I can sway her. I'm getting three other classes and teachers into the act. Maybe I can influence them as well." "I want to invite her. Her mind can be worked on. I wouldn't try with other teachers, but she can be opened. Maybe the word will get around when teachers see what I do." Clearly, Betty has an agenda beyond merely teaching her students. Importantly, this agenda includes influencing teachers about ideas on difference, community, and sharing. In short, this becomes what I will describe as her cultural politics—those values that challenge dominant, oppressive values in our society. Thus, a curriculum and school that focuses more on difference, community, and sharing begins to counter dominant values of rampant competition and individualism. It is this form of cultural politics that Betty conveyed to both students and other teachers when possible.

Of importance is that various teachers and their students enter group presentations at different times. These teachers seem to be more open minded to learning and teaching about difference. One teacher in particular seemed very inquisitive about the student activities. She took notes constantly. Other teachers seemed interested as well.

*Barry*: What did you think of the presentation?

*Teacher*: Great, they did a fine job. I may adopt some of Betty's ideas and do a global education project. It's important for students to learn about cultural differences.

*Barry*: Will you adopt this next year?

*Teacher*: I'm seriously thinking about it. I need more experience as a teacher. I'm new here, but I like Betty's ideas.

Another teacher commented,

*Teacher*: The kids did a fine job. I like the idea of sharing and community Betty builds here.

## CONCLUSIONS

Although Betty does have an influence on other teachers, unfortunately
my study stopped here. The end of the year was approaching and I was
already planning my next study. A lot has been left unsaid in this study.
For example, did these teachers adopt ideas of difference into their pragmatic curriculum? Did they become more daring and/or risk takers? Did
they challenge stereotypes and a deterministic consciousness? Although
these questions cannot be answered fully, it is important for now to note
the potential for teacher transformation, critical appraisal of difference,
and the building of self and community. What this study did confirm to
me was the undeniable construction of self within community. Additionally, how difference and understanding of others were used to counter
dominant trends was of paramount significance for the cultural politics
of critical pedagogy.

At this point in my personal intellectual growth, it seemed obvious that
at least one way to begin to build a counterhegemonic platform in
schools for critical theorists in education was to consider bridging the
gap between self and community by viewing them theoretically and connecting their constructs to dominant hegemonic values such as individualism, negative competition, and stereotypes. Only then, I thought,
could critical pedagogy assert itself despite the controlling effects of the
dominant culture. Genuine acts of intellectual resistance that begin to
redefine ways in which roles and subjectivities are constructed may be
met and serve concurrently as the base for a collective reinterpretation
of the lived world. It is this reinterpretation, at least in part, that Betty
was concerned with regarding her students.

Obviously, in this study I have provided a brief and schematic outline
of what must become a much fuller set of proposals for critical ethnog-
raphers in education. I will elaborate more on this in the final chapters.
To continue with an emancipatory, educational, and social agenda had
clearly become a priority for me, however. As a young academic enthusiastic about the cultural politics of critical pedagogy, many questions
entered my mind. What was difference? Do teachers act in solidarity over
issues of difference? Do teachers similarly agree on differences? How is
democracy conducted, if at all? Readers should be aware of these questions as, in Chapter 5, I enter a high school of 3,000 students with a large
minority population in Southern California.

## NOTES

1. By this I mean that what must be understood is how students, administrators, and teachers seek to find equitable arrangements in schools regarding race,
class, and gender.

2. George H. Mead, *Mind, Self and Society* (Chicago: The University of Chicago Press, 1934), 135–226.

3. Parkview is the fictitious name of this elementary school.

4. Jeannie Oakes (1985). *Keeping Track: How Schools Structure Inequality.* New Haven, CT: Yale University Press.

## CLASSROOM ACTIVITIES

1. Groups of students, divided into their specialty content area, will create an activity they could use in their classroom settings focused on difference. This exercise should be made understandable to the rest of the class through open discussion among the respective groups and then shared with the rest of the class.

2. In a class debate, discuss various forms of individualism—the good and the not so good. The debate should revolve over which sort(s) should be adopted in schools.

3. Individual class members build mock lesson plans around values such as individualism, community, and competition. Verbally explain how these values will be taught and how their contradictions will be dealt with in class.

## QUESTIONS FOR DISCUSSION

1. How is the self transported across difference in Betty's class?

2. How do you see yourself incorporating difference and self and generalized other into your curriculum?

3. What is a counterhegemonic framework for Betty?

4. How would you further Betty's counterhegemony?

5. How does Betty reskill her students? How is Betty reskilled?

6. In the modern (as in modernism) curriculum—be it hidden or overt—how is contradiction dealt with in Betty's class?

7. Is there potential for Betty to move out of a modern framework? If so, how?

8. Would you classify Betty as a modern or more postmodern teacher? Explain your response.

9. What could the postmodern self look like?

10. Given the structural limitations of using your postmodern self in the curriculum, where can it be accounted for in the school day?

11. What does a modern and postmodern curriculum look like to you?

12. What methods exist for you to undercut negative forms of competition?

13. How does Betty's view of teaching Hispanics differ from her principal's view?

14. How would you handle ideological differences among yourself, other teachers, and the principal?

15. In what ways does Betty empower her students?

16. Discuss the role of history and curriculum use. Does Betty make this connection? How could it be furthered?

17. How would you connect your history to curriculum use?

# 5

---

# Multiculturalism and the Politics of a Democratic Imaginary

## INTRODUCTION

In the first case study (Chapter 3), the pragmatic curriculum was paramount in establishing teacher autonomy. Teacher resistance to authority reigned supreme, in large part because teachers viewed administration work as inept. Issues of sexism certainly became a part of one or two teachers' immediate concerns but was not of that much importance to other teachers. This study also showed that teachers, despite their dislike for each other, formed group solidarity over various issues at the school site. In the postmodern tradition, it was difficult to define resistant acts. Were these acts that I have formerly labeled as institutional resistance (challenging structural constraints, like time management, challenging authorities through language, simply deviating from a set curriculum, and so on), or were they acts of cultural resistance (challenges to cultural essentialisms, like excessive competition, stereotype, racism, and sexism)?[1]

We also learned of the limitations of that study. Teachers were by and larged deskilled. I didn't learn how they were reskilled. Moreover, fascinated by these teachers, I often lost a grip on possible sites of transformation. I was enmeshed in their lives. By the end of the study I began to wonder who I was observing—these eighth-grade teachers or a combination of me.

The second case study (Chapter 4) considered the impact of a pragmatic curriculum. Within this context, a theory of self and community

was developed. It was built with the intent of viewing a potential emancipatory framework for critical pedagogy. Clearly, my focus was on the
postmodern-type literature. And with that in mind, a few questions
piqued my curiosity. What is the connection of the other to differences?
How or what role does intersubjectivity (that socially accepted and communal understanding between people or groups of people) function
within the framework of differences? What particularly interested me was
what a multicultural education can be, why we needed one, and if indeed
teachers were consciously aware of the dire need for transformation
around multicultural difference and diversity in schools.

Postmodernism, with its infinite deconstruction and never-ending
struggle for meaning, certainly provides a means to hear the other voice
and thus brings us closer to a form of multicultures or what I termed in
Chapter 1, similarities within difference. In my mind, Mead provided a
context by which to view the other as those attitudes and values that are
incorporated into pragmatic curriculum activities. Additionally, through
an understanding of how the I and me were constructed in the last case
study in Chapter 4, we saw how the intersubjective me allowed for pen-
etrations and insights to dominant ideological values such as individualism and what I also described as negative forms of competition.

The other within a postmodern discourse lends itself to an emancipatory framework which furthers Mead's definition of I and me and con-
notes listening to both the subjective and intersubjective voice of
marginalized peoples—those people oppressed, alienated, and subordinated by the structures of society (race, class, and gender configurations).

Voice, seen in the above context and as interrelated with the other,
refers to the placement of the subject (person or persons) within a social,
cultural, and economic order. As a reminder to readers, to hear one's
voice is to view it as shaped by its owner's relationships to power, cultural
history, and experiences.[2] Thus, one's voice becomes a relationship to
one's own race, class, and gendered background. Voice is that subjective
element of one's ego—what makes my identity, what I believe in, how I
live my life, and what particular values I adhere to. My voice, for instance,
includes my patriarchal background, mired in patriarchal-type teachers
and embedded within the institutionalization of a patriarchal-type, authoritarian school system. Additionally, my voice includes my immigrant
adventures in Israel and my feelings of social inadequacy, alienation, and
subordination. My voice also includes my multiple social roles and the
actions under which these roles are formed and guided, such as being a
father, brother, son, teacher, professor, and white middle-class male.

Mead's use of the term *other* becomes both a political tool and emancipatory referent for critique on dominant value structures. It also allows
postmodern theorists to understand further the subjective and intersubjective conditions that underly singular and multiple voices, realities, and

power structures—particularly as related to race, class, and gender issues. With that in mind, the conditions for what can be defined here loosely as a democratic imaginary—those struggles that both simultaneously and in different form, time, and place, try to overcome subordination—become a theoretical consideration of what counts toward a critical postmodern theory of education, as well as a practical endeavor for teachers struggling within a multicultural society for forms of equality.

In this chapter, I present the politics of what I described in Chapter 2 as similarity within difference and other particularly as viewed through the stories and teaching of five teachers in a heavily populated minority school in urban southern California. *Other* in this chapter will refer in particular to the postmodern use of the term. That is, *other* will refer to the marginalized peoples, peoples who are underprivileged, minorities who have less than the average American citizen. Within the concept of other, there is no singular reality. No single person is oppressed similarly. To understand this is to begin to view social struggle for individual and community democracy and, in large part, human tolerance and dignity.

## ACQUIRING TEACHER STORIES

For the 1989/1990 academic year, there were five teachers (four English as a Second Language (ESL) teachers and a chemistry teacher) who volunteered to be a part of this study.[3] I had originally sent letters to the 120 teachers at Chapel High,[4] explaining the intent of the study. My thoughts were that teachers would line up at my office wanting to be a part of this research endeavor. How wrong I was! Only two weeks before school started, the principal informed me that no one had volunteered. I was thunderstruck. Eventually I learned from one teacher that my letter got lost somewhere in the other notes sent to teachers and some teachers never received it. I then began to acquire an inkling of the kind of bureaucracy involved in a large-size school. For instance, one teacher admitted that she just throws away all the garbage she receives in the mail. That letter, she recalled, was also thrown away. I shouldn't have been surprised at all this. How short my memory was about similar experiences I had had as a high school teacher.

At the time the letter was sent, the general problem I was thinking of researching was the critical and complex role of female teachers in schools, particularly as it related to curriculum issues. Each teacher eventually chosen (there were a few teachers the principal suggested that I ask to be a part of this study), as well as the principal of the school, was aware that my initial interest in the study was how gender was connected to what I call the gendered curriculum. Although my good intentions were to study this, any qualitative researcher collecting naturalistic data will inform you that one cannot with any sure accuracy predict what will emanate from teacher or student dialogue and what theory or theories will underlie those words.

Initially, I hung out at the school for a month, just talking to teachers, getting the feel of the teachers' room, lunchroom, library, and student career center. In general, I talked to teachers during this period and tried to learn some of the politics of the school. This was probably the hardest part of the study. Not knowing which teachers to talk to (despite the principal's leads), I often seemed like a stranger in unknown territory. It took that month to feel secure within myself. I built good rapport with some teachers. Often, these teachers mentioned that they wanted to become a part of this study. Once I felt that I had enough allies, I gathered teacher and principal life biographies through interviews that were both tape recorded and transcribed. I learned during this period a lot about the student population, particularly about the daily influx of immigrants into the school. I was offered information about different teacher groups at the school—for example, the "socios," those teachers with the "easy jobs, nice clothes, and husbands who made money." Their hearts, some teachers complained, weren't with the students who were particularly problematic or in dire need of personal help.

I was impressed with the principal of the school. He was born in San Bernadino, California. His grandparents were from Mexico. He had, as he described, "Mexican blood in his veins." Importantly, I asked him about his students, with whom he identifies in part:

It is important for these students not to give up their culture for the mainstream. But they're going to compete with the mainstream and they have to know the rules, how to play the game better than the rest of the mainstream. I try to influence these students never to abandon their culture and bring across to them never to lose their individual identity.

Clearly, the principal's consciousness integrated his and his students' identity. He struggled with his success and his students' eventual assimilation. The struggle between keeping one's authentic voice (culture) and not losing it to the mainstream was of particular interest to the principal. I was happy that there were some progressive administrators. Concurrently, I remained skeptical at how schools can structurally smother any hegemonic forces and allow for progressive or even possibly radical changes. So in this study I could be described as cautiously optimistic.

During my first month at the new site, I was struck by the frantic pace at Chapel High. There was little time for teachers to eat and relax away from the furious pace. I also realized that, unlike my previous case studies, I would not be able to catch teachers together for any one extended period of time. The five teachers I chose to follow had different lunch periods—some at 11 A.M. and others at noon. Schoolwide meetings were held once a month and sometimes canceled. One teacher commented, "There is no way you'll get to know everything in this school. There's too much going on." Of course, my knee-jerk reaction to this teacher was that she would be wrong. Little did I know that this was good advice and that I should concentrate on one or two aspects of this monstrously large campus.

As in the previous two chapters, I became the classic participant-observer. Each teacher was observed for extended periods in the first semester. I developed rapport with both the students and teachers of each class. Additionally, in two of the classes, I taught ESL to Hispanic students and conducted a lesson on Australia in another class. In yet another class (chemistry), I was often called on for answers—to my chagrin, I was never correct in my responses or couldn't respond at all because of my lack of chemistry knowledge. At least I was made to look human! This period of time was also used to gather data with gender issues in mind but to remain open-minded to other emerging themes that were becoming apparent. After these initial observations, a review of the data suggested emerging themes of similarity within difference and other. In addition, the issue of multiculturalism was becoming increasingly significant.

As the study proceeded, a further phase consisted of more observations. Each teacher was observed for extended periods in the second semester. My intent in these observations was to capture moments of the dominant, emerging themes and questions I was generating at the time, such as what is similarity within difference, the other, and multiculturalism.

As in the other studies, I became attached to these teachers. I had to begin to balance my relationship as a friend and as a researcher. At the same time, though, I was able to see events based on my experiences as a teacher (much like in Chapter 3 in the first case study). By concurrently involving teachers in the study, I was always struggling to maintain some distance from the data and thus gain a fresher and newer perspective. I believe that I succeeded in doing this.

I also conducted long interview sessions both with teachers involved in the study and with the principal. There was no time limit to these interviews. I felt that the teachers who invested their time in this study needed to feel secure that their views would not be undercut, shortened, or the like. The interviews were tape recorded and transcribed. Additionally, teachers and I talked about emerging themes, particularly revolving around the new immigrants and the role the school and teachers had in beginning the assimilation process. In my view I needed a systematic observation period in teachers' natural surroundings. Thus, teachers were interviewed in their classrooms and at their convenience. This could best determine how teachers used the emerging theme of similarity within difference and other to meet the challenge of trying to assimilate minority cultures into mainstream America.

## CHAPEL HIGH SCHOOL

Chapel High School is an urban, unionized high school situated in a predominantly Hispanic city in southern California. The street on which this large high school campus lies is lined with dilapidated houses and old, beaten-up cars. As I approach Chapel High, though, I see luscious green grass, old but well-cared-for trees, and tall school buildings.

The school library is extremely well kept. The teachers' lounge is shabby, with torn sofas. The lunchroom has nine large, round tables in it. There is a courtyard outside the lunchroom where teachers also eat and then relax in the southern California sun. The hallways are lined with large pictures of varsity basketball teams and cheerleading squads of past years. As I walk the three flights of stairs leading to a class I will be attending, I witness boys and girls necking on the staircases. I walk by embarrassed but often glance up just to see what's going on—to see just how far they will go in school. I then recall vividly my school days from the eighth grade onward—the sexism that we guys sported, taking girls to the back of the school football field, taking turns necking. It is unfortunate for me now to recall that not only did I glow in my accomplishments, but so did the girls! Walking up these staircases, I remember Mr. Twomey. I also remember an episode in my life when I was with a girl and lied to my friends about sexual accomplishments. The next day my opponents broke my jaw in an Australian rules football game. That incident spoke to me. It shut me up for a while. I learned never to brag.

Chapel High has approximately 2,800 students. Student population varies, depending on student entries and dropouts (which are especially Hispanic). Sixty percent of the students are Mexican-American and 20 percent Mexican. The rest of the students are from Southeast Asia and Indochina, and 2 to 3 percent are white. In most classes that I observed, the macho guys sat at the back. Female students sat in the front, quiet, mostly unheard from during the class period, subdued under the noise of guys joking and mocking each other.

There are 120 teachers—ten Hispanic teachers, one black teacher, and one Hispanic administrator (the principal). Some teachers describe the school as a "dumping ground for minorities." Others believe that this is the kind of school where "the real teaching takes place." I remind my students in my foundations classes that in suburban schools, most students will succeed no matter who the teacher is. These students receive the cultural capital needed to succeed (knowledge, skills, values, and attitudes). In urban schools, I remind my students, teachers for the most part can make a difference. When I assigned my predominantly white college students to visit Chapel High School for observations, many of them shuddered at the thought, often commenting, "Will our cars be safe?" Indeed, I also fell into stereotypical traps. On one particular day I came back to my car after a morning of observations. My muffler was making a lot of noise. I shouted in the car, blaming the area, kids, gangs, anything but the car. But when I took the muffler to be replaced, I was told that the muffler just died and needed replacement. I felt ashamed.

Chapel High is caught in a particular stereotype, one that I fell right into. Viewed by teachers as a "dumping ground," a low-income, low-intelligence, low-socioeconomic, and high gang-related area, the principal in the school and the teachers I observed are both committed and determined to reverse this stereotypical image. Perhaps this is exemplified by the principal's comments:

I identify from the standpoint that I am of Hispanic descent and they are too. I think the biggest criticism that I have heard from students on me is that sometimes I am overly critical and overly punishing on the Hispanic students. I tell these students that we have a reputation to uphold and we all have stereotypes we need to break.

The major stereotype is that because you're Hispanic you should be going toward a vocational occupation.

We have to communicate with the parents of these students to inform them of the stereotypes their children fall under. We have definitely been able to get more parents involved over the last two years with these kids and us in these issues.

After observing five teachers over the period of a year, it seems that the notions of similarity within difference and other have important implications for understanding how critical theory (and critical pedagogy) can be seen both in theory and practice in schools. In some part, through the teachers in particular, the principal has succeeded at his attempts to carve out equitable terrain for students at this school.

## TEACHERS AND THEIR PERSONAL HISTORIES

Chapter 1 and other chapters in this book have connected my past to my present. As I proceeded to this case study and matured as an adult, faculty member, and critical theorist, I began to see the importance of history to subjectivity, particularly as it related to oppression, subordination, and alienation. Just as in Chapter 4, in which I connected Betty's past to the reasoning of her present global education curriculum, I felt it important to do the same with the teachers who both volunteered and were chosen for the case study in this chapter.

### Sarah

Sarah is one of many ESL teachers at Chapel High. She was born in Egypt (interestingly, I spent ten years in Israel, and this did not interfere with our relationship, which was extremely professional and warm) and at the time of this research had been in the United States for twenty-two years. She is so committed to her students that the principal commented to me, "She is extremely enthusiastic about helping kids, and she sometimes forgets to look at things within the context of the entire school." Despite this, Sarah believes how great the students are because they are immigrants and face insurmountable assimilation problems. Immediately I am reminded of my own immigrant experiences. Sarah comments,

I tell these kids they're great. It takes a lot of guts to leave one's country and start anew in another one. To go somewhere where you don't know the language, you don't know the culture. At the beginning it seems wonderful but later you get depressed because you are confused and caught in many things. You find yourself thinking you don't belong anywhere. They're not 100% American; they left their country of origin. I can foresee the problems in learning a language, cultures, the understanding, the misunderstanding of things because I've gone through that.

Sarah expects students to complete their homework and succeed. She expects them to make something out of themselves, to overcome their oppressed situations. She comments,

There are things you can change. You can change the situation and your appearance. The first step is to accept what you cannot change. Students have to have courage to change the things they can. But it requires courage, perseverance, guts. They don't have to be a member of a gang, don't have to resort to alcohol. There are other things they can change.

Sarah often tells her students that they will have a test the next day. Yet if it were up to Sarah, "I wouldn't give tests because I hate them." She is caught in a bind: "I hate tests and if it were up to me I wouldn't give them. I give a lot of tests at the beginning of the school year because if you don't tell them they are going to be tested, they don't study."

Sarah can be both humorous and stern. Her students like her. Sarah empathizes with her students. She is able to do so, I believe, because she too is an immigrant. She is well aware of a new immigrant's assimilation problems. She links her history to her students' lives:

Let me share something with you now that you are just new immigrants. A home is never the same once you leave it. Finding a new home is like transplanting a plant. This is what happened when you left Mexico and I left Egypt. Everything would look different to me. It doesn't mean you are going to be less in the new place. It only means you are going to be different. Don't forget your good qualities. Choose the good things America has to offer you. Then you'll be unique. This is how I feel. Just because you are different doesn't make you worse. We are richer because of our differences.

Additionally, Sarah connects her own experiences as a female to her female students' experiences: "I do encourage females and I've had a lot of success with them going on to do their own thing. As a female I had it hard. Not only was I a female but also an immigrant. I want my female immigrant students to have it easier." She connects her role of the female within the larger culture. She comments to me,

I came here [the United States] in the 1960s. The values have changed a lot. But the values are WASP, puritanical, work, no fun, strict, fun is sin. I was shocked at the position of the woman in America. The American woman is abused, used. A lot get married and work to get their husbands through school. They are portrayed as sex symbols, made to look cheap. Women should be able to be responsible for their own actions and not market themselves as objects. This is the challenge I faced as a female immigrant. I would not let anyone abuse me . . . I do encourage females. I've had a lot of success with females going on and doing their own thing. I tell them to go to college. I tell them that my mother was against going to college. My mother said that a woman's job was to stay home and to take care of the husband and children. And that if I had a successful career I would sacrifice my marriage.

As I enter Sarah's class, I am struck by the large, colored poster hung above the chalkboard. It says, "We take pride in the differences that make us unique. As individuals we find joy in the sameness that makes us all sisters and brothers." I recall how Sarah commented to me about the connection of immigrant problems to other problems in society:

Immigrants are not only different. They are also similar in many things. Society is suffering from very similar problems to the immigrant's problems. Because this is a very mobile society, immigrants move from one place to another and they don't know anybody and they also have to adapt. They're away from families, friends—it's very hard. This is a lonely society. I like to bring out the similarities between people, especially as they relate to hardships.

To the general passerby, Sarah's students may seem unruly. This is due to the loud noises of the students who jeer at latecomers, or Sarah's high-pitched tone, demanding work to be completed, or even louder laughter at Sarah's or another student's humor. Prolonged observation in Sarah's class, however, shows a teacher who is committed to mainstreaming students into the regular curriculum, expecting time-on-task work. She rarely uses cooperative learning groups, like some of the other teachers have. I ask her why, and she answers:

There is always cooperative learning in this class. We just do not break into groups. But you see how everyone helps each other. The exercises we do aren't just individually done. Friends help each other. Besides, when we joke, we laugh together. We can kid each other in this class. Cooperative learning is not just breaking into groups.

In short, Sarah is committed to community. And her classroom is the avenue by which this is developed. She comments, "We must all help each other. If I make mistakes you help me. We are all working together on something. And some of these kids are smarter than I am, and I'm stronger in some areas than they are. We must attack problems together, not people. We must not laugh at each other, but value what we have to say."

### Nancy

Nancy teaches next door to Sarah. Also an ESL teacher, Nancy gets the beginning students. Her basic philosophy for teaching the minority Hispanic population is "to understand their psychological background; that they are strange here, in a new environment. I will not laugh at them or be too demanding. I want to make the classroom a safe place for them. Additionally, I want them to learn respect, to be polite to one and other." Nancy believes that she understands the Hispanic culture well because "I have lived all over—I lived in Mexico where I have gotten along without one word of Spanish. I identify especially with the Hispanic kids." She also believes that she empathizes with the Hispanic population: "I also try to speak Spanish and they see how many mistakes I make. So we both are learning together. We aren't alone. We are both learning another language." This empathy with the culture, plus Nancy's commitment to teaching a minority culture, prompts her to comment about the ESL teachers she identifies as we and the other teachers at the school, whom she identifies as they: "those other teachers have no empathy. We're here trying to save these kids. They are just teaching college-bound kids. Most of the school ignores ESL. Teachers think everyone in ESL is a dodo. They have no empathy." In large part, Nancy prepares kids for the outside world "so that they can support themselves with some type of job and get along in our culture." Also, Nancy is aware that there is a tremendous amount of conflict for her students. She comments,

There's a lot of conflict within races: black and brown, brown and white, black and white. For instance, it's hard to get Mexican kids involved in cheerleading, band, music. Mainly because it takes a year or so before they know what's happening at their school. They run back to their ESL classes constantly for security. They don't know what's happening out there and if they could be assimilated sooner, I'd push for that. These kids don't know when school dances are going on and they have to hear through the grapevine what events there are—someone has to tell them in Spanish. They feel very uninformed—they feel discriminated against. They ask me why they don't know any stuff that's going on. They feel it's an Anglo thing.

With this information in mind, I enter Nancy's class. I am struck by the informal nature of teacher-student relationships. Nancy is easy going, gently motioning her students to be quiet, but never demanding them to be quiet. She comments, "I try to involve my students, particularly those who are apathetic . . . I notice out of the corner of my eye their good work or that they are good at something like art . . . so I ask them to make a poster using some words. I like to involve them in what they like to do."

Nancy's class is colorful. There is room for a TV and a library. The class is male dominated, both in numbers and voices. A group of females sit together at the front of the class. I am introduced to the class as Mr. Barry, and as time proceeds I become friendly with many of the students. I even teach a couple of ESL classes.

Nancy does not follow a strict time frame for her curriculum. She is flexible so that students can "do what they want, such as talk about news items." Nancy comments,

My kids never come to class bored. They never know what will happen. They look forward to an open classroom. There are times when I hear some quote on the radio and change my whole lesson plan to teach on any news item that I think is important. I'm not rigid at all. I don't believe in it. My kids never come to class bored because they never know what will happen next.

As in Sarah's class, there is little cooperative learning. Nancy comments that "kids just learn without needing groups. They have their own groups."

### Pearl

Pearl is the only credentialed female chemistry teacher at Chapel High School. As a child, Pearl attended an all-girls school and "received a distorted view on women—to grow up, marry, and have kids." Pearl grew up in a troubled household. A brain-damaged brother and an alcoholic father prompted Pearl into "my critical outlook on the world." Pearl's "critical" reaction to the school and the students is reflected in her comments about who she is: "I'm not a status quo type of person. I believe in standing up for one's rights. I teach kids that as well. I take action. Chemistry has taught me to be very self-disciplined." As a woman, Pearl sees her role as generally in a state of constant conflict:

I think like a man but feel like a woman. I think that chemistry has affected my whole life and the way I deal with the world. It has taught me to be very self-disciplined and somewhat ruthless—like many males I have met. In terms of my own femininity it overlaps with the masculine side of me . . . I don't think that thinking is gender related. I think that our society thinks of certain qualities as gender related (male or female). I think it's an insult to be told you think like a woman or a man—it's all a stereotype. In my life in and out of school, I'm simply being assertive and protecting the integrity of my own students. For anyone to stereotype gender puts me into a conflict situation.

Pearl's philosophy of teaching minorities remains the same as for non-minorities:

The person I meet in September will be changed at the end of the year. I want all my students, whether male or female, to succeed. I see a lot of potentially homeless people, lots of have and have nots . . . I realize that people of all walks of life have similar abilities and potential . . . like one of my best students last year. Her parents were migrant workers, and she's very bright and she's going to The University of California at Irvine on scholarship. She doesn't even have a home; she lives in a tent. The poverty is incredible!

Pearl is very opinionated about life at Chapel High—particularly about male/female relations within the science department and in her class. She does not believe in stereotypes. She comments, "No matter the culture we are speaking about, our society thinks of certain qualities being either masculine or feminine. I think this is wrong. We all commonly share being human and having responsibilities." The principal is full of praise for Pearl, calling her "one of the most intelligent teachers we have at Chapel High." This intelligence reflects, on at least one level, in Pearl's teaching.

Pearl's classes are Asian and Mexican dominated. All these students have been mainstreamed. They speak and write English fairly fluently. As I enter Pearl's classroom, I am struck by two different sets of phenomena. First, Pearl's lab sessions are equally gender divided, based on cooperative learning. Cooperative learning is a part of Pearl's philosophy of teaching. To Pearl, cooperative learning serves many functions:

Placing unruly kids together . . . kids think better in cooperative learning groups. Cooperative learning groups always work unless students don't want to think. I divide these groups into one good student and two poorer ones, usually male and female. Kids get real mad at each other sometimes . . . they show real prejudices as to who they would rather be with. I just try and break those prejudices with cooperative learning.

Pearl often comments on the cooperative learning groups: "Remember, you're representing your groups. Make sure and hand this in collectively. This is a collective effort . . . we do things together."

Second, upon observing Pearl's class at length, I am constantly amazed at the emphasis Pearl places on students to think. In fact, Pearl demands that homework be completed, or "there will be a detention and hopefully I will get you to pass. Anyone else can stay for a review as well. You have to think about your questions and your responses." Additionally, Pearl places great emphasis on grades. She is often heard warning students that if they don't study they'll receive an F. Often, Pearl walks into class and announces an upcoming exam schedule. Pearl is very achievement oriented, demands work, and often speaks to her students in a forthright manner, "Come on, you guys. I'll smack you if you don't do your work, there's a big test next week. Miguel, I'm not going to let you waste your brain." This seeming rigidity (often a product, I believe, of Pearl's hardened view of her past), however, does not displace the humor Pearl has in class. She jokes a lot, "to relieve the tension in the classroom." I ask students what they think of Pearl, and all comment that "she's great to learn chemistry from." Pearl's commitment to her chemistry profession involves many after-school workshops. This commitment, along with her assertiveness concerning social issues at the school (particularly as related to gender), make her an interesting teacher to observe and learn from.

### Joan

Joan is the mentor ESL teacher at Chapel High. She is highly respected by the principal and other teachers. Joan could best be described as extremely involved in her students' lives. She often stays after school to help needy children. She is always on the move. She believes firmly that all minority students deserve to be treated like valuable persons to "preserve the way of life that I like living and that I want my child to have . . . these students deserve an equal opportunity to work toward progress to solutions of problems we have in our society . . . to preserve democracy, freedom, and choice."

Joan empathizes with her minority students. She comments,

I have been looked down upon because I was a woman, looked at as a minority . . . I was taught in schools that I couldn't really become qualified or improve myself. I grew up in a very ethnic area in New York . . . I picked up on different cultures. Additionally, through my experiences from elementary school I've been looked down upon because I was a girl. I felt like a minority. I was told that I couldn't sing in elementary school so therefore I couldn't be in the choir, and I found out that as an adult I had a very good voice. So I know that educators can really turn someone on to something or close the doors by a simple statement like, sit down, you're off key, and thus eliminate the possibility of really improving oneself in a particular area. So I empathize with minorities when they are having a problem today. It doesn't mean they are stupid—it means they need care and attention to their particular issues.

Empathizing and valuing different cultures prompted Joan to send her children to Chapel High: "My kids even go to this school and are some of the very few white students."

In class, Joan is dynamic, relating much of her personal experiences to her students. She is committed to her students and ongoing relationships. She comments,

When you work with high school kids that you help, they come back so you know in the long run they won't forget you. I go to many students' weddings. I'm a godmother to many of their kids. I have them come back as role models to show minority kids that indeed you can better your position. I have some of my former students who have been teacher aides while they're working their way through college.

Joan's class is filled with pictures of black and white authors. There is a well-kept library at the back of the class. Students' written material is hung up on the walls of the classroom.

Joan's students are well behaved and, for the most part, work cooperatively. Joan was the coauthor of a grant that brought cooperative learning to her high school (the Spencer grant). Joan simply builds community in her classroom. She comments, "Cooperative learning does a lot to help cultures learn about each other. I often have different cultures (students) working together showing them that all cultures are an integral part of a community." In fact, the first day I walk into class, the daily journal writing theme written on the board is, "Why do people have to learn to work together in society, in school, in our neighborhood, and at work?" This theme of oneness and doing work together is evident in Joan's class and an integral part of Joan's insistent informal rule—that students respect and treat each other with dignity. Even though students "require grades more than I do or even the system does," Joan "hates them" and wishes she could eliminate them. In her class, there is even the negotiation of grades in reply to students' desire to know what their grades are. So Joan often asks the group who asks for grades, "What do you think you deserve to get?"

Joan's class is always divided into cooperative learning groups. She connects cooperative learning with life. Various comments to her students include the following: "If you mess up in your group and don't work well together and disturb each other, you won't get any points . . . some of you guys are acting silly in your group and not allowing others to work . . . you've got to all work to get this problem right because it's really hard." Joan comments that only by working together will students be able to reach their potential. Besides, she comments, "if they are to be mainstreamed they have to work together . . . three or four heads are better than one." Additionally, the role of the school, says Joan, is not only to prepare kids for the workplace:

The school has a vital role in everything. It is to prepare them for the workplace, to handle conflict, to give them the basics for both those things. The school must lay a foundation to build on, values to confront. For instance, when I teach *To Kill a Mockingbird*, I'm not teaching them how to read it—I'm teaching them how to take any book and analyze its characters and analyze the situation and work from there. It means the same in life. You take any situation, any person and analyze that person and work from there. That really is what the importance of education is. We have to teach kids the basics, to communicate with a variety of people to understand many cultures. I regard my class as a training ground for life. To do this is also to be critical of who you are as well as critical of others. Life is about problem-solving strategies for these issues. And that is what my class represents.

Joan places great emphasis on getting on in life. She comments to her students about a recent test, "Guys, I wasn't thrilled with the test. Please, you have to keep in mind that if you want to move on you have to do this work. Some of you know you can get out of this class. You've got to be here for a purpose—to get on." Even though there are tests, Joan hates grades. She comments, "I hate grades. I wish I could totally eliminate them. Unfortunately it's oftentimes not the system that requires it, it's the kids . . . and if a kid isn't doing well on an IQ test, it doesn't mean they're not good."

In general, Joan has a fine rapport with her students. Even the misbehaving males sitting at the back of the class clamor for answers to some of the exercises Joan conducts.

### Leora

Leora teaches English literature as well as ESL. My observations revolve around one of Leora's English literature classes—her tenth-grade classroom. There are at least two unique aspects about Leora. She is the only black staff member at Chapel High. She has also lived in Germany and Spain. As a minority in a school dominated by minority students, Leora has a deep and unique understanding of their personal situation. And because of her experiences living abroad, Leora exhibits empathy for her students. She comments, "In living abroad I became the foreigner. I can relate to my students coming from a foreign country and being considered an outsider. I can appreciate other cultures and customs. Many of their socioeconomic problems are those that I share in the black race." Leora's high empathy level propels her to question dominant stereotypes. She comments,

Some staff here seem to equate the cultural and racial background with intellectual status, but there's no connection at all. Maybe some minority students achieve poorly, but this is not a result of their cultural and racial backgrounds. The idea that people believe in intellectual differences is a self-fulfilling prophesy. When students start out in primary grades regardless of their racial or ethnic backgrounds, students are usually the same. When they reach sixth or seventh grade, things change. When students come to school they are faced with a bombardment of different media—sports, movies, commercials, music, etc. Unconsciously, students pick up on who is supposed to achieve and who is not. Students fall into patterns, and tracking and tests don't help solve these problems. The key to overcoming some of these issues is to involve the family more—get them involved in believing that their students can succeed, especially parents who are minorities themselves. They have to be educated.

Concerning tests, Leora believes that they are only "one way of measuring what has been given to the student. It doesn't measure intelligence or potential." Leora believes that "each individual is unique and deserves a fair education." She comments further, "Everyone has the right to a fair education. Educational opportunities aren't equal. We all have potential in us to succeed. As an educator it's my responsibility to facilitate this as much as possible." This, according to Leora, is her main goal as a teacher. To facilitate her beliefs, Leora developed a Unity Club whose primary function was to open its doors to all races for different school activities, such as International Food Week.

A close look at Leora's class shows almost bare walls. The class contains no door. The floor is fading in color or dirty! The library is in the back of the room. As I sit at the back of the classroom, I hear clearly the teacher next door instructing her class. At times this disrupts my concentration. The classroom walls are thin. The number of students in Leora's class is high. The class is extremely male dominated; male voices dominate. The ten females out of thirty-three students sit passively at the sides or front of the class. The males sit at the back or in the middle, usually in groups of four or five, usually disruptive and rarely quiet.

Often, Leora divides the class into cooperative learning groups. Usually these groups are gender divided; they are male dominated due to an excess of males in the classroom. Even though the students are noisy, Leora is able to gain control when she wants to by announcing that there will soon be a quiz. Leora utilizes cooperative learning strategies so that students can produce one product, cooperatively as a cohesive unit. She comments, "When I use cooperative learning strategies, I generally want the students to produce one product, one student the writer, another the reviewer, etc. This is a collective process."

Embedded within the concepts of similarity within difference and other are the themes of empathy and conflict. The following sections will portray their interrelatedness.

## THE BUILDING OF EMPATHY AS CONNECTED TO SIMILARITY WITHIN DIFFERENCE AND OTHER

Empathy as connected to student similarities, differences, and other are related to in-classroom interactions by all teachers at some point in their curriculum, but empathy often takes on different forms.

Joan builds empathy in two ways. First, she never shies away from telling her class about her own life story—how when she was a child she faced situations similar to theirs, how she had to "work hard to achieve as well," particularly as a woman. Second, Joan places a great emphasis on understanding the other. This is understandable given her female position in society. This can be seen in two separate class discussions—one about slaves in a class discussion about civil rights, and the second in a discussion about disabled persons. In the first discussion Joan comments, "Slaves had no rights. Just imagine yourselves . . . coming home and one of your family was sold. It's unbelievable to think that happened." In the second discussion there is more student interaction, especially as students have role-played a person with a physical disability.

*Joan*: What is a disability?

*Student 1*: Something mentally wrong.

*Joan*: Yes, it could be something mentally or physically limiting. What are some disabilities?

*Student 2*: Can't talk or hear.

*Student 3*: When you can't speak English.

*Joan*: Yes, when you are in a country and can't speak the language . . . something you all faced when you came to this country.

*Student 4*: [Smiling] Right.

*Student 5*: [Nodding] Yeah.

*Joan*: I'm going to have you think in a room alone, just try to cover your eyes and walk across the room to the other side to get the feeling of limitations and what others may feel.

The beginning of empathy building in Sarah's class is exemplified when emphasis is placed on one's home in a poem the students have read.

*Sarah*: What does a home represent?

*Student 1*: A place.

*Student 2*: Mexico.

*Student 3*: A place we can feel good at.

*Student 4*: Where you can be peaceful.

*Student 5*: Mexico, I belong. Love and warmth there.

*Student 6*: I feel alone.

*Sarah*: What does alone mean?


The concept of loneliness as related to the students has great personal meaning for Sarah and her students. Sarah empathizes with her students and comments once more on the connecting aspects of difference: "Just because you are different doesn't make you worse. Differences make us richer—we have so much more to offer others. We share our differences and can understand each other better. By understanding differences, we can see in what ways we are the same, too."

Another example of similarity within difference and other can be seen in Nancy's class. We recall that Nancy's major social commitment is to help assimilate her students into mainstream America—"to get along in our culture." Motioning different students to speak in English to the class, Nancy comments to one of her students who laughs at another student's sentence: "Some people have similar accents but other people have different accents—we must recognize this—their accents are different from yours. No one accent is right. They are just different." To gain appreciation of the other student, Nancy often includes females in a conversation that is started by males:

*Male 1*: Finished, teacher.

*Nancy*: I know, then read the sports page. You can review it and see what happened. Who won the hockey game last night?

*Male 2*: The Canadian team.

*Nancy*: Claudia, do you like hockey? What do you like?

*Female 1*: I like basketball.

*Nancy*: Do they play ice hockey in Mexico?

*Males*: No, No, No!

*Nancy*: Why?

*Male 1*: There is no ice. The climate is too hot.

*Female 2*: They play basketball.

*Nancy*: I guess we do different things here. I also see similar things we do.

Additionally, Nancy often motions her female students to write on the blackboard. In one such activity, Nancy comments,

*Nancy*: Edith, thank you very much for taking the risk of putting this on the board. That was nice of Edith to write on the board and see her mistakes. Thank you, Edith. It takes a lot of effort to get up in front of all your friends. How do you feel about it?

*Edith*: Different.

What follows is a barrage of students who also want to relate to what Edith just experienced.

Similarities within difference and other can be seen in different forms at Chapel High. To help facilitate Leora's beliefs in what I call being fair and understanding of the other, she guides the *Unity Club*. The club's functions are multifold. First, it is not a particular racial or ethnic group. It opens its doors to different ethnic groups so that all can participate in its activities. One of the students in one of the club's initial meetings comments, "I'd like to let people know outside the school that our school isn't just gangs but we are a responsible school. We have a lot of minorities. We should be looked up to, visit disadvantaged schools, tutor needy kids." Another student comments, "We are all from different ethnic backgrounds. We must talk about our concerns, get out into the community, come together to voice our opinions. . . . There should be no discrimination here." Leora comments, "We're not a large group, but in terms of being effective, we are. We've had several functions. We emphasize cultural diversity."

To empathize with difference through understanding similarities between students becomes a major theme in most of the classes I visit. Similarity within difference and understanding the other has other major components besides empathy. Not unrelated to empathy is the theme of conflict, so prevalent in nearly all the classes I visit.

### Conflict and Empathy

Teachers in this study both consciously and unconsciously see conflict and empathy as part of their day. The major conflict areas that the teachers face are divided into two teaching areas: (1) inner conflict and empathy, and (2) gender-related conflict and empathy.

#### Inner Conflict and Empathy

Sarah believes that conflict must be related to students' personal lives. We recall that as a woman and as a minority, Sarah was thrown into conflict situations. She connects conflict with empathy for her students lives. She comments,

I give them a conflict situation before we read about conflict. My two ways of solving conflict are presented—fight or flight. So I say it's better to work things out and fight out conflict. They have many of the same conflicts I had when I came from Egypt. I am a role model for them. I also suffered . . . just like these kids. I was in a similar situation—had to make a choice—fight or flight. I know what they go through. I interrelate personal conflict with the general conflict they face every day. As immigrants, they will always have conflict.

To exemplify her desire to deal with conflict, much of the literature curriculum that Sarah chooses has to do with various conflict situations. In one of the stories (Fred Stockton's "The Lady and the Tiger"), Sarah asks this question:

*Sarah*: What is the meaning of conflict?

*Student 1*: A problem.

*Sarah*: A problem that arises from what?

*Student 2*: A difficult decision.

*Sarah*: Very good, a conflict comes from a difficult decision.

After elaborating on the conflicts in the story, in which the students learn about plot, theme, characterization, and place, Sarah continues the intense interaction with her students on the nature of conflict:

*Sarah*: There's one thing very important about this story. What is it?

*Student 3*: She's an individual.

*Student 4*: She's independent.

*Sarah*: Oh, wonderful, yes, she did what she wanted. She was disobedient to her father.

*Student 3*: The king didn't approve of the relationship . . . his daughter and the slave.

*Sarah*: So what conflict do we have here?

*Student 5*: Inner conflict.

Students begin to understand the nature of their inner conflict. If anything, Sarah raises students' consciousness about the phenomenon of conflict. When I ask students if they know what conflict is, they comment, "a problem," "a gray area," "something we don't like to feel," "an uncomfortable situation," "something to solve," and "about our lives." Additionally, only a week later, Sarah connects this conflict to the nature of what a theory is:

*Sarah*: What is a theory?

*Student 1*: An idea.

*Sarah*: Is the idea always correct?

*Student 6*: No!

*Sarah*: Yes, someone has to prove it's right or wrong. Let's see, Christopher Columbus had a theory.

*Student 7*: Yes, the world is round.

*Sarah*: Did people believe him?

*Student 8*: Not everyone.

*Sarah*: Then we have a conflict between what's right and wrong.

Joan realizes the problems conflict creates. She comments,

We always have conflict—in the family, in the neighborhood, in our views on cultures. I think that conflict starts with one's personal biography. In *To Kill a Mockingbird*, Atticus did what he felt he had to. He taught his children right and wrong, to stand up for their rights, even if there may be consequences, in an intelligent, educated way.

Joan is well aware the conflict is external to the school as well as internal. She places students in conflict situations. She doesn't believe in the philosophy of teams, but in cooperative evaluation and community-related activities in school. She still, however, places the students in conflict situations: "OK, guys, yesterday I graded the test and I wasn't thrilled. You have to keep in mind that if you want to move on you have to do this work." Thus, students are taught contradictory values. This becomes, in part, a conflict they have to deal with. And Joan's insistence on cooperative learning and tests, be they individual or group related, places students within value conflict.

### Gender Conflict and Empathy

In different ways, all teachers in this study are affected by gender concerns, some teachers out of class (as we noted with Joan) but some teachers in class as well.

Pearl has had a troubled and conflict-ridden personal family background. In Chapel High, she has also had an ongoing battle with the science department, especially with its former head—"a male chauvinist, married five times and an abuser of women." Pearl feels that for at least five years she has been verbally abused by this person and denied the "materials necessary for safe conditions of the class." She commented, in a memo sent to the former principal at Chapel High, on one particular attack: "[He] attacked Betty and me at another meeting and all the science department congratulated me on my counterattack. I don't accept cursing or slamming fists into the wall. As my principal, I know you won't accept such behavior." As the gender battle over classroom rights continued, Pearl gathered interdepartmental support as well as campuswide sympathy for her conditions. Finally, the science department head was replaced with a female head. And now the principal admits that "there is a more cooperative effort now, thus the change of department heads was needed. The former head wasn't addressing the needs of the minorities or all the teachers in the department." Pearl comments that only now, after the five-year-long battle, the science department has settled down. She comments, connecting the aforementioned personal gender-related struggle to the struggle of women in general: "We must question authority; otherwise where will we be? Additionally, women who question in general will go into areas that are non-traditional—such as science."

In class, Pearl carries with her the notion that females can and must succeed in the sciences. One class in particular is male Asian dominated. They answer all the questions. In another class, comments Pearl, there is a preponderance of females who partake equally in chemistry. She calls these students "the hope for females in an area that is not traditionally female oriented." Pearl constantly relates her subject area to gender:

Male or female stereotypes should be a mixture, people are just people, not stereotypes—there's not thinking like a woman or a man . . . I think it's an insult to be told that I'm aggressive or a bitch. I'm simply defining my own, protecting my integrity. Chemistry should be enjoyed by all, male or female. It shouldn't be gender defined!

Often, Pearl can be heard telling her students that "there are so many jobs out there. Not everything has been discovered yet. Anyone here could make a career out of chemistry." Additionally, due to the stereotype that Pearl feels is placed on females who do chemistry, she empathizes with this inequity: "I was given the message that it was not in my place as a woman to succeed. In a sense, for the females in my classes, I represent the role model to rise above this stereotype. I know that some of them experience oppression. I am a vehicle to change that cycle."

In Joan's class, cooperative learning groups are in progress. The groups are divided equally. Joan is committed to helping assimilate her students, irrespective of gender. Even so, Joan believes that "guys represent the stoic stereotype and girls learn to trust early on and therefore get hurt to a greater degree. In order for girls to get on in this society, they have to learn how to adapt." Joan's main goal, then, although in part driven by the inequity she faced as a young female student, is driven by her desire, irrespective of gender, to "work together to get the problems solved and respect each other, so that we can all see each other's unique qualities." This feeling of empathy through cooperation works well to lessen gender conflict in Joan's class.

Gender conflict and empathy is evident in Leora's class as well. We remember that Leora is the only black teacher at Chapel High. In her class, males outnumber females three to one. In one activity, one male from one group comes over to another group with one female and promptly asks

*Student 1*: [Smirking] Can we use your secretary?

*Student 2*: [Laughing] Yeah, of course.

*Student 3*: [Mockingly] We are waiting for the secretary.

Disturbed by this incident, I ask Lupe (the girl secretary) why she allows this, if in fact she enjoys this. She candidly comments, "I don't mind doing the work for them. I want to be neat, so I do it for myself so I understand. In the end, when there's a test, I have everything here." I relate this to Leora. She doesn't seem shocked at the interaction of the male and females, who often, she says, "exhibit these stereotypes." She continues, "I've been in the seat of the female in this class. I know what they are going through. I can't keep my finger on everything. These groups are an attempt to equalize things—neutralize the gender inequities if possible. It's obvious, though, that they don't always work."

## CONCLUSIONS

It seems clear to me that the issue of multiculturalism is indeed a complex one. It is complex because a part of the multicultural agenda involves understanding not only different cultures and their particular norms, values, attitudes, and forms of knowledge but our own (particularly, white middle-class America) value structure. Multiculturalism is also tied into what I described earlier in this chapter as the democratic imaginary. Clearly, this study intimates that teacher struggles are personal as well as connected to the wider culture. Also, teacher experiences connect empathy with minority students. Underlying this, these teachers do not act in conscious unison. Individual assignments, curriculum, values, and opinions make sure that this does not happen.

With this in mind, what counts as conflict in the kind of democracy I am advocating must be looked at from various cultural angles. Gendered conflict will differ for different cultures. (For example, Sara, Joan, and Leora all have Asian, Hispanic, and black students in their classes.) Thus, it can be argued that multiculturalism and understanding of the other is about understanding differences as well as similarities within a democracy. The differences lie in each individual culture's unique response to values (individualism, patriarchy, competition, success, etc.) as well as each individual's response to these values. Within this democratic imaginary, teachers begin to make headway by not obliterating stereotypes of minorities. Leora is antideterministic in her assumptions of the black culture. Cooperative learning in all classes undermines such stereotypes. Sarah as well as other teachers temper assimilation into the mainstream with a commitment never to forget one's roots or "home" as Sarah puts it. And on another level, Pearl is engaged in a gender struggle of her own—in some part to change the role of the stereotypical female teacher.

How different cultures and various individuals respond to the deskilling process that involves tests (be they IQ or other standardized tests) or stereotypes (such as jock, nerd, dweeb, brain) can and must be related to different cultures to gain a sense of what they stand for both as a culture and as individuals in that particular culture.

This particular study at Chapel High points to the theoretical insight that although there are cultures and individuals who are indeed different, there is the possibility that we all have experiences that may alienate, subordinate, or oppress us. This was the case with the five teachers in this study. All, through their experiences, admitted some form of personal oppression. All admitted a need to help the minority cultures. All began to empathize with the minority culture. In a democracy, it seems to me that a critical multiculturalism existed when teachers connected their personal subordinative experiences to their students' particular subordinative experiences. That is, once students were able to understand their oppressed position in this society, a critical multiculturalism began to take shape. Similarities within differences became that border[5] to create this possibility. And, within this possibility, we can learn to understand similarity within difference and other as supportive of this democratic imaginary. At the base of this vision is a commitment to citizenship, affirmation, possibility, and hope. Moreover, this vision provides a context in which critical social theorists and critical pedagogists can begin to consider seriously the theoretical and practical framework of a counterhegemonic agenda.

At this point in my intellectual development, it became important to focus on how not only a critical multiculturalism but also a critical modernism and critical postmodernism could be incorporated into the classroom. This agenda becomes a theoretical as well as a pragmatic endeavor. For too long now, critical theorists in education and critical pedagogists in particular (like myself) have often been criticized for not making the dream of equality come true.[6] Our language and ideas have seemed, for most teachers, too far removed from the everyday pragmatic world of teachers. What I will propose in the following chapters is not equality for all, but rather an attempt to view possibilities for a critical pedagogy platform to exist. Although I have cited previously what teachers can do generally to help in this endeavor,[7] the agenda I set forth in the following chapter will, I hope, begin to lay the foundations for teachers to understand the possibility of adopting critical pedagogy ideas in their own classrooms. It is to this possibility that I turn in the next chapter, which provides an example of a unit for secondary teachers that includes the pragmatic elements of and for a critical pedagogy.

## NOTES

1. Barry Kanpol, "Institutional and Cultural Political Resistance: Necessary Conditions for the Emancipatory Agenda." *Urban Review*, 22 (3) 1989: 163–179.

2. Henry Giroux, *Living Dangerously* (New York: Peter Lang Publishers, 1993); and Peter McLaren, *Life in Schools* (New York: Longman, 1989).

3. All these teachers' names are fictitious.

4. Chapel High is the fictitious name of this school.

5. Henry Giroux, *Border Crossings* (New York: Routledge, 1992). Especially pp. 54–59 for more on borders.

6. Henry Giroux, *Living Dangerously*; all chapters; Jesse Goodman, "Towards a Discourse of Imagery: Critical Curriculum Theorizing." *The Educational Forum*, 56(3):269–289, 1992; and Barry Kanpol, "Critical Theorizing as Subjective Imagery: Reply to Goodman." *The Educational Forum* 57(3):325–330, 1993.

7. Barry Kanpol, *Towards a Theory and Practice of Teacher Cultural Politics: Continuing the Postmodern Debate* (Norwood, N.J.: Ablex, 1992).

## CLASSROOM ACTIVITIES

1. Each student is to complete a lesson plan in his or her particular content area with the democratic imaginary as the hidden goal. Justify to the class in a general discussion how this lesson is democratic.

2. Discuss in groups according to content specialty what a democratic imaginary must consist of to be democratic.

3. Divide the class into a principal, vice-principal, counselor, secretaries, teachers, custodians, and student representatives. Debate what democracy would look like in your school. This school must be chosen by the class (inner city, urban, suburban, etc.).

4. As the feminist principal of a school (male or female), discuss the advantages and disadvantages of this position. What would a school look like under this person?

## QUESTIONS FOR DISCUSSION

1. How do the teachers discussed in this chapter connect their personal histories to their pedagogy?

2. In what ways were the teachers in this study empowered?

3. Was there a counterhegemonic force in operation in this school? What did it

look like and how could it be enhanced and/or broadened?

4. What would you say that critical literacy meant for these teachers?

5. What would a critical literacy look like for these Hispanic students?

6. What is the pragmatic curriculum that these teachers use?

7. Can the democratic imaginary be postmodern? If so, how, and what does this mean for our classrooms?

8. What are some of the tensions of struggle that these teachers face?

9. What does group solidarity look like in this study, even though teachers do not act together?

10. What is difference in this study?

11. When the phrase *similarities within differences* describes our views on the other and us (me, you, white or black, etc.), what does this mean?

12. Would these teachers be classified as more traditional or critical? Elaborate on why you chose a particular position.

13. How do you view yourself as a teacher as compared to the teachers in this study?

14. If there is a hidden curriculum that these teachers employ, what does it mean?

15. What kinds of gender struggles do you anticipate? Connect your history to these struggles, if they exist.

16. How do these teachers connect Mead's notion of the I and the me to their social identity?

17. What would democracy look like for different class-structured schools (e.g., in the inner city, or in urban and/or suburban districts)?

# 6

---

# A Critical Interdisciplinary
# Platform of Possibility

## INTRODUCTION

The last three chapters have provided readers with glimpses of what possibilities there may be for teachers in public schools to implement critical
pedagogy. Whether it be teachers like Ms. Y and her activism, Betty and
her commitment for students to understand difference, or the teachers
discussed in Chapter 5, such as Sarah, whose pedagogy was tied closely
to her immigration history and gender, there is a sense that critical pedagogy is to be found in different pockets, and at different moments, during the school day and over different parts of this country. I am proud
to report that there are some very committed socially and critically conscious teachers who struggle for justice every day of the school year.

Readers of this text should note that there is no one correct way to
"do" critical pedagogy. Critical pedagogy is about teachers (in this particular case) struggling for some semblance of control in their lives—
control that has to do with achieving a qualitatively better life for students
and teachers; control that has to do with finding a democratic path that
begins to alleviate forms of oppression, alienation, and subordination.

As a critical pedagogue, however, I find myself caught in a particular
bind. On the one hand, critical pedagogists (whether female, male, white,
or nonwhite) have continually advocated language as a defining critical
momentum, despite critical pedagogy's obscure terminologies. The argument for this side of the coin remains that any new movement must
search for its defining language within its own struggle for a new para-

digm. And, as a strong advocate of critical pedagogy, I cannot refute this argument. Within critical pedagogy, however, there are multiple constituencies (feminists, some liberals, white middle-class males, minority intellectuals, teachers in various content areas in the public schools all of whom share critical pedagogy as a part of their personal world view, with similarities and differences). The list could go on and on. Thus, even though the language of critical pedagogy has been criticized for its obscure and hard-to-define messages, critics fail to tell me which kind of critical pedagogue they are talking about.

The argument on the other side of the coin is that if critical pedagogues are to make inroads into schools of education and public schools, something must be done about making critical pedagogy's ideas at least pragmatically accessible. Of course, this is not a call to simply lay out a formula of how to "do it." This is totally against the tradition of critical pedagogy and would simply be an act of deskilling. But what must finally be realized by critical pedagogists is the necessity to find alternatives to a stultified and standardized curriculum. There is a need to attempt a critical platform on some operational manner if we are to begin to grasp any sense of a democratic dream that critical pedagogists strive for. To me, the alternatives are simply unspeakable and are probably best described by Jonathan Kozol (1991) in his devastating critique of inner-city schools in the United States. Put simply, poverty, social class division, unequal distribution of labor, poor teacher working conditions, poor student learning conditions, and gender and race divisions run rampant in the United States.

I will not apologize for presenting a unit plan with general or specific objectives. These objectives may be offensive to some critical pedagogues. I do not apologize for attempting to present a unit with structure and form. I think that critical pedagogy needs structure and form despite its antistructural and more postmodern approach and underlying philosophy of endless deconstruction. I would like the reader to keep in mind that the unit I present here is merely an attempt by myself with the aid of five graduate students, Jill Deimler, Jaci Keagy, Tanya Kissell, Michele Graham Newberry, and Angela Ryan, to formulate what Stanley Aronowitz and Henry Giroux have called a "language of possibility."[1]

## UNIT PLAN

*THEME*: Similarities within Differences through Multiculturalism

*THEME DESCRIPTION*: The unit will attempt to uncover, explore, and critique the multiple identities of students, their similarities and differences, and the stereotypes prevalent within these cultures. Within trying to foster an acceptance of difference and similarities of these cultures (Asian, Hispanic, African American, and European American), literature, drama, and the fine arts will be the major content areas. The structure of the unit looks like this:

Similarities within Differences
through Multiculturalism

in

Literature
Drama
Fine Arts

with

Asian American
Hispanic
African American and
European American Cultures

This unit can be used anywhere from grades 7 and 8 onward; levels of materials would have to be modified or enhanced depending on the class make-up, class size, and age level.

## UNIT LENGTH

This is a three-month unit.

## MAJOR GOALS

1. To break the cycle of stereotypical thinking and cultural prejudice and to demonstrate the similarities within our differences of various cultures.
2. For students to find their own cultural voices so they can begin to empathize with others.

## MAJOR OBJECTIVES

1. Students will learn to critique themselves.
2. Through self-critique, students will learn to appreciate the worth and dignity of others.

3. Students will empathize with and respect the contributions of the Asian, Hispanic, African American, and European American cultures as they contribute to the richness of their personal culture and our national culture.

4. Students will learn about differences as they relate to their own lives and others' lives.

## CLASS MAKE-UP

The class is made up of thirty students in grade 10: twenty females and ten males. Race: eighteen white, six African American, three Hispanic, and three Asian. Socioeconomic status: working-class school in working-class industrial neighborhood.

## MONTHLY OBJECTIVES

### FIRST MONTH

1. Through the vehicle of literature, students will compare values and attitudes of the four cultures selected for learning.

2. Students will explore how literature simulates the lived experiences of different cultures.

3. Students will recognize the validity of multiple realities.

4. Through literary examples, students will attempt to overcome stereotypical cultural judgments and prejudices.

### SECOND MONTH

Same objectives as for the first month, except that drama will be the medium for exploration.

### THIRD MONTH

Same as for the first month, except that music and art will be the medium for exploration.

Each month has four objectives. Each objective relates to at least one week's lessons. Thus, there would be twelve to fourteen weeks to this unit. However, flexibility is needed so that anyone attempting such a unit will realize that these objectives are intertwined and may overlap at times. The following lesson plans and weekly and daily objectives are exemplars and suggestions that can be used in such a critical pedagogy unit. These lesson plans are not correct or perfect! They have been created to be critiqued.

Students will develop an awareness of self and other classmates.

### Lesson Plan Outline Week 1, Day 1

*Daily Objective 1*: Students will assess their own level of competence in dealing with cross-cultural education and multicultural awareness.
*Procedure*: Individual activity. Students receive self-assessment sheet (to be prepared individually by teachers). Students will place each of the terms on the appropriate place in the continuum based on their self-assessment. These sheets will be collected and placed in each student's portfolio.

*Source*

Adapted from *Multicultural Education: A Cross Cultural Training Approach*, Margaret D. Pusch, Intercultural Press, Yarmouth, Maine, 1979.

*Daily Objective 2*: Students will determine how we select what we see, and how one's background and attitudes could impact on a perception of an object or an event.
*Procedure*: Multiple-level picture interpretations are shown in the class for ten seconds (each teacher to choose picture). Each student writes what he or she saw. Students share responses with a partner. Volunteers demonstrate through dialogue different interpretations of pictures. Follow-up discussion in groups of three or four using cooperative learning techniques.

*Questions for Discussion* (in groups of 3 or 4)
1. How do we select out of our perception the things we want to see?
2. Why is it sometimes difficult to see things that are obviously there?
3. How does our attitude influence our perception?
4. How can we open our minds to see things that we may not have seen before?

*Note: This discussion should be allowed to continue for as long as it needs to accommodate all cultural voices.*

*Materials*: Photographs, pictures, transparency, overhead projector, cards with discussion questions (one card per group).
*Assignment*: Students write a one-page autobiography.

**Lesson Plan Outline Week 1, Day 2**

*Daily Objective 1*: Students will attempt to learn to praise themselves and increase their self-esteem.

*Procedure*: Using the cooperative learning technique think-pair-share, students are asked to think of:

1. Two physical attributes about themselves that they like
2. Two personality qualities that they like
3. One talent or skill that they possess.

After completing think-pair-share, a follow-up discussion in class will focus on these questions:

1. Did you find this a difficult assignment? Why or why not?
2. Is it more difficult to praise yourself or someone else? Why?
3. Are more people quick to give a negative comment about themselves or others than they are to compliment them? Why or why not?

*Daily Objective 2*: Students will recognize the importance of individual differences and sensitivity to personal characteristics.

*Procedure*:

1. Distribute an orange to each student. Each student is to examine, inspect, and get to know his or her fruit. Have students name their fruit and identify strengths and weaknesses in it.
2. Collect and mix up the oranges in front of the class.
3. Students write a short autobiographical paragraph about their fruit.
4. Ask students to come forward and collect their own fruit.

*Questions for Discussion* (in groups of three or four)

1. How many of you are sure you claimed your original fruit? How do you know?
2. What role did skin color play in getting to know your fruit?
3. Why can't we get to know people as quickly as we got to know our oranges?

Share answers and reflections in class using the cooperative learning technique stand and share.

*Materials*: One orange per student, cards with discussion questions for each group.

*Assignment*: Introduction to use of student journals. These journals will be used throughout the unit to encourage students to write feelings and personal interpretations of class activities. The journals will become a part of the student evaluation.

*Student journal reflection for today:*

- What parallels do you see in differentiating between oranges and between people? What differences exist?
- What was important in helping you to differentiate your orange from the others?
- Personal reflection on this exercise

*Evaluation:*

- Participation in discussion
- Group participation
- Completion of journal entry

*Sources*

Kagan, Spencer. *Cooperative Learning*. (San Juan Capistrano, Calif.: Kagan Cooperative Learning, 1992).
Newstrom, John W., and Edward E. Scannell. *Games Trainers Play*. (New York: McGraw-Hill, 1980).

**Other Suggested Activities for Week 1—Lesson Plans to Be Prepared by Reader or User of This Text**

1. Students prepare an autobiographical collage of photos, magazine pictures, fabric, etc.—anything that has meaning to them in their lives. Hold a class discussion of beliefs, backgrounds, and attitudes that help determine students' personal realities.
2. Students explore their own values and the values of other cultural groups. This can be done with value charts, ranking a list of values generated by the students, or using parables or anecdotes that illustrate different value systems.
3. Class building and community building activities should be included to facilitate group development, inclusion, trust, and respect. Numerous activities of this type are included in the following sources.

*Source:*

Pusch, Margaret D. *Multicultural Education: A Cross Cultural Approach*. (Yarmouth, Maine: Intercultural Press, 1979).
Shaw, Vanston. *Community Building in the Classroom*. (Kagan Cooperative Learning, 1992).

**WEEKLY OBJECTIVES, WEEK 2**

Students will compare their own attitudes and values to those found in Asian literature. In addition, students will become aware of stereotypical judgments and their harmful effects.

**Lesson Plan Outline Week 2, Day 1**

*Daily Objective:* Students will recognize the collective voice in the poem "We the Dangerous."

*Procedure*: Students will read the poem at first to themselves. Students will then, in groups of three, take a part (I, we, they) and read the poem aloud, utilizing a choral approach.

*Materials*: The poem "We the Dangerous."

*Assignment*: After discussing the different identities of the I, we, and they of the poem, students will write an explanation of their voice within American society, specifying the I voice, we voice, and they voice.

*Evaluation*:

• Participation in choral reading

• Participation in class discussion

• Completion of voice assignment

*Source*

Mirikitani, Janice. "We the Dangerous." In *American Mosaic: Multicultural Readings in Context*. (Boston: Houghton Mifflin, 1991).

**Sample Daily Objectives for Remainder of Week 2**

1. Students will sensitize themselves to the concept of culture. They will list several ways the short story "In the Land of the Free" represents the fears and loss of culture and identity that plague many new immigrants to the United States.

2. Students will identify in a journal entry ways in which their culture has lost some of its identity, either intentionally or unintentionally.

3. Students will analyze the motivation and behavior of James Clancy.

4. Students will write a poem about an experience that has affected them strongly, or write a journal entry discussing the benefits of writing as an emotional outlet.

*Source*

Far, Sin Sui. "In the Land of the Free." In *American Mosaic: Multicultural Readings in Context*. (Boston: Houghton Mifflin, 1991).

*Additional Optional Sources*

Anonymous. "Immigration Blues." In *American Mosaic: Multicultural Readings in Context*. (Boston: Houghton Mifflin, 1991).

Okada, John. "No-No Boy." In *American Mosaic: Multicultural Readings in Context*. (Boston: Houghton Mifflin, 1991).

## WEEKLY OBJECTIVES, WEEK 3

Students will compare their own attitudes and values to those found in Hispanic literature. In addition, students will become aware of stereotypical judgments and their harmful effects.

*Suggested literature titles and activities*: Read the short story "Ropes of Passage" and poems "Milagros" and "Napa, California."

*Sample Daily Objectives*:

1. Students will learn about the concept of alienation by naming and discussing examples of alienation from "Milagros."

2. Students will sensitize themselves to injustice by comparing the struggles and injustices Hispanic immigrants found in "Ropes of Passage" to those of American immigrants.

3. Students will identify different belief systems by understanding how incidents from "Ropes of Passage" illustrate how society's beliefs and attitudes influences Santo's life. Students will create a list of their family's beliefs and attitudes.

4. Students will analyze the correlation between the we in the poem "Napa, California" to the we in the poem "We the Dangerous."

### Sources

Castillo, Amy. "Milagros." In *American Mosaic: Multicultural Readings in Context*. (Boston: Houghton Mifflin, 1991).
Castillo, Amy. "Napa, California." In *American Mosaic: Multicultural Readings in Context*. (Boston: Houghton Mifflin, 1991).
Rivera, Edward. "Ropes of Passage." In *American Mosaic: Multicultural Readings in Context*. (Boston: Houghton Mifflin, 1991).

### Additional Optional Sources

Thomas, Piri. "Puerto Rican Paradise." Colon, Jesus. "Stowaway."
Mohr, Nicholassa, "A Thanksgiving Celebration." In *American Mosaic: Multicultural Readings in Context*. (Boston: Houghton Mifflin, 1991).

## WEEKLY OBJECTIVES, WEEK 4

Students will compare their own attitudes and values to those found in African American literature. In addition, students will become aware of stereotypical judgments and their harmful effects.

*Suggested Literature Titles and Activities*:

• View the video of Martin Luther King's speech "I Have a Dream."

• Read the poems "Any Human to Another" and "A Black Man Talks of Reaping."

• Read the short story "Sweat."

*Sample Daily Objectives*:

1. Students will learn about the concept of a dream as it related to Martin Luther King and as it relates to themselves. Students will discuss whether Martin Luther King's dream has come true for African Americans in today's society and whether it has come true for them individually.

2. Students will analyze how the painting *Big Meeting* reflects the ideas presented in "Any Human to Another."

3. Students will learn the similarities and differences of the cultural artifact of sowing and reaping. Students will compare the view of reaping from "A Black Man Talks of Reaping" to the ways all people of all races and creeds sow and reap.

4. Students will learn about the concept of choice. Students will analyze Delia's choice of asking white people rather than black people to help her. Discuss what choice reveals about power and race relations in Delia's community and in students' personal communities.

*Sources*

Teacher to choose videotape of Martin Luther King.
Bontemps, Arna. "A Black Man Talks of Reaping." In *The American Experience*. (Englewood Cliffs, N.J.: Prentice Hall, 1991).
Cullen, Countee. "Any Human to Another." In *The American Experience*. (Englewood Cliffs, N.J.: Prentice Hall, 1991).
Hurston, Nora Zeale. "Sweat." In *American Mosaic: Multicultural Readings in Context*. (Boston: Houghton Mifflin, 1991).

*Additional Optional Sources*

Fauset, Jesse Redmon. "There Is Confusion." In *American Mosaic: Multicultural Readings in Context*. (Boston: Houghton Mifflin, 1991).
Hughes, Langston. "The Negro Speaks of Rivers." In *The American Experience*. (Englewood Cliffs, N.J.: Prentice Hall, 1991).
Locke, Alan. "The New Negro." In *American Mosaic: Multicultural Readings in Context*. (Boston: Houghton Mifflin, 1991).

## WEEKLY OBJECTIVES, WEEK 5

Students will compare their own attitudes to those found in European American literature. In addition, students will become aware of stereotypical judgments and their harmful effects.
*Suggested literature titles and activities*: Read the short story "The Life You Save May Be Your Own." Read the poem "Mirror."

*Sample Daily Objectives*:

1. Students will learn about the concept of handicap as it relates to their own and others' lives. Students will discuss the ways in which Shiflet's handicap

affected his behavior and the ways in which it affected other people's behavior toward him.

2. Students will compare the way Mr. Shiflet affected the Crator women tragically to ways in which someone affected their own lives either tragically or beneficially.

3. Students will analyze how the dialect in "The Life You Save May Be Your Own" may cause a reader to stereotype people speaking a different language as inferior.

4. Students will discuss the woman's attitude in "Mirror" to most people's attitude toward aging.

### Sources

O'Connor, Flannery. "The Life You Save May Be Your Own." In *The American Experience*. (Englewood Cliffs, N.J.: Prentice Hall, 1991).
Plath, Sylvia. "Mirror." In *The American Experience*. (Englewood Cliffs, N.J.: Prentice Hall, 1991).

### Additional Sources

Justice, Donald. "Poem." In *The American Experience*. (Englewood Cliffs, N.J.: Prentice Hall, 1991).
Tyler, Anne. "Average Waves in Unprotected Waters." In *The American Experience*. (Englewood Cliffs, N.J.: Prentice Hall, 1991).

## WEEKLY OBJECTIVES, WEEK 6

Students will compare their own attitudes and values to those found in Asian drama. In addition, students will become aware of stereotypical judgments and their harmful effects as related to Asian cultures.

*Suggested Drama Titles and Activities*:

• Read portions of the play *Teahouse of the August Moon*.
• Listen to the song "American Dream" from *Miss Saigon*.

### Sample Daily Objectives:

1. Students will be exposed to stereotypes in the play. Students will compare these stereotypes to others they have come across in earlier weeks.

2. Students will define the concept of the American dream from their own perspective and as expressed in the song.

3. Students will compare the Western idea of democracy and the Eastern idea of democracy as expressed in the play.

4. Students will identify the elements in Okinawa community and the culture that Americans in the play grew to appreciate and tolerate, despite obvious differences.

*Sources*

Avian, Bob (lyricist). "The American Dream." *Miss Saigon.* (New York: Geffen Records, 1988).
Patrick, John. *Teahouse of the August Moon: A Play.* (New York: Crown Publishers Inc., 1963).

## WEEKLY OBJECTIVES, WEEK 7

Students will compare their cultural values to Hispanic cultural values. In addition, students will become aware of stereotypical judgments about the Hispanic culture.

*Suggested Drama Titles and Activities*:

• Read portions of the play *West Side Story* and watch portions of it on videotape.

• Perform selected cross-cultural mini-dramas from *Enucuentros Culturales.*

*Sample Daily Objectives*:

1. Students will compare the idea of the American dream found in last week's song to the idea of America found in the song "America" in *West Side Story.* Discuss similarities and differences.
2. Students will learn about the gangs in *West Side Story.* They will compare the gangs' similarities and differences to students' knowledge of gangs today.
3. Students will discuss the idea of gangs as related to racial prejudice. Students will also discuss the role of females in gangs, especially as related to *West Side Story.*
4. Through *West Side Story,* students will identify what machismo is within the Hispanic culture. They will compare the similarities and differences with machismo in European American culture.

*Sources*

Laurents, Arthur, Leonard Bernstein, Stephen Sondheim, and Jerome Robbins. *West Side Story.* In *Introduction to Theatre and Drama.* (Skokie, Ill.: National Textbook Company, 1982).
Snyder, Barbara. *Encuentros Culturales.* (Skokie, Ill.: National Textbook Company, 1977).

## WEEKLY OBJECTIVES, WEEK 8

Students will compare their attitudes and values to those found in African American drama. In addition, students will become aware of stereotypical judgments about African Americans. Students will familiarize themselves with the "American dream."

### Lesson Plan Outline Week 8, Day 1

*Objective*: Students will identify their own dreams, hopes, and aspirations as compared with those of the characters in the play *A Raisin in the Sun* (which will be read before class). Similarities and differences will be noted.

*Procedure*: Students will read portions of the play aloud.

*Materials*: The play *A Raisin in the Sun*.

*Class Assignment*: After identifying the two lists of dreams (their own and the character's in the play), students will mark similarities in the two lists and compare the Younger family's dream to the concept of the American dream discussed previously.

*Evaluation*:

• Participation in discussion

• Completion of written assignment

### Sample Daily Objectives for Remainder of Week 8

1. Students will identify and list their values. They will compare and contrast those values to adults in their own families (journal can be used).

2. Students will identify conflicts of old and new in this story's family structure. They will identify similarities and differences and compare them to conflicts in their own family.

3. Students will explain how Walter's definition of dignity changes from the beginning to the end of the play. They will discuss the similarities and differences of Walter's definition of dignity compared to their own sense of dignity. In a journal entry, students will talk about their own sense of dignity.

4. Students will list examples of prejudice that the Younger family experiences. Students will compare the similarities and differences with their own lives (their perception of their own, their family's, and their community's prejudices).

*Source*

Hansberry, Lorraine. *A Raisin in the Sun*. In *Introduction to Theatre and Drama*. (Skokie, Ill.: National Textbook Company, 1982).

### WEEKLY OBJECTIVES, WEEK 9

Students will compare their own attitudes and values to those found in European American drama. In addition, students will become aware of stereotypical judgments about European Americans.

*Suggested Drama Title and Activities*:
Read the book and watch portions of the movie *Ordinary People*.
*Sample Daily Objectives*:

1. Students will identify the family dynamics of the Jarrett family. Students will compare and contrast similarities and differences with those of their own families.

2. Students will examine Conrad's struggle between what he feels he should be and what he actually sees himself as. In a journal entry, students will write about personal similar and different struggles of what they feel they should be versus what they perceive themselves to be.

3. Students will discuss Conrad's reaction to his brother's death and his attempted suicide. In cooperative learning groups, students will discuss why suicide has been an option of escape for people in general.

4. Students will define Jarrett's family's version of the American dream and how it was shattered. They will discuss the similarities and differences between Jarrett's family's, their own, and their family's version of the American dream. They will complete this exercise in their journals.

*Source*

Guest, Judith. "*Ordinary People*." *Literary Cavalcade*, 33 (6), March 1981.

## WEEKLY OBJECTIVES, WEEK 10

Based on previous discoveries concerning cultural attitudes and values, students will interpret Asian art and music.
*Suggested Art/Music Titles and Activities*:

• Listen to the song "Living in America" by the group Hiroshima.
• View *The Great Wave of Kanagwi*.
• Critique *Fugin Tomari Kyaku No Zu*.
• Interpret *In Sinking Pleasure Boat*.

*Sample Daily Objectives*:

1. Students will compare and contrast similarities and differences between Asian art and music and popular art and music.

2. Students will be able to distinguish between gender roles in art and music within the Asian culture. In journals students will write on gender differences in art as they see them. This becomes a week-long assignment with library work and a possible museum trip.

3. Students will respond to Asian values through a discussion of Sinici Suzuki and his philosophies (this will take at least two classes).

*Sources*

Hokusai, Katsushika. *The Great Wave: A History of Far Eastern Art*. (New York: Harry N. Abrams, 1964).
Kuramoto, Dan and Cortez, Dean. "Living in America." *East*. (New York: CBS Records, 1989).
Teraokas, Masami. "In Sinking Pleasure Boat." *Portfolio Magazine*, 11, February/March, 1980.
Utamaro, Kitagawa. *Fugin Tomari Kyaku No Zu. The History and Process of Printmaking*. (New York: Holt, Rinehart and Winston, 1978).

### *WEEKLY OBJECTIVES, WEEK 11*

Based on previous discoveries concerning cultural attitudes and values, students will interpret Hispanic art and music.
*Suggested Art/Musical Works and Activities*:

• Critique *Si Se Puede* and *Somos Azatlan*.
• Interpret *Rope and People*.
• Critique *Saint Francis Road Mural*.
• Listen to and then discuss *Sinfonia India*.
• Listen to and then discuss Hispanic rap and folk tunes.

*Sample Daily Objectives*:

1. Students will discover their own stereotypical judgments and prejudices through Hispanic art and folk music.
2. Students will respond through dialogue to the emotions evoked in *Rope and People* and *Sinfonia India*.
3. Students will interpret the values and attitudes found within Hispanic rap and mural paintings. In a journal entry, students will respond to the similarities and differences between Hispanic rap and rap found in their own culture.

*Sources*

Chavez, Carlos. *Sinfonia India*. (New York: Schirmer, Inc., 1950).
Martinez, Ernesto. "Si Se Puede." Aquayo, Emilio. "Somos Aztlan." *Chicano Art Resistance and Affirmation, 1965–1985*. (Los Angeles: UCLA Wight Art Gallery, 1991).
Miro, Juan. "Rope and People." *Galeria Hispanica*. (New York: McGraw-Hill, 1971).

### *WEEKLY OBJECTIVES, WEEK 12*

Based on previous discoveries concerning cultural attitudes and values, students will respond to and interpret African American art and music, comparing it to their own culture's art and music (similarities and differences).

*Suggested Art/Musical Works and Activities*:

• Critique *Figures Drumming*.
• Interpret *Christmas* and *The Dress She Wore Was Blue*.
• Listen and respond to the spiritual "Didn't My Lord Deliver Daniel?"
• Listen and interpret *Jump for Joy* by Duke Ellington.

*Sample Daily Objectives*:

1. In a journal entry, students will interpret the emotions found in the spiritual "Didn't My Lord deliver Daniel?".
2. In a journal entry, students will respond to their own personal experiences in relation to the aforementioned spiritual.
3. Students will respond to and interpret and Harlem renaissance through viewing *The Dress She Wore Was Blue* and *Jump for Joy*.
4. Students will interpret the values and attitudes found within African American rap and graffiti and discuss the similarities and differences to their own culture's music styles.

*Sources*

Hayden, Palmer. "Christmas." *Harlem Renaissance Art of Black America*. (New York: Harry N. Abrams, 1987).
Hayden, Palmer. "The Dress She Wore Was Blue." *Harlem Renaissance Art of Black America*. (New York: Harry N. Abrams, 1987).
Muntu, Mode. *Figures Drumming. African Explorers; Twentieth Century African Art*. (New York: The Center for African Art, 1991).

## WEEKLY OBJECTIVES, WEEK 13

Based on previous discoveries concerning cultural attitudes and values, students will respond to and interpret European American art and music.

*Suggested Art/Musical Works and Activities*:

• Write a story based on *Billy the Kid*.
• Draw a picture based on *Putnam's Camp, Redding, Connecticut*.
• Create a rap song based on real-life experiences.
• Critique *In without Knocking*.
• Respond to *Untitled (Woman with Softdrink)*.

*Sample Daily Objectives*:

1. Students will critique *In without Knocking* in relation to the stereotypes of the European American culture.

2. Students will discuss similar and different responses (their feelings) to experiences in *Putnam's Camp, Redding Connecticut*.

3. Students will create their own rap utilizing their personal similar and different experiences. (This can be a group activity.)

*Sources*

Copland, Aaron. *Billy the Kid—Ballet Suite*. (New York: RCA Records, 1988).

Ives, Charles. "Putnam's Camp." *Three Places in New England*. (New York: Mercury Records, 1958).

Ruossel. "In without Knocking." *Artists of the Old West*. (New York: Doubleday and Company, 1965).

Unknown. *Untitled (Woman with Softdrink). (Spiritual America, IVAM— Colleccio Centre del Carme, 1989)*.

### Lesson Plan Outline Week 13, Day 1

*Daily Objective*: After listening to Aaron Copland's *Billy the Kid*, students will interpret the music by writing and discussing their own story or descriptive narrative in response to the music.
*Procedure*:

• Students will listen to an excerpt from *Billy the Kid* and will write what they feel is happening in the music.

• Students will share their responses with the rest of the class and will compare and contrast them.

• Students will write how or if the stories reflect their own reality.

• The teacher will discuss the name of the music and the story behind it.

*Materials: Billy the Kid—Ballet Suite*, Aaron Copland
*Assignment*: Students will write a journal entry describing what they discovered about themselves through their interpretation of the music.
*Evaluation*:

• Completion of the story or narrative

• Participation in class discussion

• Completion of journal entry

### Lesson Plan Outline Week 13, Day 2

*Daily Objective*: By critiquing *In without Knocking*, students will respond to and interpret the art in relation to attitudes, values, and stereotypes of the European American culture.

*Procedure*:

- Review of critique and critique procedures
- Introduction to the art work *In without Knocking*
- Students will write individual responses concerning attitudes, values, and stereotypes of the culture.
- Class discussion focused on the following:
  - Describe the feelings and emotions in the art work.
  - What are some of the thoughts and attitudes portrayed in the art work concerning the European American culture?
  - Are there any stereotypical judgments and prejudices attached to this culture? Are they visible in the art work?
  - What are the reasons for the stereotypes and prejudices?
  - How do you think the people of this culture feel when categorized in such a way?
  - How do you feel about your prejudices? Does everyone feel this way?
  - What are the similarities and differences in the way we feel about this art work?
  - What changes can occur, and how, in society today, can we foster less prejudice and stereotypes?

Students should respond to some of these questions in a journal entry.

*Assignment*: Students will respond to the class discussion and will relate similarities and differences within their life experiences in their own ways (words, drawings, paintings, etc.).

*Evaluation*:

- Participation in class discussion
- Completion of the artistic sketch

*Other Sources*

Anderson, William. *Teaching Music with a Multicultural Approach*. (MENC, 1991).
Floyd, Samuel A., ed. *Black Music in the Harlem Renaissance: A Collection of Essays*. (Westport, Conn.: Greenwood Publishing Group Inc., 1990).
Hermann, Evelyn. *Sinichi Suzuki: The Man and His Philosophy*, Athens, Ohio: Accura Music.
Koskoff, Ellen, ed. *Women and Music in Cross Cultural Perspective*. (Westport, Conn.: Greenwood Publishing Group Inc., 1987).

*Additional Art Sources*

Berliner, Nancy. "Chinese Papercuts." *American Craft*, 45(2), April/May, 1985, pp. 16–21.

The Bronx Museum of the Arts. *The Latin American Spirit: Art and Artists in the United States, 1920–1970.* (New York: Harry N. Abrams, 1988).

Glueckert, Alan. "Sumi-e Painting." *School Arts*, May, 1989, pp. 27–29.

Lee, Sherman. "Realism in Japanese Art: Things of this World and No Other." *Portfolio Magazine*, 5(2), March/April, 1983, pp. 62–67.

Mendelowitz, Daniel M. *A History of American Art.* (New York: Holt, Rinehart and Winston, 1970).

Schuman, Jo Miles. *Art from Many Hands: Multicultural Art Projects for Home and School.* (Englewood Cliffs, N.J.: Prentice Hall, 1981).

Sugimura, Yuzo. *Chinese Sculpture, Bronzes, and Jades in Japanese Collections.* (Honolulu: East-West Center Press, 1966).

### WEEK 14, UNIT CONCLUSION

Upon completion of this unit, students will synthesize their heightened awareness of self, stereotypes, prejudices, and the various voices within the four cultures into a group presentation. The focus of the presentation will be similarities within differences and multiculturalism. Sample activities may include poetry readings, skits, vocal selections, slide shows, and dance performances. The presentation will be performed first in the school and then possibly within the district, if arranged. If possible, performances in other school districts and for community groups will follow.

### CONCLUSION

On one level, this curriculum development attempt at critical pedagogy has been a humbling experience. In a curriculum document of any sort, no mention is made of the conscious intent of teachers to challenge race, class, and gender disparities as well as to end various forms of oppression, alienation, and subordination. On another level, curriculum development of this sort can provide some guidelines on what it might take to incorporate critical pedagogical elements into a curriculum.

Clearly, any teacher who views this curriculum project as an ultimate truth misses the opportunity to create a critical pedagogy that speaks to different student subjectivities, identities, and entitlements. This curriculum attempt is in no way an attempt to deskill teachers, but rather to help teachers tool themselves with reskilling opportunities. Again, I as the author cannot do this. I have no authorship over curriculum. But you teachers do.

In any curriculum it is up to the teacher to install critical pedagogical elements that on the surface meet state guidelines and are cultural and political as well as critical, open, democratic, and nurturing. The language of possibility in this curriculum, then, begs teachers not only to teach content about different countries, customs, and habits but to teach a project of this sort for reasons that have to do with social justice and the human state as central to the teaching endeavor.

I did not want to provide lessons but just provide some examples. I cannot control the class make-up or the district in which such a curriculum will be taught. Thus, the hidden agenda, often referred to as the hidden curriculum, becomes of paramount importance. While constructing this project for yourselves, reading this project, or even teaching something similar to this project, refer to the concepts discussed in Chapter 2. Within the hidden curriculum I will ask myself continually if what I am teaching and constructing is counterhegemonic. Or I will be consciously aware of the hegemonic process that as a teacher I undertake with such a project. I will ask myself in what ways have I empowered the students: Is knowledge presented in authoritarian ways or are students allowed the space to be both critical and transformational about knowledge? I will continually be conscious of the democratic intent of the knowledge I impart and the individuality that I want to foster in class. My hidden agenda is one that aims to challenge existing structures of oppression, alienation, and subordination while simultaneously teaching students the required state-mandated curriculum. In other words, my curriculum is far from objective or innocent. In it lies the cultural politics of knowledge that attempts to challenge students to reformulate their thoughts on self, difference, and other. Within this cultural politics lies the modernistic notion of community as a core concept with the postmodern notion of difference, not in opposition but seeking common harmony—a common faith, if you will.[2]

There is no doubt in my mind that teachers who undertake such a mission become social architects, visionaries (and in some senses missionaries), and futurists. Teachers of this sort will struggle to make themselves understood in a meaningful way, will be rebuked, challenged, and often neglected. When one of my colleagues at a former university I attended said that she didn't like what I taught in class, I stated that my conscious intent was to teach "democracy, if that's OK with you." Critical pedagogists' intents are noble and worthwhile, but they are challenging to existing social structures of oppression and alienation.

For teachers who read this chapter, my intent is for you to take my ideas into your area of expertise. I am convinced that areas such as social studies, arts, music, humanities, history, English, math, and so on can use social activists as teachers who incorporate critical pedagogic elements in their content area.

As I head into the final chapter, I would like readers to keep in mind that all critical pedagogists are different. We all have our own view of reality. This is why the next chapter is so important. The interview in that chapter with another critical pedagogist, Svi Shapiro, will highlight some of these differences as well as their similarities.

## NOTES

1. Aronowitz and Giroux, *Education under Siege*, for more on resistance, critique and languages and discourses of possibility.

2. John Dewey, "Christianity and Democracy." *Religious Thought* (Ann Arbor, Mich.: Inland Press, 1893), p. 63; and John Dewey, *A Common Faith* (New Haven, Conn.: Yale University Press, 1934).

# 7

---

---

# Continuing Issues and Trends in Critical Pedagogy: An Interview with Svi Shapiro and a Student

**INTRODUCTION**

For over seven years now, ever since I completed my doctorate at Ohio State University, I have been involved in teaching students from what this book has referred to as a critical pedagogical perspective. One major obstacle that I have encountered using this frame of reference is language accessibility to my students. Critical educational theorists who use critical pedagogy have often been accused of using opaque language and ideas, particularly as they relate to schools.

Some students in my foundations classes, for instance, rightly argue that critical pedagogy's obscure language makes radical educational ideas almost impossible to grasp. This becomes, they argue, a contradiction to the very argument critical pedagogists make: simply, that critical pedagogy is a means and method to undercut oppressive social relations and an attempt to end alienation and subordination. How, my students argue, can one challenge dominant ideas when the language one uses to do so is also dominant and ungraspable despite its utopian connotations and meanings?

Moreover, some students claim that the language of critical pedagogy is so obscure that it assumes an authoritarian position. This position, in a major way, also contradicts critical pedagogy's indictment. Indeed, although some of my students take on critical pedagogy as a life endeavor, for a lot of other students suspicion of its cause, both because of its language and radical message, sets in. On some levels, this book has been an attempt to make the theoretical practical and the practical theoretical.

Motivated and socially conscious students in my critical educational foundations classes are caught in a particular bind. They are trapped within the structural limits of schools to cause change. And critical theory (which offers critical pedagogy ideas and resultant teaching methods) offers little respite from this trap despite its noble messages. This is because theory is made seemingly impossible to pragmatize—despite those ideals of democracy, community, and a struggle to challenge alienation, oppression, and subordination within the school system and the surrounding culture.

Like other educational movements—call them progressive, liberal, humanist, traditional, nontraditional, conservative, and/or neoconservative—critical theory in education is also struggling to incorporate ideas and gain acceptance in the public sphere, particularly as it involves education. For instance, there are very few critical theorists in state departments of education or in high government positions. Only a few critical theorists have impacted popular culture.[1] For instance, what counts as education, schooling, excellence, empowerment, educational standards, critical thinking, and multiculturalism become of paramount importance to all involved in education. Those who impact the public will skew meaning. Critical theorists in education have *not* been successful in this endeavor; however, conservative authors such as Bloom and Hirsch blossom to record-level sales.[2]

A terrain of struggle over meaning predominates in teacher education departments and in schools over the above listed concepts. The stakes are indeed high. Whose knowledge will be incorporated into the universities and schools? Is there right knowledge? And if so, whose knowledge is most worthwhile?

Concepts such as transformative intellectual, modernism, and postmodernism have recently begun to fill the educational journals, particularly as related to critical pedagogy. Critical pedagogists writing for educational journals are caught in a bind. Who do we write for? University folk? Ourselves? Public school teachers? And while theoretical banter of critical pedagogy continues, new language is being formed. We must ask ourselves, Will these concepts, such as empowerment, become just another educational fad? Are we truly all empowered? There is no simple answer to these questions.

One thing is certain: My students are frustrated by the vast array of new and difficult language they face as they encounter critical pedagogical ideas and consider their practical import. I am sure that many, if not most, educational instructors make these ideas somewhat accessible to their students. I believe I do through stories and narratives of my personal history as related to school, sexism, and prejudice (as in Chapter 1). However, there are some students who yearn for further clarification—for ideas to be affirmed by other critical theorists' viewpoints, explanations, and interpretations, particularly as related to schools and the larger surrounding culture. Students read McLaren's[3] work and are angry at him for leaving his elementary school teaching job as well as castigating the system that has rewarded him. They read Weiler's[4] work on women as teachers and either recoil into their shells or openly deny the inevitability of sexism. Other students take on the challenge feminism has to offer us and enter the public school system armed with a feminist cause. I believe that students are both sparked and affirmed by critical pedagogy. Yet they don't face much exposure to its ideas, except only possibly in a one-semester or one-quarter course at university.

One student in a recent class of mine decided that for his final semester project he would seek out a critical theorist of repute and challenge the ideas that my course and many of the ideas in this text advocate. This student is probably typical of some new students who are exposed to, and want to learn more about, critical pedagogy. He is very bright. He is articulate. His ideas are not radical. Yet he sees the radical viewpoint that critical pedagogy has to offer as a worthwhile and noble cause, an ideal to strive for. It speaks to a language, Rocky Spino says, of "human decency and respect." On some levels Spino is understandably confused— language is just one issue. He, like many of us who live in capitalistic America, truly believes in democratic virtues. This presents him with a challenge of meaning and ideas that are confusing and often contradictory.

In Spino's questions to Professor Shapiro lie idea accessibility, scholarship, and a serious commitment to a democratic school vision of a qualitatively better society for our students in the public schools. Above all else, Shapiro is able to illuminate for us just how the complexity of such terms as *postmodernism, multiculturalism, critical thinking,* and *education* can be accessible and programmable. Spino's questions are insightful. They present a radical educator with a serious challenge both to clarify his position and talk about a critical agenda for schools in an accessible language that is mired in a quest for human decency, compassion, hope, and affirmation. My students have since found the transcript of this interview understandable and particularly inspiring as they head out into the teaching world armed with tools of critical pedagogy.

In the following interview conducted in April, 1993, I will interject as Barry. My comments relate to the information discussed in Chapter 2. It is hoped that this interview may (1) clarify any theoretical confusion, and (2) serve as another look at critical pedagogy's mission from the perspective of another critical theorist and a student in my educational foundations class.

*Spino*: We've been hearing the depressing news for a long time now. America's school system is in serious trouble. Students everywhere are struggling. But there has been change at times, too, we're told. Progressive types of curriculum have been proposed and inserted into the system every now and then. Things like whole language, the mastery approach, and, in Pennsylvania, our own beloved but battered outcomes-based education. Now, fifteen weeks into our course, Social and Cultural Foundations of Education, we're no longer talking about mere change; we're talking radical reform. In fact, according to educational theorist and activist Peter McLaren, the notion of the high school dropout may not be so much a description as a prescription. With the intolerable instruction that we have to offer students these days, McLaren writes, "dropping out becomes not so much an option as an urgent and necessary act of survival."[5]

With us today we are fortunate to have someone who has thought about the issue of educational reform as much as anyone. He's written extensively about the subject in numerous educational journals. His book on the topic is called *Between Capitalism and Democracy: Educational Policy in the Welfare State*. And he provides the foreword to the Barry Kanpol text, *Towards a Theory and Practice of Teacher Cultural Politics: Continuing the Postmodern Debate*.[6] He is Dr. Svi Shapiro.

Let me take you back to McLaren's comment that dropping out in fact for high school students today might just be a necessary act of survival. It seems to me that we've been spending years and years and much time and energy in this country pounding messages into students like "stay in school. If nothing else, at least stay in school." In view of that, do you find McLaren's advice to abandon ship responsible?

*Shapiro*: I think we're in a terrible dilemma. Because I think McLaren's description of schooling is just about right. I think schooling, especially as one gets into the higher grades, into high school, is a terrible exercise in alienation and boredom, frustration and irrelevance for adolescents today. I think that he's absolutely right as well as many others who have written about it. The real dilemma for kids, and perhaps even more so for parents, is the reality that when kids drop out of school, we punish them for it. We make life hard for them. It makes it that much harder to get a job, to get a kind of job that may have a minimal amount of interest in it. We're in an economic downturn. Interesting work, decently paying work, is harder to find. And the fact of the matter is we hold a gun to kids' heads. "If you don't stay in school, if you don't get a high school diploma, you don't go on to college, we're going to make your life very hard." Of course, even staying on is no guarantee. But the fact of the matter is it [dropping out] certainly makes the options that much less for kids. So, the way I see it is, in real human terms, there's a terrible dilemma here between the alienation of school and the penalties that kids pay for not enduring it.

*Barry*: It seems to me that much of the discussion on deskilling and reskilling can apply to all facets of the school system. School boredom ends up deskilling students as well as teachers.

*Spino*: So, we provide a strong indictment because the system is so indictable?

*Shapiro*: We provide an indictment because these are, at least as some of us see it, the facts of the situation. I think these are the facts on the ground. This is what kids face. With some kids, of course, perhaps a more pragmatic bent makes them put up with what goes on. They play the game and manage to get through it. Other kids, equally bright kids, finally decide it's intolerable to them in a personal sense, a human sense. And there are many other kids who simply recognize that school was never meant for them to begin with. Probably McLaren has written more about those kinds of kids from minority backgrounds. Schools in America were never made for these kids anyway, in terms of providing them with a route for upward mobility. That was always an illusion for the most part anyway, other than for the exceptions. So, yeah, I think the indictment is fairly aimed.

*Barry*: Yes, I think that even inner-city schools at times cover up class-bound school systems with hopeful discussion on teacher empowerment and autonomy. The fact is that teachers in inner-city schools are very autonomous, for the most part because administrators have lost control of curriculum, high dropout rates, etc. are more concerned with acquiring teachers to just fill a position in the inner-city classroom. Hegemony sets in when we realize that social practices have been about providing illusions to upward mobility. This reminds me of an inner-city school in Compton, Los Angeles. I was observing a student-teacher, when over the microphone I heard the administration [principal] mention how this middle school will have the best-behaved, smartest, highest-test-scoring students in the district. Interestingly, not one student was listening to this middle-class message. Instead, students were either loudly talking, threatening each other, hitting each other, or putting make-up on [girls]. These students' voices (their histories, subjectivities) were forfeited for an illusion of middle-class upward mobility.

*Spino*: Before we talk about some of the theory that drives your discourse and others like it, let's hang out in the school yard for a couple of minutes. I'm currently a graduate student. My fellow classmates are all pursuing their degrees of choice. Dr. Kanpol is a respected professor at a well-known university. And we have your own considerable success. It seems like, for us anyway, the school system has done okay.

*Shapiro*: Well, I really don't have a simple answer for that. I mean I have an ambivalent answer. When you say that we've done well by it, I have to say that my schooling for the most part, certainly up to high school, was an exercise in irrelevance and boredom. I put a lot of energy into it. I was, to an extent, brow beaten by working-class parents who were concerned that I not end up in dead-end work. And they were right about that. But I want to make a clear distinction here between education and schooling. I don't want to confuse them. If you say that I've jumped through the hoops and gotten the necessary qualifications and managed to succeed in the process, the answer is yes. And that is certainly true of the McLarens and various other folks of the world. There's no doubt about it. But I don't want to equate that with education. My education, in the real sense, has come sometimes in school and, very often, through what I have learned in other ways through other forms of experiences.

*Spino*: In other words, there is a certain amount of resourcefulness on your part. You have gotten where you are in spite of the system.

*Shapiro*: In spite of the system. I was fortunate in that I went to college in England in the late 1960s. I went to a college that has a radical faculty that was radically oriented in sociology. And I found a space for myself, a critical space for myself that some of us have been fortunate to find. You could not classify that experience as mainstream or typical. And in that space I found teachers who were able to offer me ideas, texts, and other kinds of experiences that were extraordinarily powerful and illuminating for me. But, again, I make the distinction here between education, which is a set of experiences that really help free the mind, that help liberate one from the taken-for-grantedness of our world, and schooling, which was, for the most part, jumping through hoops. Whether it was in England or in this country, it was a matter of grades and exams and finding ways to satisfy the curricular demands that were placed on me with very little connection to my real-life interests, concerns, and passions.

*Barry*: It seems to me that I was schooled and not educated in your sense, Svi. I even found ways to acquire grades nontraditionally [Chapter 1].

*Spino*: Let's talk about some of those powerful experiences you mention. I imagine it's those that you held onto and integrated into some of your own ideas and theories. Let's talk about some concepts, which are, in fact, very close to you. If nothing else in this fifteen weeks with Dr. Kanpol, I've got the vocabulary down: postmodernist, critical pedagogue, transformative intellectual. They're all there. Can you give any kind of a concise statement about what hopes, dreams, and aspirations underlie those terms?

*Shapiro*: Yes, I think I can. I think that what underlies these concepts is a very serious adherence to what I think of as the best and most noble ideals that we find in American society. And those ideals have to do with issues such as democracy and human empowerment, the validation of human dignity and human worth, the vision of a society and a world that's based on people helping each other and not trying to beat each other. I think the underlying moral impulse that's there in the work that I'm concerned with, I think it's guided by those kinds of basic ideals. The issues that I and others are concerned with within critical pedagogy and critical thought is really trying to highlight the dissonance between those ideals that I think most human beings in American society value and the realities by which we learn to live our lives and learn to experience our world, which are, for the most part, sharply at variance with those powerful promises and hopes.

*Spino*: You speak of a philosophy, a theoretical base, that simply stands for normal, moral ideas of human decency. If that's the case, why do you think that so many students, or so many people in general, recoil at the ideas of McLaren, Kanpol, or Shapiro?

*Shapiro*: Good question. One that I constantly struggle with. Because if there's any purpose to what we do, really, it is surely to be able to get these ideas to as wide a number of people as possible. So, if we don't succeed in doing that, and certainly we don't fully succeed in doing that, that's obvious, we have to ask ourselves why. I think that there's no simple reason for it. I think that students sometimes recoil, with some justification, from the language that's used. Some of the language we use is difficult. It's opaque. It perhaps is more about elevating our own status as intellectuals and members of the university. It becomes a language that's just not familiar to a lot of people, and I think that irritates and angers some people. I think there are other reasons that have to do with the fact that people, especially people who are teachers, have basically benefited from the system. I mean, we are, for the most part, and this I think goes back to your earlier question, we have done pretty well by the school system. We've gotten through it and we've got jobs and we've got degrees. So, of course, why shoot the goose that lays the golden eggs for us? Here you have folks who come along, the people you name, and we seem to want to tear down the system that some of us have done so well by. So there's a defensiveness that creeps in here. And, I think perhaps there's a denial. A sense that we will have to, I think, look very critically at our own work and what we do or don't do in light of these messages. And, if it's true that we're boring and alienating these kids, then it says something about what we are doing in the classrooms. Most of us don't particularly like to look really honestly at what we do if what we do doesn't seem to be producing goodness. It's embarrassing, it's disturbing, and I think, then, denial sets in.

*Barry*. How then can we deny our own schooling experiences? Don't these experiences teach us about schooling, education, deskilling and reskilling, etc.? Given the answers to these questions, how we connect our history to race, class, and gender becomes paramount to critically empowering ourselves for a democratic community or *not* as the case may be. As critical pedagogues, we must search in ourselves and in our students for our own forms of denial so as to eventually make life more tolerable for all.

*Spino*: That really makes sense. If you are coming from a message of simple human decency and value, you really need to connect this beyond the language of postmodernism to the student in your classroom. Now, the whole concept of postmodernism is something you talk about a great deal in some of your writings, particularly in the foreword to Barry Kanpol's book. You cite the emancipatory power of postmodern thought and indicate that it can be tied to education in a positive way. Yet Barry Kanpol talks about the ambiguity of postmodernism. To define it, almost, is not to be postmodern. And, when I think of postmodernism, I think of a David Lynch movie. Something very murky and mysterious. Does a movement that ambiguous have real practical value, and, if so, what would that be?

*Shapiro*: Well, obviously the whole postmodern intellectual business is a complicated one and there are many, many different ways in which one can talk about what it's really about. I've been fascinated by it precisely because of its ambiguity. But I would say this: If I wanted to pick out what, for me, is a central strand of postmodernism, central in terms of its relevance to the human condition, I think *postmodernism* is really a word that tries to capture the uncertainty of human knowing. It is the uncertainty about quite what it is that we know about the world, not only the social and the human world, but even the natural world, even the world the scientist looks at. We have come to see throughout the twentieth century, actually, especially strongly in the last, perhaps, two decades, just how limited what we know about the world really is. That is, how uncertain our knowledge about the world really is. And that is true from just about across the spectrum of human inquiry. And, of course, that unleashes both very positive and very negative kinds of phenomena. On the negative side, you have the sense that human beings are really in a world which they have to judge as uncertain, fragile. It's pretty hard to stake one's life on ideas or commitments, even moral ideas, when all about us is an accumulating amount of evidence that we have a very limited take on the world. It's limited by culture, by language, by history. This whole notion that's been with us for 400 years or so, since the Enlightenment, that we are progressively advancing toward the Truth, a certain knowing about reality, is being more or less destroyed by the kinds of inquiry that we generally tend to call postmodernism. That's a very disturbing phenomenon to human beings. I think it's not unconnected to the rise of fundamentalist thought throughout the world. Because there is no doubt about it, the phenomenon undercuts and creates human anxiety. This is responded to by some people with a kind of a battening down of the hatches, a determination to believe, in spite of everything, that we have some kind of certainty. Now, the other side of that is that there is also a freeing that comes with these concepts. As people can see, there are no certainties about the world, there are no clear-cut, for-sure prescriptions about almost anything, and there is a kind of freedom that comes from that. There's a freedom that unleashes people from determinative roles—whether it's women being freed from the mother and housemaker roles, or whether it's a minority group or a sexual minority group, whatever it is, suddenly being freed from a notion that they can be simply and clearly pigeon-holed in the world. Or just any of us. We are freed from having our thoughts, our ideas, our roles being fixed in some certain and endless manner. I think that is a freeing phenomena. So, the legacy is certainly, from my perspective, an ambivalent one.

*Spino*: Does that kind of freeing to rethink and reevaluate one's own reality have a life and a purpose outside of the college classroom?

*Shapiro*: Undoubtedly. It really is a phenomenon that infiltrates every aspect of our lives. You know, there's often a question of "what the hell do all these intellectual pursuits have to do with everyday life?" But, in fact, whether people term it postmodernism or not, we are all, especially in the Western world, affected by this growing fragility of knowledge and knowing. It affects everybody, not just the few people who actually write books and articles about this.

*Barry*: This reminds me that, as a teacher, how do I really know what knowledge is best for students and, particularly, where did this knowledge come from? These are the kinds of questions I continually ask myself in this postmodern condition.

*Spino*: Another element that comes out in your writings, Barry Kanpol's, and certainly Peter McLaren's is the idea of critical thinking. What I have come to know about being a critical thinker is acting with a certain degree of cognitive sophistication or independence. In your circle, though, the idea of a critical thinker becomes one of being a social architect or activist. You put critical thinking into a social arena. Is that a fair revision of the concept?

*Shapiro*: There's a confusion, again, of terms here. The term *critical thinking* very often in the culture, and particularly around schools today, is used to denote a very strictly intellectual task. That is a capacity to problem solve, to develop the capacity for analytical thinking on the part of students, to perhaps be able to analyze things in different ways and reach different conclusions. That's what I would call a kind of mainstream critical thinking or critical cognitive approach to education. It's fairly acceptable in broad circles and it's being promoted, I think, relatively widely. But the kind of criticality you will find in critical pedagogy is really different from this in that it's really about what I call critical consciousness. It is about focusing our critical capacities, our questioning capacity, on the everyday world in which we find ourselves with a purpose. And that purpose is rooted in a moral vision. It has to do with looking at the world, questioning the world as to whether, in fact, it treats people with dignity and respect; whether the world is one in which certain groups of people or individuals are limited or dominated, or whether the world that we live in, in fact, lives up to its democratic and humanistic promises. So, I suppose the first strand is really a strictly cognitive, intellectual orientation, and the second one is rooted in a definite moral vision.

*Spino*: So, you're not so much redefining the concept as much as putting it into a positive, operational context.

*Shapiro*: Well, I guess one way to see this is that a critical consciousness really, I think, puts those critical capacities to work in some real way. The other kind of critical capacity is basically abstracted. Let me put this in another way. The critical capacities that are developed in that strictly cognitive sense can be put to use to build better hydrogen bombs, and indeed are. They can be put to use to produce better, more manipulative advertising on Madison Avenue. And indeed they are. They can be put to use to find better ways to market products that are destructive to the environment. And they are. I mean the fact of the matter is the people who sit at the heads of our corporate board rooms and governmental agencies and so on and so forth often are extraordinarily great critical thinkers. They have very highly developed critical powers. They've been to good universities and colleges. They know how to use those things. So, critical capacity in itself really is kind of a whore. It can be put to all kinds of uses. It's an abstract idea that can be set down in many different places and put to work for many different masters. The criticality that I'm talking about, or McLaren or Giroux talks about, or Barry Kanpol talks about, is a critical capacity put into the service of a particular moral vision. And I think that's really the difference.

*Spino*: Barry Kanpol has presented his classes with words like *postmodernism, transformative intellectual*, and *critical pedagogy* and has suggested them as good concepts to become familiar with. There's another word you deal with in your writings that gets presented as something negative. That word is *capitalism*. Capitalism has provided a backdrop for, and has maybe even been in the foreground of, public education in America. What's wrong with that?

*Shapiro*: Well, I think I'm very up front about this. I mean my cultural politics are what you might call democratic socialist. I believe that capitalism is premised on moral principles that are abhorrent to me. They're based on the principles that the natural or desirable or necessary condition of human relationships is one of competitiveness, of egotism and of greed, and of exploiting one human being by another.

*Spino*: Is there no really benevolent side to the philosophy that has driven this country?

*Shapiro*: Well, you've changed the question in midcourse. The philosophy that governs this country is not simply capitalism. I think the very fact that you would ask the question in that way is a reflection of the way people are socialized into a kind of confusing sense of what this country is about. I remind you that the guiding principles of this country are not only about free market economics or capitalism or whatever. They're also about very, very different notions. Ideologically, whether or not the moral principles on which capitalism is based are desirable or acceptable, I would answer no! If you ask me if capitalism has been successful as compared to other systems in the world at providing people with lots of consumer goods, then the answer has to be, it's been pretty successful. Certainly in the First World. Capitalism has done pretty well at providing people with a certain standard of living. At the same time, we also have to bear in mind that capitalism has been a total catastrophe for most people around the world; third world people, people in Latin America, people in Africa. Capitalism has been an unbridled disaster for these people, not to speak of the effects on the environment. The problem is today that we are struck now by the tragedy of the twentieth century, from an economic standpoint. We are stuck between a system that is capitalism, which benefits relatively a small number of people, and a system that we call communism, which has been a total disaster economically, politically, and culturally. And now as we're really looking out into a coming century, I think we will have to reinvent economics, an economics that serves the majority of human beings on the planet. I certainly don't have a blueprint for that. As far as this being the guiding principle of this country, I want to reemphasize that capitalism is one half of the story in America. The other half of the story is our democratic principles, which are fundamentally based on affirmation of human dignity and human equality. And that doesn't fit easily with capitalism. I think the history of America, or at least one reading of that history, is to understand the contradictions, the conflicts, and the dissonance that has always gone on between the notion of capitalist economy, with all that's implied there, and the pursuit of a society that lives up to its democratic faith. That's actually central to the book I wrote and it's really, for me, perhaps, the central conflict that exists in American public life. How we reconcile the continuing struggle between those sets of values becomes paramount.

*Barry*: I think this notion of democratic imaginary depicts the best and noblest of these struggles. These struggles are not anti-capitalist but are, in simple human terms, about (1) challenging oppressive, subordinate, and alienating experiences and (2) struggling for a decent and qualitatively better existence than we have now.

*Spino*: So, as morally reprehensible as you find capitalism, is it not a suitable model for education?

*Shapiro*: I think that people have to make choices. For me, as I look out into the world today, the real struggle to make the world more human, in the educational sense, has to do with that form of education that promises to promote human decency, human caring, human compassion, human dignity, and human empowerment. And it's for those reasons that what I'm interested in and what I pursue and what I promote is a form of education, critical pedagogy, or whatever that seems to be most concerned with those things. Now, having said that, I don't dispute the fact that in any society that I can imagine there will be what we might call training. That is, we'll have jobs. People will have to work and people will need to be trained for that. And if, for example, we have a government in this country that wants to ensure that workers can be trained for jobs that will be there, that will decently pay them, I support that. How can any concerned citizen not be supportive of policies that promote the possibility of people having jobs that provide for them and their families? It would be very irresponsible of me to be against that. But what I want to say is that I want to go back to making a clear distinction between job training and an education that's concerned with a wider set of human values. And those things are not the same. They have to be distinguished.

*Barry*: As a wider set of values, similarity within difference comes to mind!

*Spino*: And as you talk about a wider set of human values, I imagine you certainly promote education that's for a wider set of human beings. Certainly much of what you, McLaren, and Kanpol discuss suggests that education as a tradition in this country has been centered too much on white, middle-class ideology and has left out the experiences of the other. How do we become more inclusive?

*Shapiro*: I think in that sense the critical pedagogy tradition joins together with other progressive forces in this country. I'm thinking of people concerned with multiculturalism in schools. People concerned with the role of girls, women, and other minorities in this society have begun to make some impact there. I think the very concept of multiculturalism has in it important promise. And I think that idea is that schools, education, and classrooms ought to speak much more closely to the experiences, traditions, background, and knowledge of all the students that attend our classrooms. That idea is in wider circulation than it ever has been, I think. We've made some progress there. At least the idea is in wide circulation that schools ought to attend to the fact that America is a multiethnic, multiracial society. It's not a melting pot. And that we have kids in our classrooms who really don't fit the Ozzie and Harriet mold. We've come to recognize the reality of that. Public education must cater to the needs and backgrounds of enormously diverse groups of students. I understand that in Los Angeles, eighty different languages are spoken by kids attending the public schools. In fact, I think by the year 2000 or 2010, the majority of students in our schools will be kids from minority backgrounds. We are being forced to recognize the multicultural nature of America, and I think schools, to some extent, are being forced to attend to the diverse experiences of students. I think that puts on the agenda, in a hopeful sense, the possibilities of rewriting the curriculum in directions that speak more clearly to the different experiences of students. That is, starting with the varied experiences of students, recognizing that if we don't do that we have kids in our classrooms who feel alienated, bored, and most likely will resist.

*Spino*: Perhaps in the past we have disenfranchised a large number of people who didn't fit into the majority mold. But at the same time, as the multicultural movement takes hold, how do we not go to the other extreme? What about the possibility of being so hyper-sensitive to difference that we can't make one move for fear of stepping on a different frame of reference or experience?

*Shapiro*: Well, I'll tell you something. I'm not very worried about that. The reason is because we've been trampling on people's experiences for such a long time now that people will simply have to struggle with this. And it's a good struggle. I think here particularly of my own experience as a young Jew growing up in England, going to a school where the assumption was that every child in the school was Christian. It didn't dawn on people that there may be a small group of kids in the school like myself for whom Christmas wasn't a holiday. You know, there were days when I had to take off and other kids didn't take off. And should people be sensitive to whether there should be homework given that day or exams given that day? I have to say it's okay with me if people have to stop now and begin to think about other people and other traditions. It's all right. If we have to struggle with that, it's not the worst kind of struggle that we have. It reminds me a little of this struggle going on around the military issue of bringing in or accepting gay people into the military. The very fact that Clinton has put this onto the table is a good thing for the country. It makes people uncomfortable. They have to struggle with it. But the bottom line is that people have to recognize that there are people out there who are different, and we have to struggle with how we're going to deal with these people in our society so that they feel included, too.

*Spino*: So, the dialogue is what's important?

*Shapiro*: The dialogue here is terribly important.

*Spino*: You mentioned times of feeling excluded as a Jewish student in England. Did those times, as McLaren would put it, perforate the self-esteem?

*Barry*: They certainly did for me! I felt ashamed at not only being Jewish, but being Jewish and feeling that I was excluding others or even judging others as less than because they weren't Jewish!

*Shapiro*: Oh, absolutely. Without a shadow of a doubt. I didn't have to wait until I read critical pedagogy or Henry Giroux to know that I was ashamed and embarrassed about my own tradition. I was nervous about bringing non-Jewish kids home and sharing with them the food we ate.

And the holidays we celebrated were different. I was embarrassed about it. I felt odd and strange. That goes back a long way.

*Barry*: Yes, all our histories and traditions must be connected to our present social relations.

*Spino*: As we become better teachers then, start to approach this struggle in meaningful ways, we still would seem to have to worry about academic performance. How do we revise curriculum and maintain standards as well?

*Shapiro*: That's a loaded question, really. I don't know what the standards are. I think the standards themselves are part of the issue. We have to question what the standards are and who sets the standards and who benefits from the standards. So, that's a question that we would have to decide first—who the standards are set for. Then we can begin to answer the question.

*Spino*: Let me make it more concrete. Sometimes we hear that to fail students today is to devalue or discount their own experiences or culture. So, we come up with reforms in education to avoid this insensitivity. Pennsylvania's own outcomes-based education is a way of sorts of saying we want to do better, evaluate students in a way that is more sensitive to their own experiences. Former Secretary of Education William Bennett has opined that often these kinds of reforms become ways of dumbing down the curriculum or lowering standards. What do you think?

*Shapiro*: Well, it's hard to position myself easily in that issue. Because, on the one hand, it would be hard for me to be on the same side as Bennett around this. What he calls 'dumbing down' is, on the one hand, partly an attempt to meet the reality of the diversity of students who sit in our classrooms. So, his pejorative comment in that way really comes from a person who wishes to maintain and support the status quo. His notion is that people like him, people who went to Yale, Harvard, and Princeton and so on, ought to continue to do that and ought to continue to set the standards. So, I'm not comfortable with that. On the other hand, I think there is a certain reality. And that is because kids are experiencing school as alienating and as irrelevant to them. I think that the level of resistance in schools, especially in high schools and maybe even colleges, of noncompliance to what goes on in schools, has simply accelerated, has intensified. And in order to avoid escalating conflict in the classroom, in the schools, an alternative to that is what Ira Shor talks about. And that is to accept that what's going on in school among kids is what I think he refers to as a "performance strike." That is, that kids really are just saying to hell with really working hard and doing all this stuff. And in order to avoid too much conflict, schools in America, in a sense, compromise what traditionally is called standards and accept less from kids. So, you really have the worst of all possible worlds there. You don't have much of a move toward developing the critical intelligence of kids, and, in simply conventional terms, you have schools settling for less and less. Even by conventional standards, what I find in my undergraduate classrooms is students who, frankly, know very little about the world. In that sense, I suppose I can sound somewhat like one of the conservative writers like Hirsch or Bennett. But the way in which to address that is not to intensify the stuffing down kids' throats of this information. I mean we really have to ask ourselves the basic questions about pedagogy, what it is that we are teaching, and how it is we are teaching.

*Spino.* So, where's the hope for those of us anticipating our teaching certificates? What would you tell us that gets beyond merely resisting and seeing administration or administrators or the system itself as the enemy?

*Shapiro:* This is what I have found. In my own teaching of these issues, especially with graduate students, people who are working in the schools, typically there is a process of anger and resistance and denial, perhaps, to the things I say. But for the most part, toward the end of that process, I think that the deeper message begins to dawn on teachers. That is the message that we, I think, are trying to put out. It's not simply a kind of nihilistic destruction of schools. It is really an attempt to affirm the deep moral impulses that I think bring many people into teaching to begin with. That is, that teachers don't want to go in there to become technicians and clerks or people who simply go and administer tests or whatever. What brings people into teaching and education in general is a very powerful drive to affirm human dignity, to help kids grow, to work with all students. The kinds of things that I think are at the bottom of this struggle. They are what you might call, for me, basic democratic values. I think that teachers are very strong adherents to those kinds of human goals. My struggle, I think, is really to reconnect teachers, educators with their noblest impulses, the impulses that brought them into education originally. And that, I think, the institution of schooling, in a kind of broader political context, has tried to, and continues to try to, destroy in teachers. It's not us who I think destroys the spirit of teachers, makes them feel like teaching is disconnected from those impulses. I think it's the way the institution works. So, my notion is that teaching, despite all of the constraints on it, is possible. It is possible to close the door, and despite everything else, to work with kids, to educate kids in the broader sense. We can still do it. You know, I do it, to an extent, in my classroom. And many teachers, good teachers, continue to do this in spite of everything. I think it's possible to do this. It's not simply an act of resistance. It's also an act of affirmation that goes on.

*Barry:* Yes, critical pedagogy is about affirming individuals and not necessarily *only* about social critique. I would strongly argue that to critique is also to affirm and to affirm also engages critique of the system and ourselves as we are implicated in it.

*Spino:* Dr. Shapiro, thanks for taking the time to go through this. You not only provide a critical way of extending what has been discussed in our classroom but also demonstrate your concern for teachers-to-be.

*Shapiro*: Thanks very much.

## CONCLUSION

After interviewing Professor Shapiro, Rocky Spino was sparked to investigate further the possibility of studying more about critical pedagogy and its underlying theories. Shapiro has written a clear and precise statement on the behalf of critical pedagogy.

First, critical pedagogy is a form of what others in this field have described as cultural politics. It is a form of meaning making about creating or challenging existing value structures that lead to social relations that are oppressive, alienating, and subordinative. Critical pedagogy is not innocent or devoid of choice. Thus, and second, to adopt critical pedagogy is about making a conscious choice of teaching style and teaching politics. Critical pedagogy, like other pedagogies (liberal, traditional humanistic, etc.), is not just an innocent bystander. It is partisan. It is not objective and/or value free, but subjective. It is rooted in personal histories with connections to forms of oppression, alienation, and subordination made to the present and then installed in some ways into our teaching, much like I have tried to incorporate in this book.

Third, we learn that knowledge is never a "give me." Knowledge is always negotiable and always partial. There are many realities—both yours and mine and the others. With this in mind, critical pedagogy roots its knowledge as a form of cultural politics that challenges a stymied system devoid of humanistic qualities. It is a cultural politics that interrogates the multiple realities of subjectivities with the intent to undercut oppressive situations that these subjectivities experience daily.

Fourth, we learn that critical pedagogy is not alone in this struggle to end various forms of subordination, oppression, and alienation. So as not to alienate its own movement, Shapiro argues that we as critical pedagogists must join forces with other progressive movements in the quest to further the democratic path that our leaders designated for us so many years ago. If anything, we begin to understand that critical pedagogy must become part of a common struggle rather than a separate movement. This means making our work more accessible to the public and tolerating other views with the idea to incorporate them somehow (despite what we might think them to be) into our political struggle. That does not mean that we must accept all views as truth. Ideas should be struggled over, challenged, and then incorporated for the betterment of the human condition. This challenge becomes one of meaning. How does one incorporate and live with conservative (traditional) views of standards and with critical views on challenging who made these standards? How does one incorporate the voice of the other while not excluding the voice of the majority? Another approach to this question could be, How does one include the voice of the majority while not excluding the other?

Fifth, these questions are rhetorical and will not be answered here. But they are the sorts of questions one must ask to work within the system. Critical pedagogy is not simply a platform or another meaningless discipline model to be adopted by everyone. To be a force, critical pedagogy must be incorporated into traditional and/or conservative and progressive mainstream school settings as a part of our daily teaching and living. It can be a part of any subject material. Critical pedagogy has some legitimacy as well—just like other forms of knowledge. It is not simply a critical pedagogy framework that a school must adopt. Critical pedagogy is more about human beings digging into their guts (psychology), asking and answering questions about their past, students' past, the relationship of this to the content, and how this knowledge can undercut social relations that are oppressive. Critical pedagogy can occur at all places and at all times—in teachers' meetings, on the playground, in the lunchroom, between parents and teachers, at meetings with administrators, even in the parking lot. Moreover, critical pedagogy can occur while in the confines of the classroom as well as in the quiet of the home.

Finally, if we learn anything in this book, critical pedagogy is ultimately about affirming other human beings' sense of history and self and no less. Professor Shapiro affirmed Rocky Spino by adding meaning to the difficult material Spino was challenged with in my foundations course. Shapiro exemplifies the tradition that critical pedagogy must align with to continue the uphill struggle to penetrate the schools. His language is accessible, his ideas are challenging, and his answers are not easy. Above all else, as an act of human decency, he took the time to talk to a student so many miles away—a student who just wanted clarify and further probe ideas that fascinated him. We critical pedagogists can all learn from this way of living.

With this in mind, one must understand that critical pedagogy is not only about theoretical ideas. It is also about living those ideas in our daily lives in and out of our workplace. Within a critical pedagogy tradition, then, democracy is a lived ideal, always in flux, under negotiation and reconstruction. Within this struggle, a critical pedagogy movement can rear its head as more than just progressive. Within this critical pedagogy movement, it has been argued that both modern and postmodern ideals as well as traditional and nontraditional ways of seeing schools exist. Entwined in this are personal narratives, histories, and subjectivities— stories of successes, hopes and dreams, oppressiveness and alienation.

Above all else, critical pedagogy provides us with a terrain of hope that allows investigation into furthering democratic possibilities. This kind of social commitment (and no less), I believe, is needed to carve out new spaces for teacher and student action and meaning making. Finally, critical pedagogy is both revolutionary and zealous within which the highest moral attempt to make this world a qualitatively better place for all is paramount.

## NOTES

1. Jonathan Kozol, *Savage Inequalities*. Kozol is, as far as I know, the only critical theorist to make any significant impact on the public debate on education.
2. Allan Bloom, *The Closing of the American Mind* (New York: Simon & Schuster, 1987); and E. D. Hirsch, Jr., *Cultural Literacy* (Boston: Houghton Mifflin, 1987).
3. Peter McLaren, *Life in Schools*.
4. Kathleen Weiler, *Women Teaching for Change* (New York: Bergin & Garvey, 1988).
5. Peter McLaren, *Life in Schools*, p. 215.
6. Svi Shapiro, *Between Capitalism and Democracy* (New York: Bergin & Garvey, 1990); and Barry Kanpol, *Towards a Theory and Practice of Teacher Cultural Politics* (Norwood, N.J.: Ablex, 1992).

## QUESTIONS FOR DISCUSSION

1. Discuss the differences between what Shapiro describes as "schooling and education." How does critical pedagogy lead to education and challenge schooling?
2. What kind of critical thinker are you?
3. What would you describe as the differences between capitalistic and basic democratic values?
4. Given your answers to the preceding three questions, why did you choose teaching as a career, and why after reading this book do you want to or not want to remain in the teaching profession?
5. If you had to sum up the function of a teacher as a critical pedagogist, what would you say?
6. What would a realistic vision for you look like in terms of adopting critical pedagogy as a teaching endeavor, given the structural limitations of schools?

# Select Bibliography

Anderson, G. 1988. *A Legitimation Role for the School Administrator: A Critical Ethnography of Elementary School Principals*. Doctoral dissertation, Ohio State University.

Anyon, J. 1980. "Social Class and the Hidden Curriculum of Work." *Journal of Education*, 162 (2): 67–92.

Anyon, J. 1981. "Social Class and School Knowledge." *Journal of Curriculum Inquiry* 11 (1): 3–42.

Apple, M. 1982. *Education and Power*. Boston: Routledge & Kegan Paul.

Apple, M. 1983. "Curriculum in the Year 2000: Tensions and Possibilities." *Phi Delta Kappan*, 64 (5): 321–326.

Apple, M. 1986. *Teachers and Texts*. New York: Routledge & Kegan Paul.

Aronowitz, S., and Giroux, H. A. 1993. *Education Still under Siege*. South Hadley, Mass.: Bergin & Garvey.

Aronowitz, S., and Giroux, H. A. 1991. *Postmodern Education: Politics, Culture and Social Criticism*. Minneapolis: University of Minnesota Press.

Banks, J. 1994. *Multiethnic Education*. Boston: Allyn & Bacon.

Bennett, K., and LeCompte, M. D. 1990. *The Way Schools Work*. New York: Longman.

Bigelow, W. 1990. "Inside the Classroom: Social Vision and Critical Pedagogy." *Teachers College Record*, 91(3): 437–448.

Bloom, A. 1987. *The Closing of the American Mind*. New York: Simon & Schuster.

Bowles, S., and Gintis, H. 1976. *Schooling in Capitalist America*. New York: Basic Books.

Britzman, P. 1991. *Practice Makes Practice*. Albany: State University of New York Press.

Cappel, C., and Jamison, M. 1993. "Outcomes-Based Education Reexamined: From Structural Functionalism to Poststructuralism." *Educational Policy* 1 (4): 427–441.

Chambers, J. 1983. *The Achievement of Education*. Lanham, Md.: University Press of America.

Connell, R. W. 1985. *Teacher Work*. Boston: George Allen and Unwin.

Connell, R. W. et al. 1982. *Making the Difference*. Sydney, Australia: George Allen and Unwin.

Darder, A. 1991. *Culture and Power in the Classroom*. New York: Bergin & Garvey.

Denescombe, M., and Walker, S., eds. 1983. *Social Crisis and Educational Research*. London: Croon & Helm, pp. 48–74.

Dewey, J. 1916. *Democracy and Education*. New York: Free Press.

Dreeban, R. 1968. *On What Is Learned in Schools*. Reading, Mass.: Addison-Wesley.

Dreeban, R. 1973. "The School as Workplace." In J. H. Ballantine, Ed., *Schools and Society*. Palo Alto and London: Mayfield, pp. 367–372.

Freire, P. 1973. *Education for Critical Consciousness*. New York: Seabury Press.

Ginsburg, M., and Newman, K. "Social Inequities, Schooling, and Teacher Education." *Journal of Teacher Education*, 36 (March/April): 49–54.

Giroux, H. 1983. *Theory and Resistance in Education*. New York: Bergin & Garvey.

Giroux, H. 1985. "Critical Pedagogy, Cultural Politics and the Discourse of Experience." *Journal of Education*, 167 (2): 2–21.

Giroux, H. 1990. "The Politics of Postmodernism: Rethinking the Boundaries of Race and Ethnicity." *Journal of Urban and Cultural Studies*, 1 (1): 5–38.

Giroux, H. 1992. *Border Crossings*. New York: Routledge & Kegan Paul.

Giroux, H. 1993. *Living Dangerously*. New York: Peter Lang Publishers.

Giroux, H. 1994. *Disturbing Pleasures*. New York: Routledge.

Giroux, H., and McLaren, P. 1986. "Teacher Education and the Politics of Engagement: The Case for Democratic Schooling." *Harvard Educational Review*, 56 (3): 213–238.

Giroux, H., and McLaren, P. Eds. 1989. *Critical Pedagogy, the State, and Cultural Struggle*. New York: State University of New York Press.

Giroux, H., and McLaren, P. Eds. 1994. *Between Borders*. New York: Routledge.

Gitlin, A., and Smyth, J. 1989. *Teacher Evaluation: Educative Alternatives*. Philadelphia: Falmer Press.

Godzich, W. 1993. "Reading against Literacy" in Jean François Lyotard, *The Postmodern Explained*, Minneapolis, Minn.: University of Minnesota Press, pp. 109–136.

Goodman, J. 1988. "The Disenfranchisement of Elementary Teachers and Strategies for Resistance." *Journal of Curriculum and Supervision*, 3 (3): 201–220.

Grossberg, L. 1992. *We Gotta Get Out of This Place*. New York: Routledge & Kegan Paul.

Grumet, M. 1988. *Bitter Milk: Women and Teaching*. Amherst: University of Massachusetts Press.

Habermas, J. 1981. *The Theory of Communicative Action: Reason and Rationality in Society*. Boston: Beacon Press.

Harris, K. 1979. *Education and Knowledge*. London: Routledge & Kegan Paul.

Harris, K. 1982. *Teachers and Classes: A Marxist Analysis*. London: Routledge & Kegan Paul.

Hirsch, E. D. 1987. *Cultural Literacy*. Boston: Houghton Mifflin.

hooks, b. 1989. *Talking Back*. Boston: South End Press.

hooks, b. 1991. *Breaking Bread*. Boston: South End Press.

Jackson, P. W. 1968. *Life in Schools*. New York: Holt, Rinehart and Winston.

Kanpol, B. 1988. "Teacher Work Tasks as Forms of Resistance and Accommodations to the Structural Factors of Schooling." *Urban Education*, 23 (2): 173–187.

Kanpol, B. 1989a. "Institutional and Cultural Political Resistance: Necessary Conditions for the Transformative Intellectual." *Urban Review*, 21 (3): 163–179.

Kanpol, B. 1989b. "The Concept of Resistance: Further Scrutiny." *Critical Pedagogy Networker*, 1 (4): 1–5.

Kanpol, B. 1990. "Empowerment: The Institution and Cultural Aspects for Teachers and Principals." *NASSP Bulletin*, 74, (528): 104–107.

Kanpol, B. 1991. "Teacher Group Formation as Emancipatory Critique: Necessary Conditions for Teacher Resistance." *Journal of Educational Thought*, 25 (2): 134–149.

Kanpol, B. 1992. "The Politics of Similarity within Difference: A Pedagogy for the Other." *Urban Review*, 24 (2): 105–131.

Kanpol, B. 1993. "Critical Curriculum Theorizing as Subjective Imagery: Reply to Goodman." *Educational Forum*, 57 (30): 325–330.

Kanpol, B. 1993. "The Pragmatic Curriculum: Teacher Reskilling as Cultural Politics." *Journal of Educational Thought*, 27 (20): 200–215.

Kanpol, B., and McLaren, P., *Critical Multiculturalism: Uncommon Voices in a Common Struggle*. Forthcoming.

Kozol, J. 1991. *Savage Inequalities*. New York: Crown.

Liston, D. 1990. *Capitalistic Schools*. New York: Routledge & Kegan Paul.

Leach, M. 1990. "Toward Writing Feminist Scholarship into History of Education." *Educational Theory*, 40 (4): 453–461.

Livingstone, D. and contributors. 1987. *Critical Pedagogy and Cultural Power*. South Hadley, Mass.: Bergin & Garvey.

Lortie, D. C. 1975. *Schoolteacher*. London: University of Chicago Press.

Lyons, N. 1983. "Two Perspectives: On Self, Relationships and Morality." *Harvard Educational Review*, 53 (2): 125–143.

Lyotard, J. F. 1984. *The Postmodern Condition: A Report on Knowledge*. Minneapolis: University of Minnesota Press.

Lyotard, J. F. 1993. *The Postmodern Explained*. Translation edited by Julian Pefanis and Morgan Thomas. Minneapolis: University of Minnesota Press.

Maher, F. A. 1987. "Toward a Richer Theory of Feminist Pedagogy: A Comparison of 'Liberation,' and 'Gender' Models for Teaching and Learning." *Journal of Education*, 163 (3): 91–100.

McLaren, P. 1986. *Schooling as a Ritual Performance: Towards a Political Economy of Education Symbols and Gestures*. London: Routledge & Kegan Paul.

McLaren, P. 1988. "Language, Social Structure and the Production of Subjectivity." *Critical Pedagogy Networker*, 1 (2&3): 1–10.

McLaren, P. 1989. *Life in Schools*. New York: Longman.

Oakes, J. 1985. *Keeping Track: How Schools Structure Inequality*. New Haven, Conn.: Yale University Press.

Peters, M., Ed. *Lyotard and Education*. Forthcoming.

Pignatelli, F. 1993. "Towards a Postprogressive Theory of Education." *Educational Foundation*, 7 (3): 7–26.

Popkewitz, T. S. 1987. *Ideology and Social Formation in Teacher Education*. New York: Falmer Press.

Purpel, D. 1989. *The Moral and Spiritual Crisis in Education*. New York: Bergin & Garvey.

Putnam, H., and Putnam, R. 1993. "Education for Democracy." *Educational Theory*, 43 (4): 361–376.

Rosenthal, S. 1993. "Democracy and Education: A Deweyian Approach." *Educational Theory* 43 (4): 377–390.

Shapiro, S. 1990. *Between Capitalism and Democracy*. New York: Bergin & Garvey.

Shapiro, S., and Purpel, D., eds. 1993. *Critical Social Issues in American Education*. New York: Longman.

Simon, R. 1992. *Teaching against the Grain*. New York: Bergin & Garvey.

Smyth, J. 1989. "A Critical Pedagogy of Classroom Practice." *Journal of Curriculum Studies* 21 (6): 483–502.

Waller, R. 1932. *The Sociology of Teaching*. New York: Wiley.

Weiler, K. 1987. *Women Teaching for Change*: Gender, Class and Power. South Hadley, Mass.: Bergin & Garvey.

West, C. 1990. "The New Cultural Politics of Difference." *October*, 53 (3): 93–109.

West, C. 1993. *Prophetic Thought in Postmodern Times*. Monroe, Maine: Common Courage Press.

Wexler, P. 1985. "Organizing the Unconscious: Toward a Social Psychology of Education." In L. Barton and S. Walker, Eds., *Education and Social Change*. London: Biddles, pp. 218–228.

Wexler, P. 1987. *Social Analysis of Education: After the New Sociology*. New York: Routledge & Kegan Paul.

Whitty, G. 1985. *Sociology of School Knowledge*. London: Methuen.

Willis, P. 1977. *Learning to Labor*. Lexington, Mass.: D. C. Heath.

Willis, P. 1990. *Common Culture*. San Francisco: Westview Press.

Woods, P. 1986. *Inside Schools*. New York: Routledge & Kegan Paul.

Wright, E. 1983. *Class, Crisis and the State*. London: Thetford Press Limited.

Wuthnow, R. et al. 1984. *Cultural Analysis. The Work of Peter Berger, Mary Douglas, Michel Foucault and Jurgen Habermas*. Boston: Routledge & Kegan Paul.

Yeo, F. 1992. "The Inner-city School: A Conflict in Rhetoric." *Critical Pedagogy Networker*, 5 (3): 1–4.

# Index

**About the Author**

BARRY KANPOL is professor of Secondary Foundations at Penn State, Harrisburg, Pennsylvania. He was born in Australia and lived in Israel for ten years. He has lived, studied, and taught in the United States since 1983. He is the coeditor, with Peter McLaren, of *Critical Multiculturalism: Uncommon Voices in a Common Struggle* (Bergin & Garvey, 1994).

ISBN 0-89789-393-X

90000>

9 780897 893930

HARDCOVER BAR CODE

EAN